The Genius of Freemasonry

This Edition is Dedicated to David Merchant,
member of Benjamin B. French Lodge,
Grand Lodge of the District of Columbia

The Genius of Freemasonry

William B. Clarke's
Leaves From Georgia Masonry

Edited and Introduced by Paul Rich

WESTPHALIA PRESS
An imprint of Policy Studies Organization

The Genius of Freemasonry
Williams B. Clarke's *Leaves From Georgia Masonry*

Westphalia Press
An imprint of Policy Studies Organization
dgutierrezs@ipsonet.org

For information:
Westphalia Press
1527 New Hampshire Ave., N.W.
Washington, D.C. 20036

ISBN-13: 978-0-944285-77-0
ISBN-10: 0944285775

Updated material and comments on this edition can be found at the Policy Studies Organization website: http://www.ipsonet.org/

PREFACE TO THE NEW EDITION

This book approaches Freemasonry with common sense and scholarship, which is not always the case in dealing with the world's most ubiquitous secret society. Over the centuries Masonry has provided a meeting place for many different movements as various as Rosicrucianism, Templarism, and Orientalism. It is a big old house with many rooms, full of interesting things. So characterizing all these influences will be fraught with difficulties.

The subject is firstly one that involves symbolism and the Enlightenment. Freemasonry has shaped America in many ways, but none more importantly than by providing the intellectual foundations by commuting the values of the Enlightenment: "The Masonic lodge in America epitomized the American Enlightenment and the Enlightenment became synonymous with the American Revolution...To consider Freemasonry operating in early America and ignore the potential to interject enlightened thinking would be the ultimate disregard of organizational influence in the evolution of our civil society." When a candidate is first presented in a lodge, he is asked, "In your present condition, what do you most desire?" The correct reply is "Light". Later he is asked why he is traveling through the degrees, and he replies, "in search of more light." This enduring connection between Masonry and the Enlightenment has not been discussed nearly enough, especially with regard to education.

Many of these symbols have been incorporated into the American consciousness: "...national symbols are charged with the difficult task of creating a nation." Masonry is worldwide movement, but specifically with regard to the United States, in providing unifying symbols the Masons have performed in exemplary fashion. The lodges were part of the intellectual ferment of the eighteenth and early nineteenth centuries that sprang from the Enlightenment and were the foundation of the country. Consideration of these roots might awaken us from what has been described as a coma about the constitutional and philosophical roots of the United States.

Paul Rich

LEAVES FROM GEORGIA MASONRY

LEAVES
FROM
GEORGIA MASONRY

Published by the
EDUCATIONAL AND HISTORICAL COMMISSION
OF THE GRAND LODGE OF GEORGIA,
F. & A. M.

1946

FOREWORD

A resolution adopted by the Grand Lodge of Georgia, F. & A. M., at the 159th communication, directed the Educational and Historical Commission to prepare for publication, a new and revised edition of the book, "The Story of Freemasonry," which was originally published by the Grand Lodge of Georgia in 1935.

In this new edition much of the original material has been retained. Minor changes and corrections have been made. New articles included were selected after careful consideration of available material.

We recognize the fact that there is no exclusive or absolute interpretation of any symbol, and that the reader will feel free to evaluate such interpretations offered herein by the yard stick of his own judgment.

It is the sincere opinion of your Commission that a careful study of Leaves From Georgia Masonry will bring increased understanding and happiness to the reader and also the satisfaction that every interested Mason derives from taking a progressive step in the quest for "More Light."

—THE EDUCATIONAL AND
HISTORICAL COMMISSION.

CONTENTS

SYMBOLISM OF FREEMASONRY

By John L. Travis, Past Grand Master

SYMBOLISM is the key to all mysteries, to all ancient and modern religions, to all esoteric knowledge. Without an understanding of the meaning of symbols, one will never appreciate the beauty of life, or understand what his own religion is trying to teach him. But as the knowledge of the meaning of symbols comes to him, he becomes more and more a free man, or initiate.

The letter killeth, the spirit giveth life.

Words are inadequate to carry or convey spiritual truths, for all words have a material origin, and, originally, a material meaning. Masonry does not use words to convey the deeper spiritual truths, it uses symbols, generally simple figures whose beginning are hidden in the mystic past, and whose first users are unknown, perhaps unknowable. In the old symbols of Masonry, few in number and bare of meaning to the uninitiated and ignorant, the ancient Masters concealed the Holy Doctrine and the Master's Word, yet expressed them in so plain a manner that the most humble seeker can find them.

Modern stupidity has attempted to add many new symbols to Masonry, and to explain all the old symbols in mere words. These explanations challenge the admiration of the wise by their triteness and banality, and awake the pity of the understanding by their lack of knowledge.

Modern Masons too seldom seek to discover the true meaning of the old signs and symbols of their Order, and too frequently do not know that these signs and symbols have any meaning beyond the barren and often ridiculous statements of would-be teachers—the blind leading the blind.

If you tell the average Mason that in the plumb, square and level, in the square and compasses, the cross, the circle and the triangle, are concealed the knowledge of the origin of life, of the true nature of man and his relation to the Deity, all of the nature of God that finite man can know, and the secret of controlling the forces of nature, he will open his eyes and, like a child reaching for a new toy, say in a languid tone, "Tell them to me."

And if you reply that they cannot be told in words, that this wonderful knowledge must be earned, a little at a time, by meditation, by prayer, by right-living, he turns away uninterested, and sinks back with a sigh of content to the mire of his own self-indulgences.

Tell the average Mason that the real symbols of Masonry have come down to us from the time "before the mountains were brought forth," and he will wonder what you mean. For it has never occurred to him that the mountains have not been always as they are now, that the mountains came into existence long after man inhabited this globe, or that there could be any record of anything that happened more than six thousand years ago (that being the accepted time since the creation as told in Genesis). And if you tell him that, according to ancient maps, now in existence, there were no mountains until ten or twelve thousand years ago, he will fear, if he be the ordinary professing Christian, that you are denying something in the Bible, and attacking religion, and he will shudder at your blasphemy.

Yet it is said in Genesis VII, 20: "Fifteen cubits upward did the water prevail; and the mountains were covered." What sort of "mountains" were they, if a flood of fifteen cubits upward (roughly, 22½ feet) could cover them?

Dates are not found in the manuscripts from which the Bible was translated into English, but were put into the English translation, on a pure guess, originally in England.

Ignorance and stupidity have prevented a full understanding of that wonderful book, the Bible. Job says of the earth, "It is turned as clay to the seal;" and yet Galileo was compelled to recant when he asserted that the earth moves. Passages in the Book of Books have constantly been twisted and perverted from their real meaning by a designing or shallow and superficial priesthood, to crush free thought and free speech, and to prevent the truth from being taught.

For the letter killeth, but the spirit giveth life.

Fortunately for humanity, a new age is dawning, when frankness and sincerity in the search for truth do not condemn men to the rack; when honest inquiry and open minds are tolerated; when what was once damned as heresy is given at least a hearing.

But too many men are willing to take all their opinions, all their beliefs, from some one else. This explains the power of the demagogue, who gains the hearts of his hearers by a loud voice and confident manner, who promises what any sensible man would know he cannot perform. This explains how a Mussolini can control the minds of a nation.

Few are willing to think for themselves, and most are too blinded by self-interest and selfishness to receive the truth even when they hear it.

So many Masons come to hear a lecture because they expect the speaker to make mysteries clear and easy of understanding; and so many expect the speaker to solve the unsolvable, plumb the unfathomable, and thereby save them the mental labor of doing their own solving and their own fathoming.

But they cannot get the knowledge of the Holy Doctrine from others—they must get it for themselves, as they must pray for themselves. No book or teacher can communicate the real secrets of Masonry—each must discover them for himself.

I saw a man once who was trying to find the True Word of a Master Mason in a book. I asked him if he would know it if he saw it, and he said no. I said, "Then why look in a book for what you wouldn't recognize if you find it?" He could give me no answer.

Yet we are told he could have got the Master's Word if he had been willing to pay the price.

As you may recover it if the future generation—or, rather, regenerations—of your own soul are such that you have deserved it.

For the Master's Word is a symbol. The true knowledge of God can be received only from Him. It is transmitted, not by words of mortal tongue, but by the revelation of God directly to the recipient, coming, we are told, as a blaze of glory through the top of the head, where phrenologists locate the devotional faculties.

This is the Pearl of Great Price, which is worth all that a man possesseth, and all that he can do in all his life. To have it, men of old thought it little to cross burning deserts, climb mountain precipices, endure cold and hunger and torrid heat, live in worldly poverty, bear the insults and jeers of the multitude, be esteemed as fools, and have no friend but God.

It is worth as much today as it was then.

Perhaps you think your duties to your family, to others, would prevent your making the sacrifice necessary to get the priceless gift. You are wrong. The True Word can be won only by the performance of duty. Duty is the only coin that will pay for it. You can find it in the roar of the city, amid the daily struggles for bread and livelihood, as well as in a monastery or a hermit's cave—nay, better.

Take heart, fainting one—your birthright of happiness and immortality will not be taken away from you because you are poor, or have to struggle for existence. That very poverty and struggle may form the stepping stones by which you may rise to mastership. Abolish selfishness from your heart, learn to serve, to love, and to bless.

He that would be greatest among you, let him be the servant of all.

For it is by service, by duty, by labor unselfishly for others, that we gain spiritual knowledge, not by supinely waiting for it to be brought pre-digested on a silver platter to our bedside.

There is an old saying that you will find borne out by the experience of every real seeker for Truth: "When the pupil is ready, the Master will appear." You will find this true. When you have earned knowledge, it will come to you, often through the most unexpected channels. Prison walls offer no bar, time and space furnish no limit or hindrance, to the appearance of the master to the pupil who is duly and truly prepared. John Bunyan wrote that remarkable story of initiation, "Pilgrim's Progress," while in jail. St. Paul wrote several of his wonderful letters while a prisoner and some of his greatest efforts were epistles from jail.

St. Paul, in 2 Cor. XVII, 2-4, says that he got his initiation in this manner: "I knew a man in Christ above fourteen years ago, (whether in the body, I cannot tell; or whether out of the body, I cannot tell: God knoweth); such an one caught up to the third heaven. And I knew such a man, (whether in the body, or out of the body, I cannot tell: God knoweth); How that he was caught up into paradise, and heard unspeakable words, which it is not lawful for a man to utter."

The word Paul uses here translated "unspeakable" is one which means "not spoken, or what ought not to be spoken, secret, which cannot be spoken or uttered, ineffable."

The word Paul uses here translated "lawful" is one which means "it being possible, allowed, in one's power," and of course, with the negative, it means "it being impossible, not allowed, not in one's power."

So that St. Paul said—evidently speaking of himself —this man heard words which were secret or which were not spoken or ought not to be spoken or cannot be spoken, and which it is not possible, or allowed, or in one's power to speak.

Certainly, such words cannot be found in a book.

The Master's Word contains or implies not only the knowledge of God, but also the control over all the forces of nature—the works of God. Jesus controlled the force of gravity when he walked on the water, and transmitted that power to Peter for an instant, till Peter's faith gave out. There are so-called "Cyclopean" walls in South America of such construction that no man today could erect them and fit the stones so closely as they are fitted, and the only satisfactory explanation of their existence is that the builders knew how to overcome gravity.

This wonderful knowledge seems to have been possessed by the older peoples, or at least some of them, who were the founders of our Order and the originators of the wonderful symbols of old Masonry.

What a being man must be, who can attain such powers, making him almost if not divine.

David says in the 8th Psalm: "When I consider thy heavens, the work of thy fingers; the moon and stars, which thou hast ordained; What is man, that thou art mindful of him? and the son of man, that thou visitist him?"

This is generally considered as meaning that in comparison with the moon and stars man is a very insignificant being, but if you read the rest of the passage, you will probably conclude that it means, "What a wonderful being is man, to whom Thou hast given dominion over the work of Thy hands, whom Thou hast crowned with glory and honor, under whose feet Thou hast put all things!" That doesn't sound like belittling man, does it? "A little lower than the angels" doesn't indicate a mean thing.

Job says (VII, 17): "What is man, that Thou shouldest magnify him? and that Thou shouldest set thy heart upon him? And that Thou shouldst visit him every morning, and try him every moment?"

Know, man is made in the likeness of God, and his powers and capacities for development appear to be unlimited. But he is under the great Law—he must pay for what he gets. He must earn knowledge as he earns bread—bread by labor, knowledge, by self-denial and sacrifice.

There has been a great deal of sympathy wasted on Esau, because people believe that Esau was cheated. That sympathy is probably wasted. Esau had a birthright, but this birthright carried with it a duty. If he had recognized the duty, and had prepared himself to hand down to posterity the religion which his father Abraham had, by divine appointment, he would not have needed the bean soup. But instead of marrying into a family who would respect the religion of his father, he married Hittite women, "which were a grief of mind unto Isaac and to Rebecca." Esau might know that these Hittites would bring up their children in their own religion. Too late, Esau saw his error, but his marriage to a daughter of Ishmael was not a correction of the fault which caused his loss of the birthright and came too late.

Each one of us has a birthright. The magnitude of it we do not realize. For so many thousand years men have been humbled by blind spiritual teachers who told them they were clods and slaves, not worthy to approach God except through a better informed and more fortunate intercessor. And too frequently, alas, we all today are willing to sell our birthright for what is not even worth as much as a mess of bean soup—for mere pleasures which injure the body instead of refreshing it, for things which we know are wrong. And yet, having thrown ourselves away on gambling, or indulgence in alcohol, or in still worse things, we sit up and condemn Jacob and Esau and all their tribe, although they did no whit worse than we do now.

Let us wake up and begin to study ourselves by studying the symbols of Freemasonry and the wonderful knowledge contained therein.

1. Ask your well-informed brethren, who will always be as ready to give, as you are to receive, instruction.

2. Read what books you can and get what light you can from Masonic literature. But do not forget that you will not find the priceless secrets of Masonry in books. Here and there you will get a hint or a clue, but that is all that the books will give you except such trite explanations as would not satisfy a child. There are said to be books which do contain this knowledge, but the ability to read them is acquired only after years of effort.

3. Hold all these explanations "in suspense" and do not accept anybody's interpretation as final. It is doubtful if any man living knows the real meaning, that is, all the real meaning, of any symbol. If he knows it, the limitations of language are such that he cannot communicate it all.

4. Take all the explanations you have received from others, all you have found in books, and then ask yourself if they are entirely satisfactory, if the symbol does not really mean something else. (It does). Study and meditation will bring you a new light from day to day. Remember that you are not bound to accept anybody's interpretation of a symbol, but it is your duty to formulate your own.

As you continue to study and to learn, the symbols will become alive to you and each will point out to you not one, but many, priceless truths.

The design of the Masonic institution is to make men not only wiser and better, but happier. The purpose of religion is to tie men back to God. The knowledge of the truths concealed in each symbol will be such when you have learned enough of them, to give you a serenity, a calm faith, a feeling of perfect harmony and satisfaction with life and with the universe such as you will not find otherwise.

The Master's square does not merely represent the infinite justice of God, nor is it merely a symbol of the cross, which is itself the greatest of all symbols, nor does it merely represent virtue. It is itself a symbol of the 47th problem of Euclid. That figure, the squares inscribed upon the three sides of a right-angled triangle, symbolizes another truth; that although the works of God cannot be harmonized or understood in this life, that when we are raised to a higher plane—symbolized by squaring the sides—we will find that there is a definite harmony and proportion in all that God permits to be done on this earth.

A knowledge of the real meaning of Masonic symbols will so harmonize one's life, if he uses that knowledge in his daily conduct, that the sight of each symbol will fill the true Mason's heart with joy.

If the square, the compasses and the other symbols used in the Lodge do not have this effect upon your heart, you have missed a greater part of your birthright. The Master's word is said to be itself a symbol. The fact that its communication by words is extremely difficult and perhaps impossible has its own symbolic meaning. The true light for which every Mason seeks, does not come through words at all, nor through any impressions received by the eye or any other physical sense; it comes direct from above and lights up the brain, the mind, the heart, with an indescribable radiance. It will come to you when you have earned it.

No time is too great to devote to the study of this remarkable system of knowledge. Yet, it is not intended you should neglect your daily affairs, your duties, or even a reasonable amount of recreation, to get this knowledge. You can meditate upon the symbols as you walk or drive along the road, as you wait for a train, or

at any time when your mind is not actively engaged
otherwise. If you spend thirty minutes a day in study
of the symbols, this will amount in a year to more than
three weeks' work of eight hours a day. Do not be discouraged, but learn to stand on your own feet and to
do your own thinking and remember that while you will
derive much profit from day to day in this labor of love,
you will find each day's added store of knowledge to
give you greater and greater comfort as the years roll
on. And remember this: "Whenever the pupil is ready,
the Master will appear."

But you will never LEARN Masonry until you LIVE it.

The allegory of Freemasonry applies to the individual, to the community, to the state or nation and to the
human race. The individual, blind, ignorant and in rags,
at least spiritually speaking, commences his journey toward the Light by trusting to someone to lead him; if he
is to reach the Light, he must follow a well-defined pathway; there is only one road; he must go by that road or
not at all, and as his self-improvement and deeds of
charity increase, so will his faith, until at last by the
strong power of faith, he has raised himself from the
level of the animal to the plane of spiritual uprightness
and immortality.

Likewise, the community, the state or the nation,
ignorant, brutal and barbarous, can be led, if willing,
through the same route and through the same experience
to heights of development undreamed of, and may finally
reach the point where its influence will be immortal.

We believe that the human race is traveling upward
towards the Light. From barbarism we are taught that
it has risen through semi-civilization towards general
enlightenment; through the cultivation of the arts and
sciences, through education, through organization—all of
which are taught in the second degree, a nation may rise
to commanding heights of civilization. But a nation no
matter how great its progress and wealth, is still bound
by the same laws that govern the individual. If its prosperity is not won honestly, if it is devoted to evil principles, it is bound to decay.

Here and there in the history of the human race, nations have risen by practicing the same principles taught

by Masonry, and have become centers of freedom and light. These nations have in turn decayed and at times it has seemed that darkness reigned over the world. Then other races have caught the inspiration, have raised themselves to commanding heights in literature, in art, in science, in philosophy, until they too have passed from the zenith downward to various depths of failure.

But the truths which Masonry teaches are immortal. Its allegory is of universal application. We firmly believe that the human race is still progressing towards a greater and a brighter future. Pessimism has no place in Masonry. We can see signs here and there that convince us that human nature is growing better, that humanity is advancing, stumbling, ignorantly, even blindly, but nevertheless certainly, towards a beauty and a glory which cannot be visualized.

The principles taught by Freemasonry are bound finally to succeed in making all men and all nations wiser, better and consequently happier, and if they do not do this in an instant, neither does nature do its greatest work instantaneously, but slowly and step by step.

In all times and among all peoples there have been men whose development and character caused them to stand forth like a mountain among hills, and who had reached a point where Nature was an open book, its pages clearly showing the word of God through the works of God.

To such men life, death, regeneration, and the future existence were not mysteries, for they understood much that to common men is hidden and inexplicable. Some of these Masters, as we may call them, exist in your minds today as mythical or imaginary persons, but to millions of your fellows these initiates were and are divine; some as the founders of the various religions of the world; others, as the popular heroes who will in due time return to redeem their country and restore it to its ancient glory; and yet others you have never even heard named, though their influence and teachings have largely contributed to making you and your country what the twentieth century finds you.

These men were great conquerors, but not of others; rulers whose kingdom was themselves; teachers of the

highest and most beautiful system of morality, philosophy and ethics; and, leaders of thought and of action
not only for their own times, but for all future
generations.

Whence arose their power and glory? From the fact
that they complied with the laws written by the finger of
God on the pages of the many-leaved book of Nature;
that they lived the life which the Great Creator made
them to live; and thus reaped the reward infallibly won
by the observance of those laws.

The rewards they earned by their own efforts, but
why did the few reach so exalted a height, while the
many lived and still are in obscurity and misery, and die
in doubt and darkness, leaving to posterity no single
worthy act, thought, or example? Did these great leaders
of men have teachers, and, if so who were those teachers?
And are such teachers or their teachings accessible to
common, ordinary men in the usual walks of life—men
who cannot become hermits or take long voyages to
foreign lands—men who have wives and children, who
read the morning papers, and have to work for every
cent they spend; men who, it may be, have not the advantage of a college education (so-called), nor the back-
ing of aristocratic connections?

Yes, there is a School where can be learned all that
makes men truly great; where the wisdom and exalted
learning that inspired the great teachers of the world—
Orpheus, Hermes, Prometheus, Mithra, Socrates, Plato,
Pythagoras, Moses, and countless others can be had for
the asking; where no money or price is exacted for instruction other than the price imposed by the divine Law
of Compensation.

Such a school was Freemasonry of the past; such it is
at this time to those who sufficiently desire knowledge;
and such a school will the Freemasonry of the present
more fully become when men cease to grovel like swine
in the filth for that which satisfieth not and learn to give
all things their true valuation and to seek only that which
has enduring worth and which will be at all times available. For hidden in its signs, symbols and ceremonies,
may be found the true ancient wisdom, the knowledge
and experience of the wisest and best of mankind; the

revelation made to the first men; all safely concealed from the unworthy, but freely revealed to him who is entitled to receive it.

Masonry, however has no monopoly of the truth, nor of the wisdom of the ancient sages; nor, indeed, could it or any other organization truly claim a monopoly of these inestimable gifts. This wisdom and the great truths of life are concealed about us; in every man these truths are hidden in his heart, so that when he sees one of them, he is not surprised, for he seems to recognize an old acquaintance. But men cannot see these truths when they live by false standards or darken their judgment by errors or vices.

These truths are hidden in the allegories of the world, even in the fairy tales that are told to children. But men cannot hear the spiritual meaning so plain to the adept until their ears are tuned to the harmony of the spiritual; and every fault, folly, vice, or error clogs the musical strings of the soul so that it cannot respond to its true harmonic but produces discord instead.

These secrets of priceless worth are writ large on the face of the Book of Nature, that wondrous tome of many pages made and written by the Great Creator Himself, but the worthy alone are able to learn the letters.

And even the unworthy should rejoice that the Divine Mercy has so arranged that the evil man can never see the truth, nor apprehend it, in any way but imperfectly; for whenever the evil man understands things truly, before he is freed from his evil, the knowledge of the truth would become a menace and a danger and a trouble, not only to him, but to all within the circle of his influence.

There is a way to learn the truths of Nature, the real inner and hidden mysteries concealed by Masonry. That way Masonry itself tells in plain and unmistakable language. If you cannot read its lore, it is your fault or misfortune, to be corrected by study and carefully living in accord with Masonic precepts and Morality. And as soon as you have by this course earned the right to know, you will know. Do not ask how or from whom the light will come. It is not yet for you to know. You must follow your guide, and fear not, wait patiently, and labor, and all will come right at last.

And be also admonished—become not impatient or discouraged. "There is no royal road to learning," and whenever you have earned your wages, they will be paid to you by a law as infallible as that which holds the stars to their courses. By that law, no effort for good is ever made that is not repaid in exact value to him who made it. So, whether the light shines on you today or after years of toil and struggle, remember that God is just and will in due time reward all his servants.

In that remarkable volume, "The Great Work," we are told that Freemasonry, in its modern form, represents but one of the many efforts of the Great School of Natural Science, the most ancient association known to men, to transmit its knowledge to men in definite scientific, and crystallized form. It has ever been the object of this venerable body of adepts to advance human liberty and protect human happiness, and its genius and spirit have ever pointed the way for the practice of Fraternity and Equality, and for intellectual Liberty and religious Freedom. By this Parent School of Friends and Helpers of Mankind, we are told, Freemasonry was originally intended to stand as the direct channel through which the Spiritual wisdom of the ages might be given to the world, thus rendering Masonry really Operative instead of Speculative as it is today.

The reason why this effort failed and had to be suspended until the present (or even later unless we are worthy), is told in detail in the Masonic ceremony of initiation. If you have not yet seen this reason, keep on in your study and you will in time discover it.

Also, the hidden wisdom of all the ages is open to you now, the True Word may be found by you, in this very life, if you are willing to devote the necessary time and labor and can bring the necessary ability to the search.

If you knew what are the rewards awaiting the searcher, you would not hesitate in deciding whether you would seek or not. But this knowledge is not yet for you. It is one of the prerequisites that you should enter upon this search of your own free will and accord, without mineral and metallic incumbrance, that is, free from earthly passions and attachments, without selfish desire for reward, or the hope thereof, but unselfishly and for the good of others. Neither vanity, nor idle curiosity, nor desire for Masonic honors or distinction, should be found in the breast of the true searcher. For even Masonic honors and distinction can be attained by the unworthy, and the other passions will not be gratified by truth, which humiliates and rebukes the vain, the curious, the selfish, the evil, and the impure.

"If it were possible," says The Great Work, "for the vain, the selfish and the mean, in the spirit of vanity, selfishness and meanness, to achieve Spiritual Independence and Mastership, that fact of itself would constitute a complete justification of vanity, selfishness and meanness in human life and conduct. If it were possible for the subtle trickster, the clever pretender, the vain boaster, and the morally degenerate to skulk past the Law of Compensation into the Kingdom of Spiritual Light, then would nature not only condone trickery, pretense, vanity and immorality, but would become a party to them. If this were possible, then also would there be no meaning in honesty, sincerity, humility and morality. For if nature made no distinction, why should man? If nature provided obscure bypaths whereby the vicious and the cunning might slip past the Law of Spiritual Unfoldment and, through a dark subterranean passage and a secret panel, reach the guest chamber of the Temple of Spiritual Light from the rear, such a provision would constitute 'class legislation' of the most vicious and degrading character in favor of immorality and the wickedness in human nature. In this event nature, or the Great Universal Intelligence that expresses itself to man through nature, would stand condemned as a party to fraud, injustice, dishonesty, and vice in all its hideous deformity.

"To the pure in heart it is a profound comfort to know that this is not true. In the legislature of nature there is no such thing as class legislation. The School of Natural Science has demonstrated through centuries of experiment that there are no tricksters nor moral degenerates within the 'Temple of Spiritual Light,' that there is no subterranean rear entrance, and that all who reach its sanctum sanctorum must do so by way of the front door, and then only after having met and complied with every section and every requirement of the Law of Light. Each individual admitted to its sacred precincts has come 'of his own free will and accord.' He has given 'the right knock." He has proven beyond all question that he is 'duly and truly prepared, worthy and well qualified,' and that upon his own merit alone he is entitled to 'enter and be received in due and ancient form.' "

It is a matter of congratulation that you have entered upon your Masonic career. You have entered upon a most serious and important undertaking—one in which to succeed you must exert the highest powers and faculties of your being for many years. But the reward is well worth the struggle—in fact, there is no other course open to you if you would reach true happiness here or hereafter.

It is useless to attempt to teach you any more than you wish to know and have earned the right to know. Hence, to undertake here to give you a complete exposition of Masonic symbolism and philosophy would confuse you. Besides, others have already gathered this knowledge and it is yours for the asking and the seeking. Masonry places her symbols before you—read them for yourself. She lays out her most precious treasures where the careful and worthy searcher can find them—if you cannot see them, be not discouraged, they will be there whenever you can get your sight properly adjusted. But —"Work, for the night cometh when no man can work."

And ever remember that the Great Friends and Helpers of Mankind stand ready, willing, and glad to give you all the light you can receive; while your brethren of the fraternity will cheerfully give to you of their store whenever you ask them. For they know when the final analysis is made, that it is giving, cheerful, willing, unselfish giving, that makes life worth living and leads to happiness and growth, while he who withholds more than is meet, tendeth to poverty.

THE APRON

There could be no better advise to men who are taking, their first step in Masonry, than that they should take due heed of all that upon which they enter. You have entered as apprentices into the greatest school of morality and spiritual knowledge to be found in the world by men who are as unprepared as you are. Masonry is the school in which you are taught how scientifically to live your life in accordance with the will of God, and how to regulate your conduct so that every act, word and thought shall be in harmony with the divine laws. By a cheerful and conscientious compliance with those laws and with the precepts of Masonry you will reach the point where death will have no terrors; where, when the call comes, you can, without fear and without improper regret, "draw the drapery of your couch about you and lie down to pleasant dreams!" where your ears will be attuned to the harmony of the spheres and your eyes will see the light which "never was on land or sea." By a cheerful compliance with the laws and precepts of Masonry you will reach such a point of development as you cannot believe even to exist in your present condition and with your present knowledge.

Masonry teaches by signs, symbols and ceremonies. Every word, motion, and even your very foot-prints since you first appeared at the door of this lodge room have been full of a profound meaning; and these very words, motions and steps, together with the symbols which you see displayed about you, have hidden in them that mighty wisdom which was revealed by the Great Creator to the men who lived before the flood—the primitive revelation which guided the footsteps of the ancestors of the patriarchs. When you come to see and to understand the beautiful and yet simple system of Masonic philosophy you will find a new happiness and every leaf and stone will contain for you a new delight.

It is impossible for me to give you, in a brief discourse, any explanation of many of these most important symbols. Therefore, we are compelled to leave for future study the plumb, the level, the square, the compasses, the Holy Bible, the pillars, the altar and many other of the symbols of Masonry, and we shall confine ourselves to the Apron, which is perhaps the oldest of all symbols. After the Fall, as it is called, in the Garden of Eden, Adam and Eve made for themselves aprons of leaves, and the girdle and apron have ever been used as symbols of profound truths. The deepest of these meanings you are not perhaps capable of understanding, as to know all the meaning of the apron would require a most extended knowledge of ancient religions, ancient philosophies, astronomy, geometry, history and ethnology, and as you are just come to us from the outer darkness, to throw upon you too much light would have the effect that too much light ever has—it would blind you and would be worse than the darkness from whence you came. However, some of the external meanings of the Apron can be given to you and may be the means of inducing you to seek for the further and deeper significations of this wonderful symbol. Pulling up the bib and pulling down the skirt you see a triangle with the point upward and a square. The square in this aspect of the Apron symbolizes matter, physical matter, the earth and the appetites and passions which belong to the physical body. The square in its various aspects and forms has many other meanings which you will learn when you are entitled to know them. The equilateral triangle with the point uppermost, symbolizes God in existence, while the right angle triangle, such as this is, with the point uppermost, signifies God in action and also the works of God and as man is considered to be among His greatest works it signifies the soul of man which is a spark from God. This is sometimes represented by a flame, the flame representing the triple nature of man, the fire, the light and the heat, representing the soul, the spirit and the body—three in one—and the point being upward as in a flame, indicates aspiration. To quote from the old hymn:

"Rivers to the ocean run,
    Nor stay in all their course;
Fire, ascending, seeks the Sun,
    Both speed them to their source.
"So the soul that's born of God
    Longs to see His Heavenly face;
Upward tends to His abode,
    To rest in His embrace."

In the Apron you thus see the representation of the soul and spirit in the triangle reaching upward to the highest things and the body, represented by the square, which holds it down to the earth.

It is the purpose and object of Masonry to teach you how to conform your life by the practice of the virtues of morality—honesty, charity, brotherly love, relief, truth, purity in heart and thought, so that the body may be raised to a higher rate of vibration, a higher condition, and be made a fit dwelling place for the Mighty Spirit, the spark from the divine fire which the Great Creator placed there at your birth. In order that this body may be a fit temple for God, you must cleanse and purify, removing from it every trace of intentional wrongdoing and making it clean and sweet and pure and holy, so that the glory of God may descend upon it and illuminate it, and that you may become a beacon for the guidance of all those who are seeking light.

You may think that this is an ideal and not capable of practical demonstration. You may be surprised to learn that the half has not been told you of the capabilities of the human soul for development, growth and understanding, and that in the course of one short human life you can reach to heights which in your present condition you are incapable of conceiving.

Masonry is a scientific school. It does not depend upon theory, but every single point of its instruction has been tested by the experience of millions of men in all ages of the world. Not a single man ever lived in accordance with the Masonic tenets that did not get accurately, scientifically and impartially the absolute compensation for every single good act of his life. And there can be no safe, sane or permanent spiritual growth except on the lines laid down by Masonry. Because the teachings of Masonry are founded on the eternal truth.

Masonry has known for thousands of years that the thoughts of the heart make us what we are, and that it is possible for man to control these thoughts, to keep out the bad and call in the good and by controlling those thoughts we can control every act of our lives and be no longer mere derelicts tossed about and blown hither and yon by every passing wind, but we can move forward grandly, steadily and irresistibly toward that goal of happiness which can be reached only as the result and reward of honest effort.

There is another meaning of the Apron. The square is used to symbolize the receiving faculties, and the triangle the giving powers. In this Apron you see your life history in that heretofore you have received far more than you have given. Masonry has long ago discovered that happiness consists in giving not less than we receive. Heretofore you have received more benefits than you have conferred, but by this symbol you are told that you cannot keep this up. You must confer at least as much as you receive. Emerson says in his wonderful essay on Compensation, which I would here commend to your attention: "Benefit is the end of nature. But for every benefit which you receive, a tax is levied. He is great who confers the most benefits. He is base—and that is the one base thing in the universe—to receive favors and render none. In the order of nature we cannot render benefits to those from whom we receive them, or only seldom. But the benefits we receive must be rendered again, line for line, deed for deed, cent for cent, to somebody."

Heretofore Masonry has had no concern with your conduct. It has had no obligation to you, and you have had none to it. You are now accepted into membership in the oldest society or association in the world, and from the moment of your reception here, every member of that society throughout the world owes you obligations of vast importance. Your reception here may be truly said to be the greatest benefit which has ever been conferred upon you in your whole life. Do not forget that from this moment you owe to Masonry a most sacred duty. This Apron, which is presented to you freely by the lodge to be your own property, and which we trust you will preserve and cherish until it shall be laid at last about you when your body shall be placed in the grave—this Apron, for the first time tied about your waist tonight, is the emblem of purity and innocence. Not the innocence of the infant who cannot think evil, nor, if he could, can he carry it into effect, but the innocence of the strong man, that innocence which is better expressed by the word "harmlessness;" the innocence of him who knows wrong and can do it, yet chooses the right because it is right.

This Apron you may remove when you leave the lodge room, but symbolically it will ever be tied about you, and to your dying day you can never remove the obligation which this garment symbolizes. If you disgrace it by dishonesty, stain it by impurity or by any of those things which are immoral, you will be inexpressibly base, for you will violate your own most sacred promise and also —and now since you know it, it will be a deliberate violation—of the fundamental laws of nature and of God.

But I see you are thinking that some Masons do not live as I have indicated they should, and that if they do not live right, you, too, can be excused for failure to perform your duties and discharge your obligations. Yes, my brother, some men fail to do right, and this is found not only among Masons, but among other classes as well.

But do you think it any excuse for the murderer that other men have committed murder, or to the thief that other men steal, or to the deserter that others have basely left their duty in the face of danger? No, my friend, you are now to try to live by higher rules; not to be as good or better than others, but to be better than yourself.

Purify your heart, therefore, my brother. And remember that purity of heart is a condition to happiness and spiritual growth. For when the great day of judgment shall come, if you have to offer to the Most High for a temple and dwelling place, only a mind full of lust and filthy imaginings and a body debased by impurity and evil practices, what will be your condition? If instead of a fit dwelling place, you can offer to the King of all the earth and sky but a pig wallow, will you not in that day call upon the mountains and the rocks to fall upon you and hide you from the face of Him that sitteth on the throne?

But if you can truly say on that day, "Dear Lord, here is myself, as a living temple, swept and garnished by labors for others, purified both within and without by love, charity, and truth, plumbed by the plumb of justice and right, level with the level of brotherly love and humility, and square with the square of virtue," then indeed will the Divine Spirit enter into your heart and dwell there and give you peace.

Therefore, again let me admonish you, guard thy heart with all diligence, for out of it are issues of life and death.

And may our Father help you in your efforts.

THE WINDING STAIRS

Having been passed to the degree of Fellowcraft, you have now symbolically acquired the right to enter the middle chamber of King Solomon's Temple. You start on the chart at the outer entrance. Here you see a black and white or mosaic pavement, similar to those used by the ancients in their palaces and temples. You may be told that King Solomon's Temple had such a floor or pavement, but in I. Kings, VI:15, we are told that the floor of the temple was of fir wood. It is probable, however, that the floor of the outer porch may have been of mosaic, in accordance with ancient custom.

This mosaic pavement is a reminder of the duad, the doctrine of dualism, or opposites, of equilibrium, of the dual nature of man, matter and spirit. The black and white mixed symbolize good and evil and the manner in which they are mingled in all human affairs. Two is the symbol of instability. To-day we may stand on the height of prosperity, ignorant that to-morrow we may be cast into adversity and low estate. From the contemplation of this symbol, we learn to walk humbly, ever remembering that pride in our possessions, our learning, our influence, or any earthly thing, is unbecoming, for all these things are gifts from God, and we should ever hold them as His stewards, entrusted with these blessings that we may use them for the good of our brother. For the Fatherhood of God being a tenet of our faith, the brotherhood of man follows as an irresistible conclusion. All men are our brothers, children of the same Father, and we should ever remember this in our dealings with the weak and unfortunate whom God may send to us to give us an opportunity to show our love for Him and our trust in His goodness, and, also, possibly, our worthiness to receive further favors from Him. We should never rejoice when others fall into shame or misfortune, but should humbly reflect that but for the mercy of God, we too, might be in the same condition.

This mosaic pavement also teaches us hope, for it indicates that no matter how low or miserable we may seem to be, we have but to move bravely forward, trusting in God, and we are sure to come into the light again and our happiness will be but the greater for our former misery.

On each side of this mosaic pavement, in your Masonic chart for this degree, you see the two pillars, symbolic of many things, which we will leave at this time for you to study over yourself. Passing through between these pillars you discover the beginning of a winding flight of steps, consisting of three, five and seven steps, symbolic of the course of life of those who live right, and leading upward into the middle chamber. Many are the symbolic meanings of these stairs and much delight will be yours in tracing them. Here we can, for reasons already assigned, but give you the outer or more simple meanings.

On the first three steps you see the emblems of the plumb, the level, and the square, which also belong to the stations of the Junior Warden, Senior Warden, and Master. The plumb here signifies uprightness, justice, and also has other meanings. Here it may be said to indicate that rectitude of mind and conduct which should ever distinguish the true Mason. The level teaches equality, such as should ever prevail in the lodge; brotherly love, because we are brothers; and humility, because we are all equal in the eyes of God; no matter what estate it hath pleased Him to bestow upon us. The square here teaches morality and virtue; being called a right angle it symbolizes right conduct. It also symbolizes the apparent conflict between God's will (the good of all His creatures) and God's works (the so-called evils of existence, the presence of sin, sorrow, and suffering in the world). These things cannot be reconciled by either reason or science, but by faith they can be and are harmonized and recognized as part of the plan of the Great Creator.

These three instruments are given you in this degree for use in your daily life. Whenever anything is to be done, before you act, gauge your conduct by these three. Ask yourself, first, is what I am about to do, just, according to the plumb; is it brotherly, or kind, according to the level; is it right, or what would please God, according to the square. And if the course you propose fits in with these three, you may unhesitatingly follow it, for justice, kindness, right, and truth will never lead you far wrong, no matter how poor your eyesight.

Also, you will note that things which always keep on the same level never progress, but die; for Nature shows you that to live you must move upward. But when you apply the square of right conduct to the dead level of mere animal existence, then is formed the plumb, the living perpendicular, emblem of life and upward growth, immortality. And it needs but Faith to make this combination work out for you a far more exceeding and eternal weight of glory. Note also that virtue, right living, is represented by an angle of ninety degrees, while love, brotherly love, unselfish love, the level, is twice as much. Remember, too, that "love is the fulfilling of the law."

Read now another lesson from these three symbols: Live a life of morality, kindness and brotherly love, and you will receive immortality.

And these three symbols on the first three steps also indicate to you that they are the foundation of spiritual growth, and whenever you leave either out of your life, the foundation is destroyed and your house must fall.

The number three is a sacred number, that mysterious number which "plays so great a part in the traditions of Asia, and the philosophy of Plato, image of the Supreme Being * * * to the Philosophers, the most excellent and favorite number; a mysterious type, revered by all antiquity, and consecrated in the Mysteries; wherefore there are but three essential degrees among Masons; who venerate, in the triangle, the most august mystery, that of the Sacred Triad, object of their homage and study." Three also referred to harmony, friendship, peace, concord, and temperance; and was so highly esteemed among the Pythagoreans that they called it perfect harmony. The appearances of this mysterious number in the Masonic signs, symbols, and ceremonies are almost innumerable, and it will be a good exercise for you to see how many times you can discover this symbol in them, as it would take too much time and space to undertake here to give even a part of them to you. The continued reproduction of this number three is not an accident, but has a profound meaning, and, as has already been explained to you, one that you must find for yourself.

Having climbed up the first three steps, and laid the foundation of your Masonic building, you see now a flight of five steps, replete also with profound meaning. For five is also a sacred number, ever found in connection with two, and with seven. Jesus is said to have fed the multitude with five loaves and two fishes, and of the fragments there remained twelve baskets, that is five and seven. The five steps show on one side the five orders of architecture, and on the other the five human senses. Now when you hear of a "sacred" number, you think probably that that means nothing to you personally, but stop and consider a moment. This number five is engraven in your being more than once. Examine yourself, and you find five fingers, five toes, and five avenues through which the outside world can communicate with that mysterious being who sits in the center of your consciousness and receives and translates—no man knows how—the various messages carried to the brain by the nerves from the outside world. Of these five senses two, tasting and smelling, are said to be acted on directly by material substances; while three, the most important in Masonry, are acted on by vibrations of matter, air and ether. These last are feeling, hearing, and seeing, and are said to be most important because by seeing you see the sign, by hearing you hear the word, and by feeling you can tell a brother in the darkness as well as in the light.

My brothers, he who is to rise must first learn to control himself, and must not allow those merely animal passions and appetites, the gratification of the five senses, or any of them, to govern, control, or even to affect his conduct. The soul, the divine part of man, must be the master, and must control the thoughts and not allow them to dwell on mere animal pleasures, such as we share with the brute. What happiness can there be for him who, when old age comes, discovers that he has devoted his life to cultivating and encouraging desires and appetites of the body, now weakened and enfeebled with age—a body that he must soon leave as a worn-out garment; and he has in his mind all these lusts and passions, governing his whole thought, but has not in his body the power of satisfying these appetites or even taking pleasure in them. When the servant, the body, governs the house, what do we think of the Master? What more pitiable than the old worn out devotee of pleasure. For do not forget that passion means suffering always and suffering must follow the uncontrolled gratification of any passion or appetite.

Remember now thy Creator in the days of thy youth, when the evil days come not, nor the years draw nigh when thou shalt say I have no pleasure in them.

Masonry gives you this beautiful symbolic lesson— you must put these animal appetites, your senses, your passions, your lusts, beneath your feet, and you can rise only on and over them to spiritual development. And when you have done this, subdued your passions, gained control and mastery over your thoughts, and lived a life of rectitude in thought, word, and deed, then only will

you discover what is meant by that text in Scripture—
"The stone which the builders rejected is become the
head of the corner."

You are not, however, to despise or mistreat your
body in order to control it, as some have mistakenly done
in what they thought was the practice of religion, for
Masonry considers your body a temple, the dwelling
place of that divine spark called the soul. And it is your
duty to keep that temple pure and holy and clean, that
that divine spark may be worthily housed. Masons should
therefore, learn to control their actions, their words, and
even their thoughts. For thoughts are things, and he
who encourages evil thoughts in his mind, even though
he may never intend to put them in practice, may (and
almost certainly will) set in motion an evil force, strong
enough in time to destroy him utterly. Guard thy heart
therefore with all diligence, for out of it are the issues
of life and death.

So, we learn that each appetite and passion, when
properly controlled, and wisely directed, has its own
constructive value in the building of character; and that
we can develop spiritually only by rising upon the ashes
of our dead selves to the upper heights of Mastership.

"Freemasonry is the subjugation of the Human that is
in man by the Divine; the Conquest of the Appetites and
Passions by the Moral Sense and the Reason; a continued
effort, struggle, and warfare of the Spiritual against the
Material and Sensual. That victory when it has been
achieved and secured, and the conqueror may rest upon
his shield and wear the well-earned laurels, is the true
Holy Empire." The corn, wine and oil that were anci-
ently the wages of a fellow-craft, symbolize but a small
part of the reward that is his who gains this victory, and
becomes the ruler over this Empire.

Seven steps now appear before us each bearing the
name of one of the liberal arts and sciences; and by the
number seven, as applied to the arts and sciences, is symbolized all the arts and sciences and the whole body of
knowledge, learning, science, and wisdom, and not
merely those particular arts and sciences named on the
seven steps.

Seven is a particularly sacred number, having appeared in the religious and philosophical system of the

entire ancient world. It also is engraved in your very being, for at the age of seven you first showed understanding, at the age of fourteen puberty is generally reached, at the age of twenty-one manhood is recognized, at the age of twenty-eight full growth attained, and at the age of thirty-five, physical vigor is highest, at forty-two, this begins to decline; at forty-nine man should have reached the height of intellectual strength; and at seventy he has reached the ordinary limit of human life. These figures are not merely arbitrary, but the result of study and observation of men everywhere.

So, seven days constituted the entire period of creation, seven colors are found in the rainbow, of which three are primary; seven days in the week; seven lamps in the great candlestick of the Tabernacle and Temple; the seventh year was a Sabbath of rest, and the year after the seven times seventh year was the year of Jubilee; Jericho fell when seven priests, with seven trumpets, made the circuit of the city on seven successive days— once each day for six days, and seven times on the seventh; and time is lacking to give you all the instances of the use of seven in sacred literature and in the esoteric writings. "The seven eyes of the Lord," says Zechariah, "run to and fro through the whole earth." The ladder of the ancients (supposed to be that which Jacob saw in his dream, with the angels ascending and descending) symbolized the seven mystic spheres: the Moon, Mercury, Venus, the Sun, Mars, Jupiter and Saturn; down which the souls of men came in their progress towards the earth, taking from each planet its particular characteristic; and up which men must climb back towards God, leaving at each planet the earthly or lower attraction which they no longer need; the seven-fold purification being symbolized by the seven steps of King Solomon's Temple, which also symbolized the purification mentioned in the Kabalah and the Hermetic writings.

We owe the particular methods of instruction in this degree to Pythagoras, one of our ancient Masters. He taught "the mathematics, as a medium whereby to prove the existence of God from observation and by means of reason; grammar, rhetoric, and logic, to cultivate and improve that reason; arithmetic, because he conceived that the ultimate benefits of men consisted in the science of numbers; that geometry, music, and astronomy, because he conceived that man is indebted to them for a knowledge of what is really good and useful."

"He taught the true method of obtaining a knowledge of the Divine laws, to purify the soul from its imperfections, to search for truth, and to practice virtue; thus imitating the perfection of God. He thought his system vain if it did not contribute to expel vice and introduce virtue into the mind. He taught that the two most excellent things were, to speak the truth, and to render benefits to one another." Many other wonderful things were taught by Pythagoras, and also, our modern Masonry but imperfectly reproduces his lectures, to its great loss.

These seven steps teach us that we should enlarge our minds and hearts by a study of all the arts and sciences, learning all we can of Nature, and, through it, of Nature's God; that the true Mason should have his mind polished and adorned by both useful knowledge and by those other pleasing and humanizing arts, such as music. And this can all be done if you will quit trying to treat time as your enemy, and using every art to "kill time," as the uninitiated do, and will utilize every spare moment for the enlightening of your mind and the acquisition of wisdom, for "wisdom is the principal thing, therefore, get wisdom, and with all thy getting, get understanding."

Now, my brother, having reached the summit of our journey, let us pause and reflect upon what we have learned, and impress upon our hearts the lessons taught by our recent experience. There is one God, and we are all His children, whom He loves and watches over with tender care. All men are our brothers. Our bodies are the living Temples of God, of which King Solomon's Temple was but a symbol, and we must not profane them by thought, word, or act. We must control our appetites and passions with this aim ever before us. The result will be real and lasting happiness, here and hereafter.

And now remember what I told you before; that Masonry is never dogmatic. You are at liberty, if you choose, to reject all the interpretations I have given you of the Masonic symbols, and to adopt in their place your own interpretations; or you may accept part of what I have given and take your own opinions for the rest. I have no right to criticise you for your beliefs nor have you the right to fall out with me if I do not believe as you do. It is not what we believe that counts in estimating our character, it is what we do. The Master said: "Whosoever shall do the will of my Father which is in heaven, the same is my brother, and sister, and mother."

Study the symbols of Masonry, and dig deep in the rubbish of the Temple for the great truths buried there. They are well worth your digging and search. But the study of symbols, without practically applying them to your life, is a mere intellectual exercise that will result in more trouble than profit to you if you merely seek to understand without living up to them. As soon as you learn what is meant by a symbol, you must make it a part of your life, let it be the rule and guide of your heart, drink it as water from a pure spring, feed your soul upon it, and you will grow in knowledge of a deeper meaning, while your soul will reach further upward towards the stars and the Divine knowledge they typify. For wisdom is a growth of the soul, and the reward of labor and effort, not to be bought except by its equal value in sacrifice. Each time that you have progressed, if you will look back, you have had to lay upon the altar of sacrifice, something that represented the labor of your hands and heart, symbolizing that you would repay by labor for your brethren and humanity the benefit you had been freely given.

But before you set out upon the daily application of Masonic knowledge to your life and labors, let me warn you of the dangers. It is not an idle warning when we are told: "Let him that hath put his hand to the plough, not look back." If you start out upon the discharge of your obligations to God and Nature, according to the Masonic plan, and after making the start, lack the necessary courage and determination to persist, your case will be more desperate and your punishment greater than if you had never seen the light. A river lies before you and must be crossed. If you have not the courage and resolution to cross it, if you are going up and down its banks looking for an easy place to get over, beware lest your life be lost because of your inability to prove yourself entitled to pass.

But let me beseech you, neglect not this glorious opportunity and these glorious privileges offered you by Masonry, "Happy is the man that findeth wisdom, and the man that getteth understanding. For the merchandise of it is better than the merchandise of silver, and the gain thereof than fine gold. She is more precious than rubies; and all the things thou canst desire are not to be compared unto her. Length of days is in her right hand; and in her left hand riches and honour. Her ways are ways of pleasantness, and all her paths are peace."

"Then shall thou walk in thy way safely, and thy foot shall not stumble. When thou liest down thou shalt not be afraid: yea, thou shalt lie down, and thy sleep shall be sweet."

THE FELLOW-CRAFT DEGREE

My brothers, you have been passed to the second degree of Masonry, and for the second time you have been warned to take due heed of that upon which you were entering. The warning was well given. You have taken the second step towards that light which will shine forever. You have reached the second stage on the pathway that, followed truly, leads to immortality.

Masonry, my brothers, teaches by symbols. In this it but follows the ancient method of teaching, the most ancient method known. Every man is free to interpret the symbols of Masonry for himself, more, he is expected to do so; and you are at liberty to accept or reject whatever I or any one may tell you of the meaning of our symbols.

This was the method of teaching followed by our Master Pythagoras, who in Egypt learned the ancient Mysteries.

This is the method of Nature, and is the only way to convey to every soul that exact degree of light that he is ready and able to receive.

God teaches by symbols. To learn to interpret the symbols of Nature is to know. Be careful that you do not mistake, but remember that "the letter killeth, it is the spirit that giveth life."

All around us we see this solid earth, a reality. On her bosom we behold the activities of Nature, daily working miracles before our eyes. We can weigh and measure the earth, analyze its surface, and determine its constituents; we can map out its course through the universe, and locate its place among the stars for any day in the next million years; but this is knowledge of material things; and we would really know but little if our knowledge were confined merely to the material, and we would have little happiness if we thought that all the varied changes and forces of the universe were but the effects of material causes. Those who so think have as a doctrine the denial of the evidence of their own hearts—a doctrine that never yet brought happiness or peace.

The truth, as we are told in the Harmonic Series, that all matter is but the outward manifestation of a spiritual counterpart or original, and that there is no force but is a spiritual force.

Matter is constantly changing, it is spirit alone that can defy the gnawing tooth of time and say: "O Death, where is thy sting? O grave, where is thy victory?"

Hence those who are materialists base their beliefs and found their hopes on what is sure to change and to disappoint; but the Mason is taught to fix his eyes on the eternal and unchanging truths of morality, and by the practice of moral principles to earn that wisdom which neither moth nor rust can corrupt and which thieves cannot break through and steal. Plant your feet on the eternal verities, and all the storms and spirits of Hell cannot prevail against you.

As you were told just now, Nature teaches by symbols. Every rock and stone, every tree and flower, every bird and every star, every stream and ocean, is a symbol of spiritual truth.

The brilliant butterfly, arising from its grave and prison house, woven by itself, which it entered as an ugly worm, has for ages been a symbol of the resurrection. The Greeks called the butterfly Psyche, this being also their name for the soul. From this word we get psychology, psychic, and all such terms. This is one of the symbols of Nature that has brought hope and comfort to many a weary soul.

One of the most ancient religious systems taught the sacred character of the North or Pole star, that it was divine, never changing, never moving, ever found in the center of the heavens. This religion, it is said, is dimly seen in the works of this particular degree. The Swastika is the emblem of this ancient belief. So old is this doctrine of reverence for the Pole star, that it is said to date further back than the worship of the sun; and sun-worship it is said, must have existed for more than 25,500 years, as can be ascertained by a study of ancient monuments and a comparison of their hieroglyphics with the recession of the equinoxes.

The Pole star was doubtless but a symbol of the eternal, immutable, unchanging God, as the Sun was the giver of life and light to the world and so a symbol of the Light of the World, God, who gives light to all men and to all creation.

Idolatry comes when men forget or lose the hidden interpretation of the symbols and worship the sign for that concealed by and represented in the sign. There have been North-star worshippers and for ages there have been worshippers who know not that they have for the object of their adoration but a symbol—a symbol of the Unchangeable God, the Giver of Light and Life, the Supreme Light.

However idolatry is not confined to sun worshippers, nor to star worshippers, nor to those who bow down to idols of wood and stone.

Most men are idolaters. Some worship place, power and popularity; others worship wealth and others excitement. The most foolish worship their own bodies, and devote their energies to gratifying the appetites of what was given merely as an instrument of the soul. These are slaves of their appetites and passions, and so deeply are some enslaved that they even boast that they cannot keep from eating too much of certain foods, or that they cannot stop tobacco, liquor, drug habits. In other words they seem to be proud that the servant controls what should be the master. But the more the body is pampered and its desires gratified, the less pleasure can be derived from such gratification and such pleasures will certainly pall and grow wearisome as age approaches and the body becoming worn out and decayed is preparing for its certain abandonment. Even the most unthinking man cannot escape the knowledge that one day he, too, must lay down this physical flesh, as a workman discards an outworn tool, and must take up life in another sphere; but how few are preparing for this momentous change? What then will the worshipper of his body worship? Where will he find pleasure, and where will he hide his unworthiness? What will he be able to offer as a password to the celestial Lodge, in which unselfishness and purity and self-control are the ruling principles; in which earthly power, wealth, and physical pleasures have no place or part, having been left in the ante-room—upon the earth, with the discarded physical body of the earthly existence?

One of the principal symbols of Masonry is the Temple of Solomon, on which for seven years, six days in each week, we are told, there labored faithfully 80,000 entered apprentices, 70,000 fellow crafts, and 3,300 Master Masons, and three Grand Masters. Yet, this building when completed was less than 90 feet long, 45 feet wide and 45 feet high. Here is a wonderful symbol, each particular conveying its own meaning, yet the whole symbolizing something that embraces all the rest.

An examination of the description of this wonderful Temple will show that it was a double cube. It was thus a symbol of that which was also represented by the ark of the covenant carried before the children of Israel as they journeyed through the desert—from Egypt, the land of slavery and darkness, to Canaan, the Promised Land of Liberty and Light. By following faithfully the idea of one God, supreme and eternal, the Hebrews were in a few generations, it appears, elevated from the condition of toiling slaves to that of lawgivers and teachers for a thousand generations, not only of their own people but for the whole world. The Jews never forgot that the Temple was but a symbol and so they have preserved a wonderful system of morality and philosophy and a knowledge of spiritual things superior to that of any western people.

But we must not look to our Loving All-Fadir (All-Father), as our Northern ancestors called the Great Architect of the Universe alone for light. Investigation and study will show that all the ancient nations knew more or less of the truth concealed in the symbols of Masonry; that, many divinely inspired teachers came to show the world the light, both among the ancient peoples, and that such teachers are to be found today. Seek and ye shall find. Knock and it shall be opened unto you. Ask and ye shall receive. Do not fear that you will be left in darkness any longer than you deserve, for as soon as you can give the right knock, as soon as you have earned the right to know, then you will know in that very instant.

To know the truth you have but to live right—to do always what you honestly believe is right—and to keep searching and looking for the light. Look about you and see in how many ways God has revealed His kindness and love. Never the sun went down at night to rise again upon a fairer and rosier dawn but we find a lesson of courage and hope in adversity, and a promise as strong as if sealed with His hand—as it is—that in darkness and adversity He is but preparing better things for to-morrow.

Never the winter stripped the trees of their leaves and fields of their herbage but brought us the lesson that no matter how we may fall on bleak and barren days, no matter how ragged and bitter our lot, there is already on the way a smiling and joyous spring and a flower-scented summer, and He will bring them to us as surely as the stars go on their courses. Hope and Trust are taught by these symbols.

Never a sower went forth to sow but we are reminded of the Law of Compensation: "Whatsoever a man soweth, that shall he also reap." Beware how you sow aught but good seed.

Never a flower lifts its head to the sun, shedding its fragrance upon all around, nor a tiny bird raises its hymn of praise to the Great Creator, but teaches us the lesson of sincerity and contentment. The violet does not seek to imitate the sunflower, nor the wren the eagle; so let us live our lives each day, simply and earnestly, seeking to please God rather than man, seeking to do what He made us to do, not to gratify our ambitions, our avarice, our vanity, nor our appetites. These things pass away, but Truth and Right will never pass away, and he who would enjoy life to its fullest capacity must work by the immutable principles of morality. "Morality," says The Great Work, "is the established harmonic relation between man as an individual intelligence and the constructive principle of his own being."

These simple things in Nature also teach us that we can be in harmony with the Creator: "He that made the eye, shall He not see? and He that made the ear, shall He not hear?"

The Temple of Solomon is a symbol to teach, among other lessons, that no labor or care is too great to fit our hearts and minds as living temples for the dwelling places of the Most High. That we must not profane the Holy of Holies of our own heart by bad thoughts or improper desires, but must keep it pure as He is pure.

The two pillars at the entrance signify the principles of fixity and motion, attraction and repulsion, which hold the universe together and guide the stars in their courses.

The mosaic pavement symbolizes among other things the most secret doctrine as to the constitution of matter, and teaches us that life is made up of bright and dark, good and evil, while the blazing star in the center teaches, among other things, that he who fixes his eyes on the heavens and guides his steps by the divine light will be little troubled by what goes on around him upon the earth.

The symbols upon the first three steps teach us to found our lives and test our actions by the square of virtue, the plumb of justice, and the level of brotherly kindness, without which no enduring temple of human character can be built.

When we have stationed ourselves upon this foundation we find in the five steps the lesson that until a man has learned to subdue his passions, he can never rise spiritually; that in order to rise to the heights of moral and spiritual development, we must put the body under control, under our very feet, so to speak; and that when we have learned to do so, then all the fields of knowledge and science will be open to us and all the powers of such knowledge at our command.

This knowledge of all the forces of nature is symbolized by the seven steps that come next. Seven being the number symbolical of perfection, the seven liberal arts and sciences typify all the circle of arts, science, and knowledge, of which the grandest of all is Geometry. Geometry was originally synonymous with Masonry, as our ancient Masters knew and understood the principles of design, and that God built the universe upon geometrical designs and patterns. "God geometrizes."

All this knowledge is offered you freely, upon condition only that you prove yourself worthy. How? do you say? By living each day a life of morality, in its proper sense, in virtue, brotherly love and justice towards all creatures; even including our little brothers, the brute beasts. By trying each day to make some man wiser and happier. By setting to all men an example of right conduct, rectitude and manliness. By guiding your life by the Pole star of Truth and Right. By ever remembering that God is your father and all men your brothers. By being a true Mason and true man.

THREE EXCELLENT JEWELS

"The attentive ear receives the sound from the instructive tongue, and the mysteries of Masonry are safely lodged in the repository of faithful breasts."

Here we have an epitome of Masonic duties and obligations. First, before we can teach, we used to think, we must learn; now in order to learn, we must teach. Next, we used to think, before we can give, we must receive; now, we know that in order to receive, we must first give. Lastly, in all cases, we must know to be silent. We are faithful to our duties only when we give at least as much as we receive; for there is no other way by which to appropriate Truth, or call it our own.

Works of charity, considered Masonically, are to be performed by the mouth, the ear, the hand, the knee, and the foot. Each of these has its own constructive value in building character; and each has its destructive tendency. But that charity which keeps silent as to all matters improper to be revealed, is the greatest charity of all.

The first obligation of every man who has a knowledge of truth in any degree is secrecy—not to divulge his knowledge to any who will use it wrongly; in other words, not to communicate it but to those who are duly and truly prepared, worthy and well qualified. The secrets of science, when known by bad men, increase their power to do evil. Masonry is science of the highest type; and its knowledge should be transmitted with discretion.

This duty of secrecy applies to all the transactions of the Lodge. The Old Charges say "Yee shall keep truly all the counsell that ought to bee kept in the way of Masonhood, and all the counsell of the Lodge." Masons are under obligation to keep secret all that occurs in the Lodge, unless it is illegal or against Masonic law and usage; and then it is to be communicated only to a superior body for correction. Family, friends, and acquaintances have no right to know the private transactions of the different Masonic assemblies. If this obligation were always recognized and obeyed, how many heart burnings and jealousies, how many enmities and dislikes, how many reproaches against Masonry, would not now exist.

The obligation of secrecy extends further, however, than to the mere transactions of the Lodge and the modes of recognition. Masonry, as its foremost advocates and teachers contend, is the repository of the secrets of the ancients; the fountain head of forgotten knowledge; the treasure house in which is hidden the wisdom that guided the steps of all the ancient Masters of the Royal Secret; the Living Rock from which is to flow the Water of Life for the healing of the nations. Those who have the custody of this knowledge should be very careful to whom it is entrusted. Improvement in Masonry can be effected only by learning to be silent. Pythagoras did not require five years' silence of his students arbitrarily, but from principle. All the ancient writings are full of warnings against the abuse of the power of speech. Eliphaz mentioned as the three greatest of the seven troubles that afflict mankind "famine, the sword, the scourge of the tongue." So we read in the Scriptures: "What man desireth life? Keep thy tongue from evil and thy lips from speaking guile." "Death and life are in the power of the tongue." "Whoso keepeth his mouth and tongue, keepeth his soul from troubles." "A lying tongue is but for a moment."

Likewise, the New Testament is full of warning and advice about the tongue. "It is an unruly evil, full of deadly poison." "If any man among you seem to be religious, and bridleth not his tongue, but deceiveth his own heart, this man's religion is vain." "If any man offend not in words, the same is a perfect man, and able also to bridle the whole body."

"Too much talking," says General Albert Pike, "like too much thinking, destroys the power of action. In human nature the thought is only made perfect by deed. Silence is the mother of both."

"Remember that each single word you utter will rise up against you on the day of judgment." "Though life is short, Thought, and the influence of what we do or say, are immortal." Thus Dr. Guthrie, in "Regeneration."

Speech consists of vibrations of the atmosphere. These vibrations are communicated to the solids and liquids of the earth; and through solids and liquids new vibrations are set up, transmitting the word through the ether as light and electric impulses, which go out in all directions through space. These new vibrations will never die. Nor will the sound waves ever cease to reverberate through the air. Weaker and weaker they certainly become, but mathematically it can be shown that they can never cease. Every stick and stone, every rock and tree, carries in its own bosom a record of all the vibrations of the universe. Even a small mineral or metallic body may thus become a memorial of all that has transpired around it. And to limitless wisdom and power these records are always open and legible. It is not an idle statement, therefore, to say that what we do and say are immortal in their consequences. Yet how few understand the importance of speech, the greater importance of silence.

"The spiritual man," says Dr. Guthrie, "will never utter a single word unless it be at the same time (1) necessary, (2) true, (3) loving, and (4) beautiful."

There is a deeper reason for silence. When the Divine Shining Ones, the Friends of Helpers of Mankind on the other side, vouchsafe to us spiritual knowledge through unusual experiences, the first impulse is to tell it. If we speak freely of these benefits, we are told, they will not be continued. Silence is one of the tests of Initiation, constantly repeated. Volubility is the offspring of Vanity, the greatest enemy of spiritual growth.

Moral laws, when seen by the Natural man, before he has gone far on the path of Initiation, appear inverted or reversed—backwards. They sound contradictory to human experience and to natural wisdom.

One of these laws is, that to learn we must first teach; to receive we must give; to have power to do, we must do.

So the first duty of the Mason is to teach the way of Life; to whisper words of wisdom; to give good counsel; to administer consolation in affliction; to live for others by sharing their sorrows and sadness. Many a wandering step is restrained by the timely warning, given in love and with discretion. Many a sad heart is gladdened and many a burden lightened by a fit word of sympathy. If we all spoke our sympathy instead of smothering it in our own bosoms, the world would be a much brighter place and smiles and sunshine more common. Silence is enjoined at proper times, and places, but the duty to speak is equally on all of us.

"Science is preserved by Silence, and perpetuated by Initiation. The Law of Silence is absolute and inviolable, only with respect to the uninitiated multitude. Science makes use of symbols; but for its transmission language also is indispensable; wherefore the Sages must sometimes speak. But when they speak, they do so, not to disclose or to explain, but to lead others to seek for and find the truths of science and the meanings of the symbols." So spoke our ancient Masters.

The instructive tongue, therefore conveys the message of duty to give the Truth in proper times and to proper persons,—those who will not abuse the knowledge. The attentive ear refers to the corresponding duty—to follow and obey the Truth wherever heard. For Truth not obeyed is a dangerous possession.

Now there are three kinds of obedience. The lowest is obedience from fear, or obedience to a superior force. When we obey from being forced to do so, in time obedience becomes habit. After we follow habit long enough, the principles that were first forced upon us, become part of our being, and are followed from affection. This introduces the obedience into the will, or positive principle. This explains why children should be forced to obey when young, thus forming habits of right living, which in time become changed into love for right conduct. The Truth thus sinks from the head, the mind, into the heart and breast, the daily life, and then into the bowels, the affections and ingrained principles, the very being. Only those who obey the law from love can be truly said to obey at all. "Not the hearers of the law * * * but the doers of the law shall be justified."

As man has greater spiritual powers than any animal so he has a greater range of sounds at his command, and so his affections and thoughts and sympathies are more harmoniously and clearly expressed. Likewise, his ear is attuned to a greater variety of sounds, and can more clearly differentiate and distinguish them. Many a man who has spoken rightly with his words, could not reach the affections of his hearers, because his words did not express his true feelings. The emotions of the soul cannot be hidden from the attentive ear, and no matter how moral and elevating the sentiments spoken, they fail to reach the heart if they are not felt by the speaker. This is the secret of eloquence. Also, it explains why some men speak such beautiful sentiments, approved by the mind, but fail to make converts or friends, leaving their hearers cold and unmoved. "Though I speak with the tongue of men and of angels, and have not charity (i. e., kindness and sincerity), I am become as sounding brass or a tinkling cymbal." How many public speakers have this "brassy" sound to their voices! But when the man of the heart and soul comes to speak, his words may be ungrammatical and his gestures ungainly, but the multitude recognizes the truth in his voice. The Ephraimites were detected by their voices. Many a warning of impending danger will be received by the attentive ear when not intended as such.

The breast contains the most vital parts of man, the heart and lungs, which refer to the will and the affections of the understanding. "When speaking of the natural man the breast signifies the conjunction of the natural good and truth, but, after his resurrection to newness of life upon the five points of fellowship, the breast signifies the conjunction of spiritual good and truth, which is mutual love or the lowest bond, that unites the universal heavens in one society consisting of innumerable parts, the laws and bonds of which cannot be broken."

"Mutual love, when represented by the breast, also signifies secrecy, which cannot be violated without profanation. For the foregoing reason, the secrets of a brother Master Mason are said to be as inviolable in the breast of a brother as they were in his before communicated, and, also for the foregoing reasons, no man can comprehend or be admitted by vision into a heavenly state, until he has conquered in spiritual temptations, represented in the Master's Degree."

"For these reasons, the Word of the Lord, which treats altogether of the Lord, the heavens, and the church, is written in correspondential and representative language, which at the same time treats of the celestial, spiritual and natural degrees. The natural degree only to a limited extent, being understood and comprehended by the natural man; but as he progresses in regeneration, there is an unfolding of the Word."

"As we increase in goodness and truth, our affection and understandings enlarge, and we perceive more clearly that all that is good and true belongs to the Lord, and that we are really, in ourselves, poor and destitute. To such belongs the kingdom of heaven." "Blessed are the poor in spirit; for theirs is the kingdom of heaven."

How many of our people to-day are living lives of intellectual starvation and heart poverty, filling themselves with the husks that are fit only for swine, closing their ears to the Inner Voice, forgetting that "He that turneth away his ear from hearing the law, even his prayer shall be abomination."

Far better to do as little Samuel was taught—say, "Speak, Lord, for thy servant heareth." Open your heart to Truth, let her guide you, and fear not to follow your guide. Truth never interferes with Religion, but with the interpretation of Religion by ignorance, ambition, or cunning, or by selfishness, vanity, or other unworthy motive. True Religion never fears the Light;—how can it, if it is leading us to the Light?

Science (i. e., Truth and Knowledge) and Religion ought ever to go hand in hand. Both depend upon Revelation. The only difference between them is in the manner of receiving Revelation. The Word of God is not confined to the Prophets, it is written in the Works of God, in all nature and the universe. Whenever the conclusions of Science conflict with the facts of Nature we reject, not Science, but the interpretation. All nature is composed of symbols. He who interprets these symbols for himself, humbly and faithfully, will never become an atheist. Atheists are the products of rejected Dogma.

"Revelation," said our ancient Masters, "is the WORD. The word, in fact, or speech, is the veil of Being, and the characteristic sign of life. Every form is the veil of a word, because the idea which is the mother of the word is the sole reason of existence of forms. Every figure is a character, and every character belongs and goes back to a word."

To hear, we must obey. Set your alarm clock for tomorrow, and, when it goes off, refuse to hear it; do this for a few days, and in a week, though it ring never so loudly, you will not be able to perceive the sound through your previous neglect. Take warning.

THE MASTER MASON'S DEGREE

Foreword

It is not expected that this article will give any new instructions to the wise; it is written for learners, for those seeking true light. Having recently wandered in darkness himself, the writer may be able to give some brother a hint as to the first part of the way. These lines are written in the hope of being of service to humanity and to Masonry by one indebted to both.

Let it be distinctly understood that the writer is not a Master. All statements as to the powers and capacities of a Master are made, however, on good authority. Any one doubting or denying the existence of such men and of such powers among our common humanity is respectfully referred to the blind man who never having seen the sun, moon and stars, asserted most positively that these luminaries did not and could not exist.

Do you deny the possibility that any mortal can acquire the powers that the Masters are said to have? "This is equivalent to saying," says Brother Thos. M. Stewart, in "Symbolic Teachings," "that you know all that has been acquired by any one on this subject in the past, and that you also know all that may be known about it in the future." After considering what your denial includes, do you still deny? Read Hosea, IV:17.

The following article is a compilation, the writer being indebted to Masonic writers for the thoughts expressed, but particularly to—

"The Great Work"—By T. K.;

"Mysteries of Masonry"—By L. E. Reynolds;

"Symbolic Teachings, or Masonry and its Message"— By Dr. Thos. M. Stewart;

"Morals and Dogma"—By Albert Pike;

"Restoration of Masonic Geometry and Symbolry"— By H. P. H. Bromwell.

"Whatever earthly thing thou would'st begin, lift up in prayer to God. In prayer wilt thou find a touchstone whether thy earthly purpose dares to stand before the heav'nly will."—Rueckert.

THE THIRD DEGREE

All the ancient nations had their mysteries, in which were taught science, philosophy, and morality. The ceremonies could be conferred on those only whose lives had been upright and who were thought to possess intelligence to understand and resolution to carry out the morality inculcated. Sublime beyond description, these initiations were the beginning of a better life, which it was believed would lead to immortality. Of the most sacred character, even war was suspended in favor of the mysteries, and the divine favor was thought to rest upon them. The world's greatest philosophers and teachers, Moses, Solon, Pythagoras, Socrates, Plato, and countless others, bear witness in their writings and their lives that they passed through these secret schools. Here they were taught the lofty principles that made them immortal.

Masonry may not be able to trace its origin historically and directly back to these ancient schools, but in spirit, in design, and in effects it is the successor of these venerable orders. Its method of teaching and its philosophy are the same, and it has hidden in its signs, symbols and ceremonies the same simple and wonderful truths as those inculcated at Eleusis, Elephanta, Memphis, and the other sanctuaries of antiquity.

A most important part of the ancient ceremony of initiation consisted in the candidate's being buried and brought back to life; thus symbolizing the belief in immortality of the soul and its conscious and continuous existence after physical death.

But, still more important—the candidate was shown that mere conscious continuity of existence is nothing in itself desirable; but that no happiness can be found either in this life or the next without conscious and continuous growth in righteousness, without usefulness and service. This lesson also is to be found in the apron.

The design of the Masonic institution is to make men wiser and better and consequently happier. It lays down in its symbolic instruction the principles of morality, those secret springs that have inspired the lofty lives of the truly great. He who obeys the Masonic precepts will not need to consult the opinions of friends or the public— he will find in his own breast an unerring monitor upon which he can always rely.

The student desiring to learn what these principles are must be willing to live them. Wisdom is a growth of the soul. Moral principles are worthless until they have been made alive and driven deep into the interior recesses of the soul by practice.

Knowledge is worthless unless it can be put into use. If you are not willing to live your Masonry, do not seek to know your sacred mysteries. Such knowledge carries with it the responsibility of use and obedience; and this responsibility can not be evaded.

Tubal-Cain was an instructor of every artificer in brass and iron—brass signifying natural good; and iron, natural truth.

An artificer in brass and iron represents a good and wise man; to instruct in goodness and wisdom is the peculiar duty of a Master Mason. Such instruction can be given efficaciously only by example.

The ruling principles of the human form are natural good and truth; the right side corresponds to good and the left to truth. There is a tendency to use the left hand first in all things that are done through deception, and to extend the left hand to an enemy, or where there is pretense of friendship. The right hand is the emblem of fidelity. The word "sinister" is merely Latin for "left hand." When an evil man is surprised, there is always a tendency to turn or look to the left. Masons, on the contrary, are taught always to turn towards the right.

("How shall I get to Heaven?" asked a certain man of a witty divine. "Turn to the right and keep straight on," was the answer). For these reasons, "The most vital principles of man's life are said to be contained between the right and left breasts, and the most sacred principles of his profession between the points of the compasses, one of which represents natural good and the other natural truth." These principles "can be implanted only in the contrite and humble spirit, wherein a man is said to be neither naked nor clothed, appearing to himself to be in a state in which there is neither usefulness nor truth."

To prostitute the truth to selfish purposes brings its own punishment. In the Entered Apprentice, it makes one unable to know or speak the truth. In the Fellow Craft, it leaves one a prey to the animal passions—symbolized by the beasts of the field—and to the unbidden thoughts and passing fancies of the moment—represented by the birds of the air. In such a state, like a ship without a rudder, man is at the mercy of every wind and current, no longer the master of his fate, but a hulk, a derelict, drifting aimlessly and hopelessly toward certain destruction. Bowels signify compassion, mercy; one who continues in the perversion of sacred things to selfish ends is said to be deprived of the mercy of the Lord, and delivered to the three lusts, love of the world, love of self, and love of mammon, being by them consumed and, as it were, scattered to the four winds of heaven.

The South represents the place of knowledge, or science, symbolized by the brilliance of the noon-day sun. The West represents wisdom, gained by the experience of a long and well-spent life. The East signifies the affections, or the light of Divine Truth, attained only by Faith and sacrifice.

Solomon symbolizes wisdom; Hiram of Tyre, power; what Hiram the Builder represents you must learn for yourself. To attempt to explain all meant by him in this brief article might have an effect the opposite of that intended, through being misunderstood. It is notable that in all three names appears the Grand Omnific Word of the Orient, that name by the proper pronunciation of which miracles could be worked and all the forces of nature controlled. It is also a matter for due consideration that the hero and example of Masonry was a workman, a son of toil, a man of the people. By this we are taught the dignity of labor.

Man cannot progress in spiritual growth and knowledge without temptation. The greater his progress the more severe will his trials be. This is logical. The cabinet maker applies the square to his work much oftener than does the architect of the pigsty. The finer and more nearly perfect the object to be made, the greater and more exacting the tests it must undergo. There is comfort in the thought that the greater your temptations, the greater the possibilities of progress thereby indicated, if you but stand the tests.

When trouble and danger come upon men, they naturally seek relief first through science; then as the temptations become more severe, solace is sought in experience and philosophy; these failing, we must at the last rely upon Faith in the Divine Love, that profound trust in the unseen Father by which we are enabled to exclaim: "Though he slay me, yet will I trust in him."

The three greatest enemies of mankind are Ignorance, Ambition, and Fanaticism. Of these three the oldest and worst is Ignorance. We oppose its attacks with Science and knowledge. Ambition's seductive whisper may be overcome by the lessons of wisdom and experience which teach the uselessness of worldly honors and power. Fanaticism cannot be overcome except by Faith and Love. Before we can attain what is called Immortality, we must overcome self and make the great sacrifice.

Man has in himself two principles, the Masculine, or principle of Will, and the Feminine, or principle of Desire. It is the latter that gives us our appetites and passions and is called the widow's son, meaning the natural degree of the mind before regeneration by a life of morality. This natural desire, these appetites and passions, this widow's son, must be put away, destroyed, buried as it were in a hill near Mount Moriah before we can become Masters. Christ (the divine spirit within) must be born at Bethlehem (the house of bread, i. e., sacrifice) (among the animals) in a stable (amidst our earthly appetites and passions) and so the divine and immortal spirit within us must take the place of the (animal appetites and base passions) and be laid (in their place) in the manger (where they fed). To express it differently, the earthly wheat, symbolizing for the Fellow Craft natural good and truth, must be buried, that it may, dying, rise as the divine knowledge of the Master Mason. What says one of our ancient brethren of power: "But some man will say, How are the dead raised up? and with what body do they come? Thou fool, that which thou sowest is not quickened except it die." The Master does not fear death. To him this dread messenger brings but the change from the grain of wheat, sown by the husbandman, into the new wheat, that shall grow and spread and bear a hundredfold.

The man who loves the Lord because he hopes to be saved by the technicalities of faith, or for the sake of the pleasures, riches and safety of heaven, is actuated by the principle of Desire—in other words, by Selfishness, or the widow's son; this must be slain before he can be a Master, obeying God's laws from principle, and not from interest. How true it is that we can not say of any man that he ever will become a Master Mason! But persevere in the practice of every commendable virtue, for your reward is sure, whether you reach Mastership or not.

Generally, the only way the widow's son can be done away with is by the operation called death. But this is not the only way. "It is possible to put off the body without death even now. Such was the case with Enoch and Elijah," etc. The same principles applied to-day will give the same results as those reached by the patriarchs.

Such results have been attained, we are told, by many who have lived "in obscurity, without offices, honors, or emoluments." "Natural Science," says that remarkable book, **"The Great Work,"** "has demonstrated with absolute certainty the continuity of life after physical death."

"The most profound problem of human life," says this wonderful book, "and the most pathetic cry of the human soul throughout the ages have been the problem and the cry: 'If a man die shall he live again?'" To the great majority of mankind in all times and among all peoples physical death has been a leap into the darkness * * * Now and then, however, there has been one whose vision has been clear, and to whom the other shore of life has been distinctly visible * * * What a difference this clearer vision has made in the attitude of soul of those who have come down to the River of Death at the end of life's journey! To such as these the voyage across the dark waters that stretch between the two worlds, or the two continents of life, is but a voyage from the dark Continent of Death to the Land of Spiritual Life and Light. It is a voyage toward the Harbor of Truth and the Haven of Peace.

"It is a voyage from the banks of Time to the shores of Eternity. To those who, from this side of life, have been able to look across the other shore and see the lights of the City of Life, the journey is begun with a song of joy in the heart and thanksgiving upon the lips. A definite knowledge of that which lies beyond removes all doubts and fears. Those who possess such knowledge know that the closing of this life is but the opening of the doors of the higher life. To such as these, 'Death is swallowed up in Victory.'"

Such is the meaning of the Third Degree of Freemasonry, and facts prove our doctrine to be true.

This, my brothers, is the pearl of great price. Is it not worth all that is asked for it?

Seek and ye shall find.

ARE YOU A MASON?

Are you a Master Mason?

The first time the newly raised candidate hears that question, he will probably answer, "yes." But now that you hear it after thought as to what it means—Are you?

Some years ago, a gentleman visiting scenes of interest around Richmond, Virginia, asked his colored hack driver if there were any of the Poe family about Richmond. "Yes, boss," said the negro, whose color rivalled that of Egypt's night, "Dat is my name—Poe." "Well," said the visitor, "are you related to Edgar Allen Poe?"

"Why, boss," answered the black man, "I **is Edgar Allen Poe.**"

Those who are most ready to claim that they are Masters are not always most entitled to be considered as such.

In the "Tyler Keystone" of July 5, 1912, Brother Robt. C. Wright asks: What a Master Mason is. This question should be answered, and this the writer will attempt, expressly disclaiming any pretense of reaching the standard here laid down, as well as any originality in the ideas expressed.

A Master Mason is a man who has truly learned to subdue his passions and has improved himself in Masonry.

Let us examine into this definition a little. What is this Masonry in which a man must "improve himself" to become a Master?

"Masonry is a beautiful system of morality, veiled in allegory and illustrated by symbols."

But what is Morality? "Morality is the established harmonic relation which Man, as an Individual Intelligence, sustains to the Constructive Principle of Nature." Put in other words: "Morality is Man's established harmonic relation to the Constructive Principle of his own being."—The Great Work.

Masonry throughout its whole fabric is constructive, and its allegories are based on the operations of Building, or aligning one's self with the Great Constructive Principle of Nature and of one's own being.

Before a building is erected, however, the materials are first set apart or "devoted" to the work. Hence, a Master Mason must first have devoted or set apart his own powers and capacities to the work of building a Spiritual Temple. And he must have done this freely and voluntarily. This material must be sound, hence an inward preparation, one in the heart, is the first requisite. For as out of the heart come the issues of life and death, so if the material be unsound at heart, the building erected therefrom cannot withstand the assaults of time or the attacks of the elements, even if it can bear its own weight.

The material then being examined and found without blemish and well-fitted to be used for the proposed building, all irregularities and excrescences must be removed. This the Master Mason has done by the constant use of the Gavel of his Will, guided and tested by the Square of his Conscience. By these instruments he has removed from his life all its vices and superfluities and has prepared himself "as a living stone, for that spiritual temple, that house not made with hands, eternal in the heavens."

Having proceeded thus far in the line of constructive effort, he has laid the foundation of his Spiritual Temple, using the plumb of uprightness, in thought and heart as well as in outward conduct, in feelings and desires as well as in words and professions, for the plumb admonishes him to build upward ever. He has also used the level of equality and brotherly love, by which he has not only driven out arrogance and pride, and arbitrary conduct towards others, but has also instilled courtesy, kindness, and humility. All this he has squared by the square of virtue, justice, strict rectitude, and duty, both towards his fellowmen and himself. For no carpenter would undertake a building without a square, neither can a man progress in the work of Spiritual Building without incorruptible virtue and purity of thought, word, and deed; nor without the full performance of every duty, to whomsoever owed.

And he has covered this foundation with a Mosaic pavement, reminding him to accept good and evil fortune with equanimity, that light and shadow, good and evil, prosperity and adversity, are to be expected equally by all men; that no matter what his possessions, whether wealth, intellect, knowledge, power, or health, they are but lent to him to use rightly, and that he cannot reasonably expect to enjoy them without paying the price —and if he refuse to pay, they must be taken from him.

No profane man, nor one who habitually takes the name of God in vain, no swearer, drunkard, libertine, retailer of filthy stories, no dishonest man, no man who is a glutton, or covetous, or cruel, or vain, or haughty, or intolerant, or cross, or impatient, or quick to anger without cause can properly be called a Master Mason. How can he be a Master until he can control himself?

The foundations of Masonic character are Brotherly Love and Humility, Uprightness, and Virtue. If any part of this foundation is taken away, the whole building must fall.

The foundation laid, the Master Mason has learned to rise over and upon his appetites and passions, to turn them into the columns that support and adorn his edifice. He does not despise his body, nor seek to destroy his natural appetites, but learns to turn them each to constructive uses. And it may be said in passing that when his Temple is completed, these very "appetites and passions" of the physical man (or is it not more probably their spiritual counterparts)—the Stone which the builders rejected—become the headstone of the corner, the keystone of the gateway to spiritual knowledge and real happiness.

The Master Mason has also improved himself, as far as possible, in the liberal arts and sciences. He is a man of liberal and generous mind, who is ever seeking more knowledge, not for mere self gratification or intellectual pleasure, but that he may be more useful to his fellowman.

He also knows when he comes to the river of spirituality, and can tell what he wishes to cross, and whither he is going. He has not abandoned his undertaking, as did the Ephraimites, and turned back after setting his hand to the plow, but has steadily gone forward, regardless of all temptations and despite all opposition.

He is of such tried courage that Death has no terrors for him, nor can the present and imminent threat of it deter him from his duty or induce him to betray a trust. His integrity is dearer to him than his life. For he knows that Death is but a phantom, feared by Ignorance, and to the wise man no more than the laying aside of one's garments when the hour of rest has come.

In all this labor, the Master Mason has been clothed in Innocence, as with a garment—the innocence of knowledge of the truth. He has scattered around him (and thereby increased) a love for all mankind, a toleration recognizing that each man has a right to his own opinions and that he who persecutes for opinion's sake thereby usurps the prerogative of God. He has sympathized with the sorrows of all the world and done what he could to alleviate suffering. And he has learned to look with pitying sympathy upon diseases of the spirit and intellect, as he would upon those of the body, with neither hatred nor anger, nor the desire to punish or persecute. Also, he has a profound Faith in God, which is in equilibrium with his Intelligent Reason.

Such a man will not be found seeking Masonic office, and will accept such office only as an invitation and opportunity to do more good; will not complain if the "honors" of Masonry are given to another and not to him; will be self-controlled, courteous, considerate, sympathetic, and kind to all; will understand something of the true meaning of Masonic symbolism; and will be an exemplar of what is highest and best in humanity.

Such a man may be justly called a Master Mason. Such a man is the owner in fee simple of a Spiritual Temple in that country where neither moth nor rust corrupt and where thieves do not break through and steal.

Are there such men? There always have been, and always will be, thank God. By their fruits ye shall know them.

The article from the "Tyler-Keystone" is reprinted by permission.

CORN, WINE AND OIL

By Rabbi Isaac Marcusson

A MONG ALL early peoples, we find life divided into three aspects—physical, mental, spiritual. The fully developed man was the man who considered all these aspects of life and did not develop one at the expense of the other. The gladiator or the athlete stood at the lowest of the ladder of life and the proverb, "A strong mind in a strong body," was the ideal towards which man strove.

It is not to be wondered at that throughout its whole history Masonry endeavored to keep alive this three-fold aspect of life. It was clearly understood by the founders of our order that the fully developed man was he who took heed of every aspect of his nature and body; mind and soul were to be equally guarded.

Corn. This has always been the symbol of the physical life. It represents orderliness and brotherhood. While each grain of corn stands separate and alone, yet it has its place in the line and is firmly imbedded with all the rest in one central unifying mass. Should a single grain, even for a moment lose its hold, it falls out unless supported and sustained by its neighboring grain. So man in his social life must finally realize that if he lets go of the central purpose of life, if he steps out of his place in the great march onward, "his place will know him no more;" he falls out of the orderly procession of life. But like the ear of corn there are sustaining forces which for a little while can keep him in his place if he will but cling to them until he can once more take hold of life and its deeper purposes. So while corn to the Master Mason is symbolic of the physical life, it also has for us a lesson of great and lasting value. It represents the deeper lesson for which Masonry stands—social order and a helpful brotherhood. It is the nourishing, sustaining food on which we are dependent to make ourselves felt in the higher walks of life. But it is none-the-less essential. It is the foundation stone on which the higher life must be builded if we are to erect a structure that shall be a real temple wherein man shall rise to his better self.

Wine. The cluster of grapes symbolic of the mental life of man likewise teaches us a higher lesson. As wine stimulates the physical body so learning stimulates the mind. It is the divine fire brought from Heaven to enable man to rise from the lowliest in life to the highest. It is to be used in cultivating the arts as well as providing the physical needs of man. But it, too, is symbolic—each grape holds its place in the cluster but all grow out of one central stem. A delicate weak tendril holds it to the parent vine. So man is held to the finer things in life by faith. He realizes that the physical life is but a means and not the end and purpose of existence. Material things are good only in so far as they are used for the cultural and mental advancement of man. And as from the bunch of grapes there comes the invigorating and joy-giving wine so from a full and rounded mental life there comes the happiness of a developed intellect, of a broadened vision into life, of higher values of existence. And as the wine improves with age, gaining in aroma and flavor, so the mind of man grows richer through wisdom and each added learning gives it a new flavor.

Oil. Oil is the symbol of the spirit. It was oil that kept alive the perpetual flame which burnt before the Holy of Holies in the Temple of King Solomon. It was especially prepared oil representing the toil and care which man spent upon it. It was pure oil from which all that was low and base was removed, representative of the highest spiritual truth to which man could lift himself. It was the oil extracted from the olive—good for food, it is true, but its material benefits to be sacrificed so that there might be extracted from it the precious oil to keep alive the eternal flame. So man too is taught through Masonry to give up if necessary the material gains and the physical advantages, if he can bring in place thereof the spiritual values which enrich and ennoble life. But more than that, the oil was symbolic of royalty. Upon the head of king and priest it was poured as a sign of power. The king and priest were representative of the higher virtues. This is the lesson which the Bible teaches us. King Saul, a mighty man of valor, a true soldier, rising head and shoulders above his comrades—he was symbolic of the physical, and then King David, the builder, the sweet singer, the Psalmist, representative of the mental. But he was not to build the Temple of God. King Solomon in whom were united the three qualities erected the Temple unto God.

To the Mason today this complete life should be the aim and goal. Upon his head is poured the anointing oil of service. To him comes the opportunity to erect a spiritual temple to which men can turn when seeking the higher things in life. He must be sure that the foundation symbolized by the physical is strong and clean; he must see to it that the superstructure representative of the mental is carefully planned and thoughtfully built but he must be sure that within this Temple there burns the oil of truth and from this light there shall stream forth a ray which shall guide man in his darkest hours up to the altar of faith.

Corn and Wine and Oil—these shall be the symbols by which the Master Mason shall become the well-rounded man and attain that perfection towards which we should strive.

THE REAL OBJECTS OF FREEMASONRY

By William B. Clarke, Past Grand Master

ECAUSE OF THE fact that lodges symbolize the world and the blue sky above in their symbolic covering, we are accustomed to call all Lodges "Blue Lodges." The writer, in designating Lodges, is partial in referring to them as lodges of Ancient Craft Masonry. The very word "Ancient" infers that, as Masons, we have inherited something from the past. The term "Craft" implies that we are members of or successors to an organization which was established for work. Craftsmen labor to build something. If we would learn the real objects of Masonry, let us examine into the ancient past and learn what the craftsmen of old labored to build.

The rank and file of Masonry in later years has accomplished much, but, this accomplishment appears to have resulted from the pride of tradition, the noble accomplishments of certain leaders who have inspired us in late years by their leadership, and a certain satisfaction in knowing that Masonry is an ancient and honorable institution. We might view the great body of Masons in the same light in which we may view the American Indian. Ordinarily he is a savage, but, there is a pride of race, a haughtiness of bearing, a nobility of character which would indicate a heritage from a noble past. His art, the beauty of his thoughts as revealed in the councils with the white men, would indicate that the American Indian is the last of a civilization of conquerors which has been lost over the expanse of time. And so it is with many Masons. They are proud of the Order although they know nothing of its history or from whence it came. Many men, some leaders of the fraternity, are haughty in the offices which they hold because of the honor attached to the office, yet they are not familiar with the purposes and teachings of the Order which they are supposed to lead. The art of Masonry is unknown to thousands of its members. Many Masons repeat the beautiful thoughts of Masonry but fail to know from whence these thoughts come and do not apply them to their daily lives. Many of us glory in the record of the Masonry of the past, but move no muscle or stir no brain cell to meet the responsibilities of the Masonry of the present.

It may surprise some Masons to know that the Masonry of the ancients required a mental standard. Before men could become Masters, they had to master the teachings of Masonry. The Masons of old were the master minds of their day. They led the world of their time in thought and teaching. It is for these reasons that the ranks of the Craft several hundred years ago were largely filled with the great thinkers of that day.

The Masons who formed the operative Guilds of seven and more centuries ago and who constructed the great cathedrals of Europe which are still the marvels of the architectural world of today, were not only master builders. They were primarily master thinkers, incorporating in the buildings which they designed and constructed the great principles of science, religion, philosophy, and of life which they learned from the experiences of man through the ages and have incorporated in the symbols which we use today. They associated with them in their work, as speculative Masons, the great artists, teachers, scholars and leaders of their day that they might learn their wisdom. The present system of ritual and symbolism which we use is our heritage from the past, remarkable for its depth of human emotions, clear-cut logic and fundamental philosophy. The landmarks given us by our ancient brethren are unchanging guides in life because they are of divine origin. They are unchangeable by man because man cannot change the truths of the Divine.

Because the emotional nature of the great majority of us has been stressed by religion, the logical side of our nature has not reached that development which Masonry intends should exist. Consequently, we are prone to interpret the square of Masonry as a symbol of virtue rather than as the real symbol of reason. It is the emblem of the Master, the personification of Wisdom. If we would find the real objects of Masonry, let us apply the square of reason to conditions at the present time and thus be enabled to judge things in accordance with their real value and to arrange them in their proper sequence according to the true value determined by experiences of the past.

In recent years we have witnessed the many innovations which have been used to arouse interest and to increase attendance at lodge meetings. Special nights of entertainment, musical evenings, dances, vaudeville, comedy, and almost every form of entertainment known to the professions which make a business of whooping up interest in any project. * * * Masonry of the past did not need to use these superficial forms to arouse interest and to have growth. Do the present times demand that we abandon the methods of ancient Masonry or are the present times calling for a return to the things of old which gave Masonry its birth and sustained its progress?

There is an old saying that "Hindsight is better than foresight." This statement comes from the manner in which pilots have for centuries steered ships up winding rivers at night. Beginning at the river mouth, they place the first of the channel lights in a line with the second of these lights and steer until they can line up the third and fourth lights and so on. There come times when the turns of the river obscure the lights ahead. It is then that the pilot looks to the rear and lines up certain lights behind him which are marked on the chart. He follows these until he rounds the turn sufficiently to see again the lights which are ahead. His hindsight is better than his foresight because his course is guided by experiences which he knows to be safe. If we are to attempt to determine the course of the Masonry of the future, let us be guided by the lights of experiences from the past.

So frequently do we hear that Masonry is out of date. The Mason of understanding will immediately challenge that statement. Because the majority of Masons are sadly lacking in the knowledge of the height, breadth and depth of Masonic teachings as contained in the meanings of the many symbols of Masonry, there is no reason for stating that Masonry is out of date. That which is true and which is good, is never out of date or out of demand. Truth never changes and is unchangeable. The method of teaching the truth may be out of date but the truth itself is never old.

Let us look back over the events of the past few years, use our reason for an understanding of the course of events, and see if Masonry meets the requirements of the times. We may find that the world has come to a new appreciation of the value of those things which Masonry has held most sacred and has taught for centuries in a remarkably logical manner.

Recently, the writer read an article by a nationally prominent authority on education and the public school system of instruction. This article made the startlingly significant statement that the public school system of this country would never fulfill its mission until it had incorporated in its curriculum a definite course in good citizenship. The author of that article appeared to feel that no child was really equipped to fight the battle of life until one of the great primary instincts of life, conscience, had been properly directed and developed in the schools. Thus, if we are to teach good citizenship, which is the real purpose for the establishment of the public school system by our forefathers, we must begin early in the establishment of a definite and progressive course for teaching the moral standards which govern our relations with one another, both private and public. This author discussed the reasons for failure to observe law, as stressed by President Hoover in his appeal to the American people; for the manner in which our courts and judges are held up to scorn and ridicule; for the silent consent to the grafting which is said to exist in many quarters; and for the failure to stop or protest against the commission of crime in this country. The author laid it to the door of failure to possess a national conscience.

Nearly all authorities on pedagogy agree that the conscience in the child is the one infallible guide in distinguishing between right and wrong and, that it develops fairly early in life. Masonry has never quibbled on that subject. In the logical development of its plan of instruction, the very manner of reception of the candidate in the first degree drives home the importance which Masonry gives to the prick of conscience. Masonry places conscience logically before faith.

Just recently, the author of this article was teaching a class of Sunday school teachers the fundamentals of the science of teaching. A nationally prominent divine was present and emphatically agreed with the statement of the writer that the position given to conscience by Masonry prior to the beginning of faith, was correct.

Conscience is the bed rock upon which faith builds her structure. Thus we find that Masonry has been teaching for hundreds of years that one great primary instinct with the educators of today are trying to locate somewhere in the educational system of the nation. And yet, men will say that Masonry is out of date in her methods. The world's master minds have given to Masonry her symbolism and her method of instruction, therefore it is sound, both in principle and logic.

In Masonry, we find developed one of the most fascinating and logical plans of instruction known to man. All of us should be familiar with the symbol composed of the point within the circle and with the two parallel lines tangent to the circle. In this symbol is illustrated the whole plan of Masonic instruction. The circle is the Divine Will circumscribing our every action and we are represented by the point within. The two parallel lines illustrate the manifestation of the Divine Will both in the affairs of individuals on the one hand, and in humanity as a whole on the other. The actions of the individuals form the civilizations of the race of men.

As the candidate stands within the ante-room he symbolizes a soul upon its entrance into the world. Geometry teaches him that a circle reduced to infinity becomes a point. As the circle symbolizes the Divine Power, we are taught that if we would find God, look for His revelation within our own souls. We are a part of Him and He of us. If we would find God in the world, then look for His revelations of Himself in the affairs of humanity.

Again, in the candidate in the ante-room, we see the beginning of the life of a human being and, in the three degrees we will trace the growth of that life from the cradle to the grave through all its phases. On the other hand, the candidate in the ante-room is the symbol of the growth of the human race from the days of savagery and of primitive man and, in the three degres, Masonry will reveal to us the growth of the human race in its conception of the source of Divine Power from the first promptings of conscience until the fullness of faith has come. How logically and how beautifully has Masonry taught for hundreds of years the great truths of life which the educators of today are now trying to place in our schools and Sunday schools.

Since conscience is the bed rock upon which faith is built, it will be interesting to ascertain what Masonry does with the question of faith. Masonry immediately recognizes the importance of faith by placing the expression or statement of faith second in order to conscience in its plan of instruction. It goes farther than that and broadens that faith with another principle which educators of today are agreed must be emphasized. At the end of the first part of the E. A. degree, Masonry brings in the lesson of charity. This, coupled with the profession of faith, immediately impresses us with the great principle which is the foundation of all the enduring religions of the world, the Fatherhood of God and the Brotherhood of Man. Charity is but love and love for each other is brotherhood.

Masonry is not satisfied with a simple declaration of faith on the part of the candidate. It immediately begins to enlighten that faith. In the second degree, Masonry reveals to the candidate the whole course of human life. The winding stairs of the second degree portray the pathway of life from the beginning of creation. The black and white checkerboard refers to that cosmic condition of the universe before the Divine Will was expressed. Out of that indescribable, indefinable condition which the Hebrew of the Old Testament describes as cosmic, there appears the bodies terrestrial and the bodies celestial which compose the universe at Divine Command. The first of the three steps is marked with the plumb, indicating that man was created an erect being, differing from the animals and endowed with a Divine Spark which inspired him to lift himself above the animal. In the level, we see that attribute which distinguishes the human race from the animals in another phase of his being, the dawn of brotherhood. In the square, we see the symbol of the brain power given to man, another great distinguishing feature which differentiates man from the animal world. The plumb, the level and the square in Masonry also define those attributes which we give to the Creator. Since we cannot picture the source of Divine Power, we describe by attributes, Infinite Beauty, Infinite Strength, Infinite Wisdom. In these three steps, Masonry thus illustrates that Power in life which brought the universe into being and also gave to us a part of the Divine Spark.

As we pass to the second series of five steps, we see portrayed those senses which are so vital to the life of the race and developed to a far greater degree in man than in the animals. In the third series of seven steps, the fullness of the brain power with which man was endowed is given its great opportunity of realization in the joys of life through the practice of the seven liberal arts and sciences. Those mean nothing to the animals but were ordained of the Divine Will that the faith of man might be an enlightened one. And, finally, Masonry does not cease at this point, to open to the eyes of the seeker after truth the revelations of Masonic knowledge. At the top of the stairs is the river of death but, suspended above it is the symbol of the eternal life. How often have we seen the sheaf of grain placed upon the casket of some deceased person and failed to learn the significance. It is there to teach the great lesson that, since the stalk of the grain must die before the grain is of service, thus also must the body die before the eternal soul shall reap the rewards and fruits of the life hereafter. The second degree therefore is the degree of wisdom concerning the things of life. Masonry would not have our faith an accident of birth. Masonry would teach that our faith must be an enlightened faith, built upon a knowledge of the eternal truths of the Divine.

Masonry further enlightens the candidate throughout its ritual. In the Masonic system of instruction and ritual, the Bible is the center of the lodge. The entire ritual of the three degrees revolves about it. It is the Great Light of Masonry. As the lodge symbolizes the universe, the Great Light symbolizes that source of Divine Power which is the actuating force of and the center about which the universe revolves. Again, throughout the three degrees, Masonry surrounds the Bible with the ritual and the symbols which tell the great truths of science, philosophy and religion. In his Masonic life, the interested Mason has found that in the ritual and the symbolism of Masonry, there has been pictured for his enlightenment those truths which make the Bible to him an ever-new Book. Masonry does not permit the interference of priest, rabbi or minister, holding that the relations of a man with his God are matters of his own conscience, uninfluenced by dogma, creed or theology. Because of this fact, Masonry has given to the world many of its greatest social and religious leaders, enlightened men capable of finding the great truths of religion and unhampered or unimpeded in their purposes to teach them.

From the great religions of the past, we will find that Masonry has kept that which was true and which was good and has preserved the knowledge of them in its symbols. Today, men are seeking that very religious enlightenment which Masonry has given to its members. Leaders of the church are realizing more and more each day that if the church would progress, it must do a great deal of teaching as well as of preaching.

A short time ago, the writer was present at a meeting of ministers and laymen to hear an address by the head of a prominent theological seminary. This man is a teacher of ministers. It was significant that from this leader in the Church came the statement that the Church of today cannot continue to exist merely upon dogma and doctrine. The present generation is highly educated and demands that the preacher in the pulpit shall teach not only the Bible but, the Bible as illumined by the results of science, archaeology, philosophy and world history. We have found that Masonry realized this fact centuries ago and has consistently given to the student of the Bible every source of information known to the world. The Church is but beginning to do that which Masonry has done for centuries. Yet, men will say that Masonry is out of date.

It is said the Bible differs in one outstanding respect from all other great religious books. Whereas, the other religious books teach man seeking the Divine, the Bible is the only one of the great books which teaches the Divine seeking man. Our brothers of Ancient Craft Masonry caught this conception and taught it in a masterly manner. Many of the great churches designed by them seven hundred years ago, are planned in the form of a cross. The cross upon the ground is the symbol of the Divine Presence upon earth. In the designs of these churches, the mass and height of the building, the form and ornamentation of the doors and windows, the manner of construction, and the decorations and sculpture upon them portray all the great truths of the Bible in a logical and beautiful manner. Our ancient brethren were masters of spiritual knowledge and master teachers of these truths by means of symbolism.

During the days of the Reformation, when men were bleeding and dying in the struggle for the right to worship God according to the dictates of their conscience, some, in their ignorance, sought to destroy all vestige of symbolism in the churches in order to stop the superstitious worship of the symbols themselves. The Iconoclasts wrecked so many former Roman Catholic churches that Martin Luther, the remarkable leader of the Reformation, came from hiding and risked the loss of his life in order to put a stop to these depredations, and to preserve that symbolism which was true. For more than four hundred years, some religious denominations have refused to permit either on or within the churches, any vestige of symbolism. Their churches have been but cold and severe structures, largely void of any purpose except to serve as an auditorium in which a long and tiresome sermon might be preached. Today, we find that Masonry's square of reason is leading many of these churches to an understanding that symbolism is the oldest of the languages and we find that in just a few short years there is coming rapidly back into being an appreciation and understanding of that great style of architecture, the Gothic, which was the product of Masonic mind and genius. Gothic is now the most popular and prominent style of ecclesiastical architecture because it is the richest in the truth of its conception, most perfect in the form and symbolism of its design and ornament. Thus again, men may say that Masonry is dead. The Church can say, emphatically, no.

The records of publication will show that the one book is printed in the greatest number of volumes and the greatest number of languages is the Bible. It is interesting to note that Masons have never ceased to consider the Bible the Great Book of the world. Yet, few men know that a Mason was intimately concerned in developing the opportunity to publish the Bible to the world. When Martin Luther began the great fight in Germany for religious liberty, there came to his assistance one of the noted Greek scholars of the world at that time. This man gave to Luther his active cooperation in the translation of the New Testament from the Greek into the German. From that time onward, the Bible became the property of the world and men were released of the yoke of ignorance of its teachings. This world renowned Greek scholar, we learn, became a charter member of the speculative lodge of Masons which was organized at the time of the completion and the dedication of the wonderful Cologne cathedral. When this work was finished, the old guild of operative Masons passed out of existence and a speculative lodge was organized to succeed it. Upon the roll of charter members was found the name of Philip Melancthon, the Mason who aided Martin Luther, in the translation of the Bible. With him, appeared the name of Admiral Coligny of France, who led the Huguenots in that struggle for religious liberty and who lost his life in that cause when the Huguenots were massacred on the bloody Saint Bartholomew's Eve. Thus did Masons and Masonry in the ancient days, fight to preserve the Divine Truth as revealed in the Bible and to give that truth to the world.

In the archives of the Grand Lodge of Georgia, there reposes today one of the original copies of the Bible in German as translated by Luther and Melancthon, and later used in the Lodge of which Robert Burns, the immortal Scotch poet was a member at the time of use.

We have seen to some extent that the great truths taught by Masonry are as vital to the world today as they were centuries ago. Although times and customs are changing overnight, let us not think for a moment that the square of Masonic reason applied to thought and conditions of the present will not reveal significant facts. In these facts we will find the real objects of Masonry.

Let us realize that the one room country school is almost a thing of the past. In its place, we find the handsome, complete and highly efficient consolidated schools of the present. The children in the rural districts are being given as complete and thorough an education as can be obtained in the most complete and magnificent schools of the city. The rural districts are being taught far more than the three Rs.

In the public schools, we find the system divided into the seven phases of life. The pre-school class, or kindergarten, corresponds to the phase of early childhood. The elementary school corresponds to the latter phase of early childhood and to middle childhood. The junior high responds to the characteristics of later childhood. The senior high trains early adolescence. The junior college trains middle adolescence. The college answers the requirements of later adolescence. The whole system of instruction follows the Masonic theory of the phases of life which Masonry has taught for centuries.

The rural section, through the advent of the automobile, has largely ceased to exist. The vision, foresight and experience of the dwellers in the rural districts are being broadened through intimate contact with all phases of life and manners of living, never before possible. With these things come experiences never before realized.

The church has felt and responded to the demand for thorough and detailed instruction along the lines of definite and logical plans. In the modern Sunday school, the seven departments of the school correspond to the seven phases of life just as the division of the public schools similarly corresponds to these phases of life. The methods of instruction in the seven departments and the subjects taught, respond to the characteristics of these seven phases of life. In addition to this careful plan of instruction, the teachers of the Sunday schools are being carefully taught the fundamentals of teaching, the details of proper methods and the various purposes of the plan of organization. The theory and purpose of the Sunday school is being explained to them. The writer does not state that Masonry has changed the ideas and plans of the Church but, it is not necessary to show that the logical plan of the Masonic system of education is but now being appreciated by the systems of education in this country.

Another phase of religious instruction which is rapidly being changed is the sermon. There was a time a few years ago, when the sermon was almost the entire service. Preachers in the pulpit are now faced by men and women who frequently are better educated and trained than themselves in many subjects. The sermon has been shortened to some twenty or thirty minutes length but, it is safe to say, that many of the sermons now given contain far more food for thought and far more real instruction in twenty minutes than were given in two hours a few years ago. The Church has realized that it must teach as well as preach.

Let us take a look at the number of great Bible classes for men which has been organized by the Church. Many of these classes are being led by enlightened Masons. Nearly all of them are being led by enthusiastic and trained laymen who are giving to men a man's thoughts of the Bible and are inspiring other men by word and example to follow the Great Leader of men. These laymen are bringing to the interpretation of the Bible many of Masonry's great revelations concerning the search of the human race for light and truth over the centuries.

The present generation is seeking the plain and simple truth. It is giving to all men the freedom to express the individuality of each; false modesty is being removed from the situation and thought is valued for the plain truth which it contains; false standards are being pulled down and the men are trying to give to every thought, word and deed that value which it deserves of itself. Since the various styles of architecture have in all times portrayed and expressed the geographic conditions, thoughts, customs, morals, religion, civilization and wealth of the peoples who produced them, we find a significant fact in the architecture of today. On one hand there is a rapid return in ecclesiastical architecture to the Gothic of ancient Masonry. Its conception and execution alone gives to church architecture the mystery of the spiritual. Its symbolism and its wealth of tracery alone interpret that intricacy and beauty of religious life and the delicacy of human emotions.

On the other hand, the removal of superficiality, the desire for simplicity of life and thought, the determination to esteem things for their true value, is being exemplified today in the new style of architecture of commercial buildings. Buildings are void of unnecessary ornament. Proportion of mass and line is being sought. In place of richness of ornament, natural richness of material and beauty of texture is being sought in the ornamentation of our buildings. Men are appreciating things for their real and not for their superficial value. Material must have a workable as well as an ornamental value.

As the impressions of life of the present time flash before our eyes, what do our memories recall of the things which Masonry impressed upon us? Do we remember the condition of our preparation for reception of the three degrees? Can we not recall that Masonry attempted to drive into our hearts the fact that it is not concerned with our wealth, position in life, honors, or our influence and friends? It was concerned with the things of real value only, the spiritual things. The superficialities of life were of no consequence to Masonry. It took us for what we really were and gave to us only that which we were entitled to receive and of which we were worthy. The present generation can learn much from the teachings of Masonry. It is one of the world's most logical and wonderful systems of instruction.

Having applied the square of reason to some of the fundamental teachings of Masonic symbolism and, having used our hindsight to look over the experiences and desires of the present generation, it is safe to assume that Masonry and its teachings are as vital to life today as they were hundreds of years ago. The ideals and purposes of Masonry today are the same as they were centuries ago. Since we know that the world is in demand of the things which we have to offer, we are in a position to ascertain what are the REAL OBJECTS OF MASONRY.

One great truth strikes us with startling force. Masonry has always been a TEACHING INSTITUTION. Here we have the REAL OBJECT OF MASONRY. For centuries, Masonry has taught men the great facts of life and has been one of the greatest forces in the world for good. If ever there was a time in the history of the world when enlightenment is being sought, that time is the present. The real object of Masonry today, as it has always been, is to teach men the truths contained in its symbolism. Let Masonry teach men what it has learned from the experiences of the race of man on the earth, how we came into this world, what are we supposed to do while we are here, and where we are going when we leave here. More than ever before, the world is demanding a knowledge of these things. Masonry offers in her symbolism that very knowledge in all its richness, without dogma, theology, prejudice or bias. Let Masonry teach men what it knows. That is the first object of Masonry.

In teaching, the ideal is not merely to instruct. Men can read the truths of Masonry without entering a Masonic lodge. The ideal of all teaching is to train by thought and by example so that there is aroused in the pupil the desire, the will, to do things learned so that there is developed in the pupil a personality, a character, which of itself is an example of the truths learned. Here is the second REAL OBJECT OF MASONRY. Here is the real and fundamental truth behind the fact that we come into Masonry of our own free will. Masonry has no intention to force us to do the things desired. It wishes us to come with a fundamental "will to be a Mason." If that voluntary desire is not present, Masonry can do nothing with the candidate. It cannot teach a man to be a Mason against his will. The will to live the things and truths learned is the ideal of teaching. Authorities on pedagogics are now emphasizing the development of this "will to be." It is the great fundamental in all teaching. Yet, Masonry has known it and recognized it and used it for centuries as the basis of Masonic teaching. It is the second REAL OBJECT OF MASONRY.

Particularly, throughout the history of the last five hundred years, when Masonic efforts largely brought about liberty and religious freedom, there have frequently come before the eyes of the world men of intellect, vision, will power and faith. The thoughts which these men put forth and the translation of these thoughts by them into action have frequently changed the course of civilization. It is interesting to learn that many of these great men have been Masons, trained at Masonic altars, inspired by Masonic principles, and, in accordance with the ideals of Masonic teaching, of their own free wills offering their services and their lives for the uplift of humanity. Wonderful men in whom a Masonic personality had been developed by Masonic teaching. Personalities which inspired other men to higher ideals and noble deeds. Their lives have illustrated what Masonry has attempted and is trying to do. In the furnishing of these leaders we have the third REAL OBJECT OF MASONRY. It is to supply men of true faith, of courage, of will power, of intellect and of vision who will lead the Craft and the world of men to higher and nobler thoughts and deeds. Men who seek not honor, wealth, glory or power, but men who serve because the truths they have learned inspire them to a noble service.

It has probably occurred to the readers of this article that the accomplishments of the three objectives named will require a high degree of leadership. That is true and the truth of it is becoming evident every day, both in lodges and in Grand Lodges. A growing number of lodges is now being led by young men, the products of a new system of education. They are men of education, men of intellect and men of vision. They are not men to be swayed from their logical and sound purposes by appeals to the emotions. Their actions are being based upon a logic resulting from the wide experiences in life furnished by the automobile and the motion picture. They are being trained in organization and service through school, church and civic club. We must remember that their experiences are far greater in their youth today than were those aged men of a few years ago.

From these young masters and past masters are coming the grand officers of tomorrow. The men who would lead them, must have a deeper experience, a wider vision, a greater intellect. They will demand it and Masonry should at once recognize that fact and begin to put its house in order. Shall Masonry change what it has? No. Masonry needs but to teach carefully and logically through a definite plan of instruction in the lodges. The candidate of the future must be given something besides the ritual. Albert Pike says that symbolism is the soul of Masonry. The mechanically learned ritual can then be but the fleshy body of Masonry. The candidate of the present is but demanding his Masonic soul. Let Masonry give that to him, and the three REAL OBJECTS OF MASONRY as outlined will be achieved. * * * The number of Masons in the state may decline, but it will be the natural result of the removal of the wheat from the chaff. That which remains will be fruit and will bear fruit. Let Masonry immediately begin to attain the three REAL OBJECTS.

THE SUPREME ARTIST

By Rev. Gilbert Dobbs, Past Grand Chaplain

THE NINETEENTH division of the Psalms bears a message to every true Masonic heart. Here the harp of David vibrates with celestial music as though swept by a seraph's wing:

> "The heavens declare the glory of God;
> And the firmament sheweth His handiwork.
> Day unto day uttereth speech,
> And night unto night sheweth knowledge."

The dual revelation of God is the theme of this inspired ode. God is gloriously revealed in His Works and in His Word. The sun that rules the day, the moon that governs the night, and the stars that are chanting though to mortal ears inaudible, litanies to the Most High God.

The heavenly hosts—the solemn armies of the night in brilliant array are marching on to their mysterious destiny under divine command.

Vast galaxies of flaming suns, the spiral nebulae of worlds unborn and all the unapproachable glories of a boundless universe proclaim His infinite wisdom and power.

The Supreme Architect of the Universe is a Supreme Artist too.

Dr. Mackey calls attention to the striking coincidence that the letters forming the English word G-O-D, are the initial letters of three Hebrew words that mean respectively, Wisdom, Strength and Beauty, those three pillars of Freemasonry. We often speak of the God of Omniscience, Omnipotence and Omnipresence; but not so often of the God of Beauty.

Perhaps the very first impression that comes to us as we witness the glories of the day and the witchery of the night is one of the infinite and overpowering beauty of creation.

From his bridal chamber in the East the sun comes forth bringing with him the ineffable beauties of the dawn. His unseen painters brush his pathway over hills of gold with emerald, saffron and rose; and as he travels toward the west and the purple pavilions of the night he leaves behind the unearthly splendor of sunset skies.

The very Earth itself with its unique and multitudinous life is the beauty spot of the universe. God could have made a cold and cheerless world, but it dropped from His creative hand a thing of beauty divine.

Why did He spread over it by day its tent of azure blue with its miracle of floating clouds, and its purple canopy of night jeweled with stars? Why did He clothe her in the wondrous robes of the umbrageous forests and hang on her breast the breastplate of limpid lakes and seas; and hang about her neck such chains of silver streams? Why make the earth a paradise of birds and trees and flowers? And why vary the waters of the world with indigo blue of gulf and sea, the green of flowing rivers, the white of foaming cataracts, the prismatic colors of the sunbow, the sparkle of the diamond dews and the lacy beauty of the frost?

Why? Because He is the Supreme Artist. Because He is the God of Beauty, and because He made it to be the habitation of His masterpiece—esthetic MAN.

That beauty he has woven into the very fabric of man in his body, in his mind, in his soul.

"From harmony from heavenly harmony
This universal frame began
From harmony to harmony
Through all the compass of the notes it ran
The diapason closing full in man."

Then the glory of God is seen in the beauty and blessing of his Word. The works of God proclaim His wisdom and power; the Word of God his justice and mercy. The one His glory, the other His grace. The one is a challenge to the intellect, the other is a chalice for the soul. The one may arouse us to unspeakable wonder and awe; the other moves us to adoration and love.

The Universe may invite us into the wide fields of speculation, the Word defines for us the vaster issues of life. The one is the playground of science; the other is the laboratory of religion. No conflict here. Science deals with the facts and phenomena of the material world—religion with the no less indisputable facts and phenomena of spiritual experience. The one guides our minds to behold the glittering thrones of power; the other leads the soul into the sanctuaries of prayer and the Shekinahs of divine love.

The Word of God is a "lamp unto our feet and a light unto our path." It is more to be desired than much fine gold. It is sweeter than the honey in the honeycomb. It converts the soul, and in the keeping of it there is great reward.

"The proudest works of genius shall decay,

And reason's brightest lustre fade away,

The sophist's art, the poet's boldest flight,

Shall end in darkness and conclude in night,

But faith triumphant over time shall stand,

And grasping the sacred volume in her hand,

Shall back to its source the eternal gift convey,

Then in a flood of glory, fade away."

GENESIS AND GENIUS OF FREEMASONRY

By N. H. Ballard, Past Grand Master

THAT PERIOD in the history of Europe beginning with the downfall of the Roman Empire and lasting for nearly one thousand years is commonly known as the Dark Ages.

Great barons boasted that they could neither read nor write; such accomplishments belonged to poor clerks and scriveners. Theirs was the strong arm to strike down their enemies in battle. While the church did exert some feeble effort to educate the few in the simplest humanities, yet so engrossed were the clerics in their own assumptions of power and their conflict with great barons as to forget entirely the masses and leave them in almost total darkness.

There lived in Northern Europe a race of people fair of skin, blue of eyes and light of hair, who were destined to play an important part in the future history of the world. These people were brave and courageous. One among many of their noble characteristics was their respect for womanhood. It may well be said that from this people comes woman's liberation from the slavery of inferiority and the establishment of her civil and political freedom.

This people were being pressed by the Slavs from the east, who in turn were being attacked by the hordes of nomadic tribes in Central Asia. These Teutons had already gone as far north as possible; the ocean on the west had already been reached; to relieve this pressure they were forced southward toward the three European peninsulas—the Grecian, the Italian and the Iberian.

They came down on Italy like an avalanche and left imperial Rome a wreck, and established their own kingdom of Lombardy in the valley of the Po. They gave name to France and empire to Spain. They crossed the channel and gave everything, laws, language and customs to the British Isles.

In their southward course they came in contact with a new influence and the life of Him whose advent had been proclaimed by "peace on earth, good will toward men." While this people was not entirely subdued, yet

the mixing of the free, liberty-loving characteristics that
the forest life had taught them, with the teachings of
the gentle Nazarene so blended their traits as to make
of them an important factor in the future history of the
world.

The state of society developed after the downfall of
the Roman Empire is known as feudalism. It was based
on land tenure and the weak seeking the protection of
the strong. We will not here enter into the different
phases of its development, but if you would know and
understand medieval history, you must acquire a knowledge of its development and progress. The system resulted in a great number of comparatively small
baronies. The center was a castle or manor house in
which the lord lived with his family and retainers. About
this manor house were cultivated fields, woodland and
pasture lands. Most of the fields were the lord's; these
were planted, tilled and the harvest gathered and stored
in his barns by the tenants. The villiens and serfs were
assigned a very small piece of ground upon which they
labored when not engaged in the lord's work; yet the
small amount of grain that their little lot produced must
be carried to the lord's mill, where a heavy toll was
exacted. They toiled for others and received but little
reward for their labor.

These manors were little worlds in themselves. The
flax was raised in the fields and the wool was clipped
from the sheep, which they wove into cloth in their own
handlooms. The raw hides were tanned with the oak
bark from the forest and made into shoes and harness.
Every home had its ash-hopper that was leached for
alkali and by mixing it with the refuse grease, they
manufactured their own soap. There were carpenters,
blacksmiths and millwrights who made all the imple-
ments and machinery of the farm. The chief and almost
the only products they had to buy from the outside was
iron and salt.

This state of affairs was in itself an education. The
children reared in the atmosphere of farming, grazing
and manufacturing acquired a basic knowledge of the
three foremost occupations of man.

These people possessed a store of common sense.
They had acquired those simple yet ample rules of con-

duct and expressed them in pithy adages and sayings, many of which may be found in Poor Richard's Almanac and John Ploughman's Talks, such as: "Honesty is the best policy;" "A bird in the hand is worth two in the bush;" "An idle brain is the devil's workshop."

The village priest moved among the poor, a benediction as sweet as "the dew that falls on Hermon." He taught the children the catechism, the creed and the simple principles of religion, preparing them for confirmation by the Bishop. He sat at their frugal board and around their firesides in the evening. He held before the eyes of the dying the crucifix and made them look and live. To the survivors he spoke words of sweet consolation, and told them of Him who said: "Come unto me, all ye that labor and are heavy laden, and I will give you rest."

Yet one thing they lacked—freedom, liberty. As the caged bird beats its wings against the gilded bars, and peering out into the open space beyond, strives to regain the freedom of its native haunts, so in disconnected movements and ununited efforts the masses strove ineffectually against the bonds that bound them, in servitude.

"God moves in a mysterious way
His wonders to perform."

Complete freedom whether bestowed on individual or nation when they know not how rightly to use it, often is more harmful than good. They needed a long term in the school of experience before they could really appreciate its value or use it to their own advantage. In God's proper time and way it came, and being rightly prepared to receive it, they have been helped to the fullest measure.

The seventh century witnessed the rise of Mohammedism, Islam or the sword. With an insignificant beginning in the desert city of Mecca, it spread with a rapidity rarely equaled. Its victorious spread was only stopped by the Himalayan Mountains on the east, and its armies thundered against the walls of Vienna in the west. From the south they moved victorious through the Iberian Peninsula, crossed the Pyrenees and were effectually stopped at Tours by Charles Martel.

The eleventh century witnessed a return visit by Christian Europe to this Moslem foe. Rarely in the world's history has a people been so united in a common cause. With great faith and wonderful enthusiasm, with a heroism unsurpassed and courage undaunted, they pressed in surge after surge against this Saracen foe, but in the end they failed to accomplish their objective. Yet in their very defeat there was a grandeur unsurpassed, a heroism unequalled, and dauntless courage without a parallel.

Like a mighty river that leaps uncontrolled over the precipice and loses itself in spray and mist, so these mighty surges of Christian Europe against the Moslem were dissipated and only glorious memories left—memories that will last as long as mankind cherishes the deeds of the brave and the heroic.

We may have great faith, our motives may be as pure as the mountain snow, with a determination that knows no defeat, yet unless our efforts are rightly directed and correctly planned, our fondest hopes are dashed unrealized, against the walls of opposition. We may have faith that would move mountains, yet without work it availeth nothing. We are taught this truth in the rugged phrases of Masonry when we say that to achieve real success, God and the square must be present and we must be governed by the square and the rule.

While the Crusaders did not obtain that which they sought, yet their defeat was turned by God into a victory. While not at all what they expected or anticipated, yet they achieved a more enduring victory than if they had won their objective.

Rome conquered Greece, and copied bounteously from this country the products of her pencil and chisel, both in architecture and arts. The empyric rules of her grammarians and rhetoricians were bodily absorbed, but not the products of her philosophers and mathematicians. These were to find a safe retreat in Arabia, where they were eagerly cultivated and preserved. As a result of the Crusaders, there seeped from Arabia to Europe a knowledge of the sciences, philosophy, medicine and mathematics that here and there took root and was the direct cause of the Renaissance, the rebirth of Europe, the revival of learning that once had been hers, but long lost and now restored. Europe felt deeply this impulse and moved forward to the greatest accomplishments in the history of the whole world. It was not accomplished without bitter, blind and unrelenting opposition. The history of the fifteenth, sixteenth and seventeenth centuries tells the story of this conflict and final dawn.

Thousands of the villiens and serfs were released from the bondage of the manor to join in these crusades. On coming back they did not return to this bondage, but many became itinerant journeymen; others settled together, often around the seat of the king, thus forming what was to be future cities. There was a growing demand, both in the palace and in the castles of the barons, for fineries and such things as they could not manufacture on the farms, or else their home-made wares lacked the artistic appearance of the imported articles. Thus there grew up a system of commerce with these cities as the center of activities.

Thus there came an increasing number of people under the direct government of the king. The king used this power against the increasing demands of the barons and was finally able to crush them. Of course the invention of gunpowder helped this, for no longer could the baron raise his drawbridge, flood the moat about his castle and be secure. The cannon could tear down the wall of the castle and leave it subject to easy attack.

Someone has said that man's progress is like a pendulum, swinging from one extreme to another, yet ever upward and onward. The destruction of the power of the barons gave the king supreme power, and thus there developed an absolute monarchy, in which the king recognized that he governed by divine right and not by the right of the barons or the people. This development is represented in the Bourbons of France and the Stewarts of England.

The seventeenth century marks the culmination and final defeat of the Stewart dynasty. Freemasonry's birthday is just four years after the accession of George of the house of Brunswick to the English throne, a complete acknowledgement of right of Parliament to elect their king and define his qualifications and limitations; that he should govern not by his own will, but through ministers responsible to Parliament.

Thus Freemasonry is coeval with popular government in England. It breathes the spirit of the rule of the people and can only prosper in such an atmosphere. It perishes under tyranny, both of Church and State. It is the very embodiment of freedom and liberty. Well might its motto be: Liberty, Equality, Fraternity!

At the same time with the growth of cities there grew up a system of guilds, both merchant and craft guilds. These were organized for self-protection. One of the most important features of the guild system was apprenticeship. The young man would bind himself to a master, usually for a term of seven years, to be taught the particular trade of the master. He lived usually in the master's home and was furnished both food and clothing. When he had completed his apprenticeship and received the endorsement of the master, that he was a skilled workman in his particular trade, he was then accepted as a fellow of the craft. As such, he could travel, work at his trade and receive the wages of a craftsman.

Masons should be very much interested in one of these guilds, known as the Freemasons' guild. It could with all propriety be called the churchbuilders' guild. From this guild Freemasonry can show a direct descent.

For some time previous to the year one thousand there was a general belief throughout Christendom that the world would come to an end at that time. But the time came and passed; the sun continued to shine and the seasons followed each other in order. In the meantime, no new churches were built and the old were permitted to fall into decay. There soon came a revival of church building, not only in repairing the old churches but in erecting new ones.

It seems that when great changes and revolutions are in progress that will affect the destiny of mankind, great men appear on the scene fully prepared for the emergency. If the American Revolution had not occurred, Washington would have been only the Potomac farmer, Jefferson the lawyer at Williamsburg and Franklin the printer at Philadelphia; whereas Washington led victorious armies, Jefferson with great skill composed the declaration of rights and constitution, and Franklin became a great diplomat.

So there slowly developed a corporation, a guild of builders, who within the next four centuries were to send Strasburg's spire to conspire with the clouds, to make Cologne the most beautiful building in the world, and to fill hill and moor of Europe with the most wondrous works of art.

They chiseled in granite block the sweetest story ever told—a story of love, devotion and sacrifice. They sent their temples to heights never before attempted by the builders of art. The soft light of the interior had about it the repose and stillness of the forest primeval. These builders were imbued with a deep religious zeal. They toiled not for meat and bread, but with a sense of worship. They glorified God in Gothic temples. These craftsmen portrayed in stone the life and passions of their Lord and Master whom they devoutly served. They carved Bibles out of stones and made marble blocks speak a language of love and adoration.

In the course of time a new form of expression was invented. With a few movable types and a little ink, thousands of Bibles could be printed and read and re-read by millions, whereas beautiful Cologne, on which a large number of craftsmen labored through many decades, and on which countless treasures had been expended, could be read and appreciated only by those comparatively few who lived in its vicinity.

Victor Hugo, in his Notre Dame, depicts a wonderful scene. He represents the King of France in disguise, visiting a priest in a cloister adjoining the famous cathedral of Notre Dame. Before the priest was a printed book, one among the first ever published. Pointing his finger at the new printed book and then toward the somber walls of the great cathedral he said: "This will destroy that." He did not mean that the printed books would destroy religion, of which the great cathedral was a symbol, but this new form of expression would supplant architecture that had been used by man from time immemorial to record his prayers, his hopes and his fears.

This new form of expression was destined to revolutionize the thoughts of a great people and bring to the masses Liberty, Equality and Fraternity.

Architecture declined. The genius and labor that had created these wonderful works of art was to be directed into other channels. The ravages of war and ruthless time will gradually destroy the buildings; but the thoughts of love, devotion and sacrifice will continue to live in the printed page throughout countless ages and be a sweet benediction to the millions that the stone edifice could never have reached.

The creative genius and skilled workmanship of this craft was no longer needed; but from its dying embers Freemasonry lights the torch of freedom of thought, liberty of speech and equality of opportunity, and presses onward to new accomplishments. It will build with legends and symbols temples in the hearts of men, temples not made with hands, eternal in the heavens. It raises high its banner of white upon which is inscribed in letters of gold: "For God and Humanity." With a prayer upon its lips, with eyes to the front, with lofty ideals and noble purpose, with malice toward none and charity to all, it moves onward to final victory.

When Martin Luther nailed to the door of Wittenburg his ninety-three theses and successfully maintained his contention against the sale of indulgences, he opened a new vista in the world's history. In the doctrines enunciated, Freemasonry does not take sides, either with Luther or Rome. The adherents of either may sit side by side in a Masonic Lodge and each respect the beliefs of the other. But in the fundamental doctrine of free thought and free speech Masonry makes no compromise. Upon this foundation stone it builds and confidently awaits the final victory.

This protest of Luther gave to the individual the right to think and form his own opinions. It resulted in the translating and publishing of the Bible in the vernacular of the people. It increased the desire of thousands to learn to read that they might themselves peruse and study this book that told of the history of an ancient people who through many vicissitudes of fortune preserved the idea of the oneness of God and that He should be worshipped in spirit and in truth.

The ruling hierarchy of the church asserted that this Book of Books could not be understood by the layman. On the other hand, it was asserted that if the book really be of God, then any human soul that places itself in the right position and earnestly seeks God, to it will the God in the printed pages be revealed.

Masonry teaches that the individual may obtain God if he rightly seeks Him, that the attainment of God's kingdom is based upon an individual choice. Hence Freemasonry stands for universal education and enlightenment, that each individual may have the opportunity of interpreting God not only to himself but to the fellow man.

* * * * *

You have a birthday. It marks the beginning of your individual existence, but not your real beginning, for you are the product of countless generations. Indeed, the pulsation of your heart, is but the rhythmic beat caught from a mother's heart, and so on back to the first mother.

Freemasonry's birthday is St. John the Baptist's Day, (June 24th) 1717. The place is London, at an insignificant alehouse known as The Goose and Gridiron. At that time and at that place was organized a Grand Lodge of Free and Accepted Masons, the first Grand Lodge of speculative Masons ever organized. From this organization every body of Freemasons of whatever name or rite, must show either directly or indirectly its origin, or else it is not Masonic as we know Masonry.

It was born of poor but honest parents. No herald proclaimed its advent. For the first four years of its existence there was no Secretary, hence no records. No contemporaneous diarist or scribbler even mentions its existence. Just what was done during those four years, we wish we knew, yet the world-wide ramifications of Freemasonry today tell us that it was built on a firm and sure foundation.

While we know less than a dozen names connected with these four years of the beginning of Freemasonry, yet three stand out in bold prominence, and every Freemason should know not only their names but their contribution to the beginning of Freemasonry.

The first and foremost of these three is John Theophilus Desaguliers, the father of the Masonic ritual and chief founder of Masonry. His father and family were driven from France after the revocation of the Edict of

Nantes, for no other offence than that the elder Desaguliers was a Protestant minister and preached justification by faith. We like to think that Desaguliers kept in
remembrance the wrongs that were done to his family
and thousands of other French people by the unholy
combination and corrupt kingcraft and corrupt priest-
craft, hoping the formation of a society advocating universal education and enlightenment would have sufficient
force and power to prevent such an unholy combination
in the future.

Dr. Desaguliers was an A. M. graduate of Oxford,
and later this college conferred on him the degree of
LL. D. He took orders and was a learned theologian. He
was a most excellent mathematician and indefatigable
in his research in natural philosophy. In each of these
lines he achieved some distinction. You will be interested in studying the effect of this trinity of accomplishments (theology, mathematics and philosophy) on the
Masonic ritual.

The second name in this trio is George Payne, an
eminent antiquarian, a gentleman and a scholar. It was
he who gave the rules and regulations of Freemasonry,
and he might well be called the father of Masonic
jurisprudence.

The third was James Anderson, D. D., a Scotchman
and a Presbyterian preacher, who rendered valuable
service in the early period of Freemasonry.

While we are not sure as to the contents of the ritual
of this period, yet there seems to be no doubt but that it
was a ritual of one degree. The operative guilds received a young man, freeborn, of mature age and of
good reputation, who during the seven years of his apprenticeship, was taught all the arts, points and parts of
the secrets of Masonry, and upon receiving the endorsement of his master as to his proficiency in the arts, was
accepted a Fellow of the Craft and could travel where
his services might be needed and receive the wages of a
Craftsman. So the first period of speculative Masonry
had but one initiation, that conferred upon the candidate
all the rights and privileges of Freemasonry.

Especially during the seventeenth century these Masonic lodges in a decadent condition were fast losing their operative character and becoming merely social organizations. Many men other than Craft Masons were being introduced into their organization. The Rotarians, Kiwanians and like clubs will give you a general idea of the recrudescence of this period. Amid innocent mirth and around the festive board serious questions may be discussed for the general good of the community.

It was during this period that some form of initiation or ritual was introduced into the decadent Lodges. It appears that this ritual had a German origin, perhaps from Cologne. Its source seems to be from a Lodge dedicated to St. John the Baptist. This gradually developed into the idea of a mythical Grand Lodge of St. John from which they derived their authority. The phrase "at Jerusalem" was added much later and should be disregarded. The addition of St. John the Evangelist to this dedication, while of late origin, yet satisfactorily completes the dedication.

While this ritual was simple and crude, yet it forms the basis of the highly organized ritual of the Masonry of today. While we can only surmise just what this ritual was, yet we may be reasonably assured that it is the present day ritual of the Entered Apprentice degree, with a few omissions and additions and many refinements. This we know: that the penal sign, grip and pass-word of an Entered Apprentice is the same now as then, and is in universal use among Masons.

This period, 1721-1725, marks the transformation of Masonry from a one degree system to three degrees. The controversy between the purely operative Masons and the speculative, or as they were then called, gentlemen Masons, had subsided. Speculative Masons were in complete control. Dr. Desaguliers was extremely cautious in the introduction of these two additional degrees. They were of the nature of higher degrees. Always remember that basically Masonry is one degree. The expansion into three degrees completes the formula: One is three and three is one.

In the same year (1721) that the Fellowcraft degree was first conferred in London, Dr. Desaguliers journeyed

to Edinburg, where he introduced this degree in Edin-
burgh Lodge. This Lodge has in their possession the
oldest authentic Lodge minutes of any Masonic Lodge,
dating back to 1598, and like the London Lodges, had
for many years been conferring Masonry on others than
operative Masons. The basic one degree system of both
was undoubtedly similar, both having had a common
origin from Germany. These Scotch Lodges held in high
veneration the patron saint of Freemasonry, St. John the
Baptist. They like London recognized a mythical Grand
Lodge of St. John, from which they derived their ritual.
Hence even to this day Scotland proclaims her Masonry
to be St. John's Masonry.

It appears that the Master's degree was not introduced into Scotland until a much later date. The first
record of this degree being conferred in Scotland is in
1737, one year previous to the formation of the Grand
Lodge of Scotland.

Scotland has always followed the English ritual. The
Mark Master's degree is the only exception. This degree
is a component part of the Scotch Master's degree. Every
Master Mason is invested with the Mark Master's degree. It is the same degree as is conferred in the Royal
Arch Chapter in America. Craft Masonry in England
has never accepted the Mark degree.

By 1723 the Fellow Craft degree had been accepted
as a component part of the Masonic system, but conferred only in the Grand Lodge in their quarterly sessions.
A new requirement was added, predicating membership
in the Grand Lodge on the possession of this degree.
Heretofore an Entered Apprentice could hold any office
either in constituent or Grand Lodge.

During this same period there is mention made of the
Master's part. But it is evidently not the Master's degree
as we know it; it was rather an investiture of the Master
at the time of his installation with the stone squarer's
or Jerusalem word. It corresponds to the Past Master's
degree of the present time; the password is the same.
The Master's degree as we know it was not to be introduced before 1725 and not to come into general use in
the Lodges for several years later.

Thus 1725 marks the completion of speculative Masonry into a system or rite of three degrees. While there

have been some additions as well as some omissions, and many refinements, still the ritual that you know today is in all essentials the ritual of 1725.

If some Rip Van Winkle had been made a Mason in 1725 and just awakened from his long sleep of two centuries, he could by the recital of his initiation theme be admitted to any Masonic Lodge of today.

There was nothing new in the first section either of the Fellow Craft or Master's degree. The changes are merely adapting the particular degree. For example, the apron is used in all three degrees, with a difference in the way of wearing it to distinguish the degree you have attained. There was transferred from the Entered Apprentice degree to the second section of the Fellow Craft, the seven liberal arts and sciences emphasizing the importance of geometry, the five orders of architecture, the two pillars and the porch of Solomon's Temple. There was added to this the legend of the winding stairs and the letter "G." The second section of the Master's degree consisted only of the Hiramic legend.

"The Constitution of Freemasons," edited by Dr. James Anderson, was first published in 1725. This was the first Masonic book ever published and corresponds to the monitors and manuals of the present day. It was in current use for the first fifty years of Freemasonry. It is divided into three parts: first, The History of Masonry; second, The Ancient Charges of a Freemason; third, General Regulations, compiled by George Payne.

The historical section is nothing more than a fairy tale. It may be disregarded entirely, except you may be interested in the great advance made in the treatment of history during the last two hundred years. The second and third sections are most important. It gives us the basis for our Masonic duties and actions. It is a source from which we must continually draw, that we may not wander from the true Masonic course.

The first paragraph of the Charges is very important. I quote the whole paragraph:

"A Mason is obliged by his tenure to obey the moral law; and if he rightly understands the art, he will never be a stupid atheist or an irreligious libertine. But though in ancient times Masons were

charged in every country to be of the religion of
that country or nation, whatever it was, yet it is now
thought more expedient only to oblige them to that
religion in which all men agree, leaving their particular opinions to themselves; that is, to be good
men and true or men of honor and honesty, by
whatever denomination or persuasion they may be
distinguished; whereby Masonry becomes the center
of union and the means of conciliating true friendship among persons that must have remained at a
perpetual distance."

Again quoting from the section headed "Behavior
after the Lodge is over and the Brethren are gone:"

"Therefore no private piques or quarrels must
be brought within the door of the Lodge, far less
any quarrels about religion, or nations or state
policy, we being only as Masons of the catholic religion above mentioned, we are also of all nations,
tongues, kindreds and languages and are resolved
against all politics, as what never yet conduced to
the welfare of the Lodge nor ever will."

Again quoting the qualifications of applicants:

"The persons admitted members of a Lodge must
be good and true men, free born, and of mature and
discreet age, no bondsmen, no women, no immoral
or scandalous men, but of good report."

The first contests among Masons had been whether
the operative or the speculative elements should control.
The contest developed some bitterness, but finally the
speculative members won complete victory, separating
themselves completely from the operative, retaining only
its glorious memories and traditions.

History records no more wonderful declaration than
this, so bold, so resolute. It has in it all the elements of
the heroic. A small band of men numbering but a few
hundred, with but a few among these whose name was
known beyond their own bailiwick, boldly proclaiming
the organization of a great peace society that would
ultimately bring warring nations into a state of friendship and concord, that would conciliate true friendship
among people who otherwise would be kept apart.

It invites all good and true men, of whatever country or tongue they may be, to unite into a great brotherhood, raising high that white banner upon whose white surface is inscribed in letters of gold the words: "For God and for Humanity!" and press on to sure victory; to join in battle array against those forces of ignorance, tyranny, intolerance, bigotry and all other forces that may contribute to man's enslavement and degradation.

Martin Clare in 1732 was authorized and directed to revise the ritual and lectures. He was a scholarly man and literary in his taste. He changed the doggerel verse in which the early ritual had been composed, into better English.

To the Entered Apprentice symbols he added the point within a circle, to the Fellow Craft the winding stairs that previously had consisted of seven steps, was changed to three, five and seven; the seven to represent the seven liberal arts and sciences; the five, both the five human senses as well as the five orders of architecture; the three, the Trinity.

He also introduced "the pass and token of the pass." It was a substitute for the true word and true grip of the Fellow Craft and the Master's degree, entrusted to the candidate in the ante room, by means of which he gained admission and was enabled to pass the different guards. The older Masons can recall the persistent inquiry: "How can a Fellow Craft enter a Master's Lodge?" Past Grand Master Thos. H. Jeffries cut the Gordian knot by suggesting that the Lodge be called to refreshment during the conferring of the second section of the Master's degree. No doubt the same question, "How can an Entered Apprentice be admitted to a Fellow Craft Lodge?" was asked at that early period, and so "the pass and token of the pass" was invented. In America it is used for an entirely different purpose, that of protecting the true word and grip. We seem to have liked the idea and so invented and introduced due guards to protect the true signs. These are in use only in America.

Up to 1732 the obligation applied only to secrecy. The many points it now contains were taught in lectures and charges. Martin Clare added several additional points that have grown today to many—perhaps too many. You weaken an obligation when you overload it.

By 1738 Masonry had become firmly established and was growing rapidly. Grand Lodges had been established in Ireland, France and Scotland. Several provincial Grand Lodges had already been established in the American colonies. It had grown from a purely local organization in London until its aspirations had grown world-wide. Its ritual had attained both in phraseology and contents practically the same standards as it has today. Its laws, rules and regulations had been firmly established.

As from a clear sky there came a thunderbolt hurled against it from Rome in the Bull of Clement XII, dated the 28th April, 1738. It condemned in unmeasured terms the institution itself. It forbade the faithful of the Pope's obedience to harbour it, to conceal it, or in any way to join with it, under no less penalty than excommunication and from which only the Pope could absolve the dying. This was amended the next year as to the papal states and adding the penalties of confiscation of property and even death without hope of mercy. Just the cause of this bitter denunciation is not clear. Evidently however it was the punishment of the whole on account of some apparent infraction of a small part. It must have been on account of the Masonry of France and the Continent. Masonry of the English Constitution contains nothing either in ritual or laws that could have possibly called forth a denunciation so bitter and so unrelenting. The renewal of these decrees has been made from time to time, * * * in comparatively recent times.

I recall at this latter time in my Lodge, Ocean No. 214, at Brunswick, there were in its roster the names of several Irish Roman Catholics. It was the religion of their fathers throughout many generations; they were devoutly attached to it; they knew well that this denunciation must have been based on misinformation, for the Masonry with which they were familiar contained nothing to justify such a condemnation; but necessity forced them to make a choice, and be it said to their credit that most of them remained faithful to their Masonic obedience, even unto their death. If in one small Lodge so many remained true and staunch Masons, how many thousands throughout the world must have remained faithful even unto the end.

In more recent years the fulmination of the Pope has been directed in bitter, unrelenting denunciation of the public schools. The very life and existence of Freemasonry is firmly bound up in the perpetuation of these schools. The hope of the future is wrapped up in their continuance. Then let us with faith undaunted in God and in humanity gird our loins for the battle and press on even unto victory.

There is nothing whatever in Freemasonry that in any way forbids Roman Catholic membership. They are even invited to join with us to battle against a common foe. In a Masonic Lodge there may sit side by side Jew and Gentile, Protestant and Catholic, Mohammedan and Buddhist, each maintaining inviolable his own peculiar faith, yet mutually respecting the faith of his companion. Separately and unitedly they strive for the final victory of Liberty, Fraternity and Equality.

The year 1738 marks the beginning of a dissension and schism that was to divide Masonry into two hostile camps and was not entirely to be healed for three-quarters of a century, but out of which grew a richer, greater Masonry.

A few Lodges in London, the membership of which were chiefly Irish, innocently began after the Lodge was closed to confer additional degrees. It corresponded to a custom in this country but a short while ago of conferring side degrees. This aroused the ire of the Grand Lodge of England, which had always been most conservative. First these Lodges were warned to desist, but they did not heed the warning, and all who persisted in this infraction were expelled and charters of at least two Lodges were taken up.

While this action seemingly for the time quieted the disturbance it did not succeed in preventing its continuance. These expelled Lodges continued to meet, make Masons and confer these additional degrees. This was to continue for fourteen years, when in 1752 was organized a schismatic Grand Lodge known as Ancient, Free and Accepted Masons. Thus originated A. F. & A. M.

in contradistinction to F. & A. M. of the old or constitutional Grand Lodge.

The principal degree conferred by these recalcitrants was the Royal Arch. It had but recently been introduced into England by Chevalier Ramsey, a Scottish Jacobite. The degree finally adopted by these schismatics was quite different from the Ramsey degree, both however based on the recovery of "the word." The Ramsey degree, now the thirteenth of the Scottish Rite, was based on the reattainment of "the word" by the three Grand Masters at the building of Solomon's Temple, which God had communicated to Enoch and preserved by him in a way explained in the degree.

The other conception of the degree, which is the Royal Arch of the American York Rite, consists of the repossession at the second building of the Temple, of "the word" which had been hidden by the three Grand Masters at the building of the first Temple. The one explains how "the word" came into the possession of Solomon, Hiram of Tyre and Hiram Abif; the other how this same word was recovered for Masonry under the direction of Zerubbabel, Joshua and Haggai.

The other degrees conferred by these Lodges were the Temple degree, now the eighteenth and thirtieth of the Scottish Rite and the Knight Templar of the Commandery; also the Knight of Babylon, which today is the fifteenth and sixteenth of the Scottish Rite and the Red Cross of the Commandery.

With the organization of a schismatic Grand Lodge during 1752 there developed a powerful contender against the old or constitutional Grand Lodge organized in 1717. From the beginning the new Grand Body was in spirit bold and aggressive. One name stands out in bold relief as its chief promoter—Lawrence Dermot. He was a man of considerable talent, but with a determination to succeed at any cost. To this end he did not hesitate to deceive and make statements that he could not but have known to be false. Yet nothing succeeds like success. This Grand Lodge became very popular and chartered numerous Lodges in America and through its army lodges sent its form of Masonry around the globe.

The main difference was the added degree of the Holy Royal Arch. It was known as the Masonry of the four degrees. It also authorized the conferring under its charter of other degrees. They changed the secret substitute word to the one we now use in America. They added the sign of distress and the words accompanying it. These appealed to the army Lodges and became so popular as to result in the invention of signs of distress both in the Constitutional Grand Lodge of England as well as the Grand Lodge of France. This accounts for the difference in these signs as used in America, England and the Continent. These three different signs of distress as well as the two substitute words should be communicated to each member at his raising.

The old or Constitutional Grand Lodge to prevent a member of the schismatic Grand Lodge from visiting any of their Lodges reversed the pass word of an Entered Apprentice and Fellow Craft. On this account they were termed innovators or modern Masons, whereas the schismatic Grand Lodge called themselves ancient. Thus the ancient Masons were the new and the modern Masons the old.

Around this date, 1772, we will cluster several Masonic events, some of which occurred just previously and others just after. We use this date because in that year was first published Preston's Illustrations of Masonry.

William Preston was a man of literary taste and considerable ability. He was an indefatigable student of the Masonic ritual. He was a constant visitor of the Lodges throughout England and even visited the Continent in his study of this ritual. Whatever may be said of the imperfections of "The Illustrations of Masonry," it was undoubtedly the most popular book on Masonry ever published, and gave direction and impulse to Masonic thought as no other book has done.

Though much abbreviated, it was literally copied by Thos. Smith Webb of America in his Monitor, which in turn has been slavishly copied by all the American Monitors and Lodge Manuals, with the sole exception of Pennsylvania. The Ahiman Rezon of this Grand Lodge bears the same title as the one first published by Laurence Dermot, the Grand Secretary of the Ancient Grand Lodge of England. It contains nothing of what we know as monitorial work. This is left unwritten—following the early traditions of Freemasonry—to be explained to the candidate by the Master at an initiation. We call a Master bright when he can glibly repeat the ritual, but under the old customs he must in addition to this be versed in the philosophy of the ritual as well as the Masonic symbolry.

William Preston undoubtedly received much inspiration from William Hutchinson, Master of Durham Castle Lodge in the north of England. His lectures on the three degrees attracted wide attention. His lectures were perhaps too sectarian to come into general use. His published work, "Spirit of Masonry," should be read by every Masonic student as the first attempt to present the philosophy of Masonry in printed form.

This period (1772) approximately marks the date of the recognition by the grand bodies of Ireland and Scotland of the Ancient or Athol Grand Lodge. They not only did this, but adopted the work of the Ancient instead of the Constitutional Grand Lodge, which had been previously in use in both of these jurisdictions. This accounts for the fact that the substitute word and sign of distress is the same in Scotland, Ireland and America and different in England and on the Continent.

Dunkerley belongs to this period. To the esoteric work of the Constitutional Grand Lodge he perhaps added the sign of pity, the sign of admiration, as well as the distress sign, all still in use in English Lodges, but nowhere else. He also mutilated that great symbol of Freemasonry, the Tarsel Board, by separating it into three parts: Jacob's Ladder, the Ornaments of a Lodge and the four cardinal virtues. He also added to the point within the circle, two parallel lines and the two St. Johns. To all of this explanations were given "so absurd as actually to excite admiration."

At the end of the War of Independence, although one or two of the Colonies had formed independent Grand Lodges, the majority of the Lodges were left without any Grand Lodge. It is significant that a majority of the Lodges chartered by the Ancients took the side of the colonists, while on the other hand the Lodges chartered by the Constitutional Grand Lodge were favorable to England, hence Tories. Grand Lodges were quickly organized in the American States and practically all adopted the work of the Ancients.

During this period there arose an apostle of Freemasonry in the person of Thomas Smith Webb. He published a Monitor that was almost in universal use in America for many years, and was as well the chief sponsor of the Webb-Preston lectures that form the basis of the catechism and ritual of all the States, with the sole exception of Pennsylvania.

In the charters of all Ancient Lodges, authority and permission was given to confer the additional degrees of Royal Arch, Red Cross, etc. When the different Lodges surrendered their charters to the Grand Lodge, the new charters issued did not authorize the conferring of these extra degrees. They thus became orphans without any central authority. It was the genius of Webb that combined these into Chapter and Commandery, thus establishing what is known as the York or American Rite. He may therefore be called the father of the York Rite.

In 1801, at Charleston, South Carolina, a few zealous Masons organized The Ancient and Accepted Scottish Rite. They used the French Rite of Perfection as the basis and added eight additional degrees, making thirty-three in all. All Scottish Rite bodies in the world derive their authority either directly or indirectly from this body. It is rightly called the Mother Council of the World.

Both the Scottish and York Rites are misnomers. The Scottish Rite has nothing to do and is no way connected with the Masonry of Scotland, and the York Rite likewise has nothing to do with York.

Today Masonry in England presents a unified front. This happy and much desired event occurred in 1813, when the two Grand Lodges combined under the title of The United Grand Lodge of England.

During this period in England the Reverend George Oliver was a prolific contributor to Masonic literature— some writings interesting, others dull. "The Revelations of a Square," purporting to be the story told of the square worn by the first Grand Master in 1717, down to 1813, is based on a diary by Dr. Oliver's father. While it may not be historically accurate, yet it is the one source from which we obtain an idea of the early workings of Masonry.

Wm. J. Hughan makes wonderful contributions to Freemasonry in his search of the old and hidden manuscripts dealing with the early history of Masonry, and the meticulous care exercised in the editing of these manuscripts. His contributions are the most important in the whole history of Masonry.

In America there were three outstanding names. If you would be a well-informed Mason, you should know something of the contributions of each. They are: Albert Pike, Albert G. Mackey and Theodore S. Parvin.

*   *   *   *   *

The first section of each of the three degrees is esoteric. The discussion of these is to be oral, within tyled Lodges. There is current a series of questions and answers that are presumed to give reasons of each act of initiation. However, they are not official and are unworthy of the dignity that belongs to the Masonic ritual, being puerile, insipid and devoid of any educational value.

Interpretation under correct guidance should be made by yourself, and when formulated should become a component part of your very being. They may be general or individual. You may interpret the ritual in terms of the human race, emerging from darkness to light, from barbarism to civilization, from ignorance to enlightenment, or in terms of the masses under the rule of feudalism, oppressed by church and state, as they gradually emerge into a state of freedom and liberty; or you may interpret it in terms of yourself, as you develop from childhood into the full growth of manhood.

Why was I required to make an application upon my own free will and accord, without improper solicitation of friends? What did I profess in that application? What did my vouchers profess? Why was the application required to lay over and not be acted upon immediately after its receipt? What was the reason for such things done to me? What was the import of such things said to me? Combine these into preparatory admission, entrance and dedication and so on. Try to give an interpretation of these when taken as a whole.

Let me illustrate: You were made a Mason because you were a man, not simply of the male sex, but a man in the full sense of the word; because your mind was free to accept the truth when rightly presented to you; because you would not let bias and prejudice control it; on account of the fact you were both in mind and body mature, capable of forming mature judgments; because the people among whom you had lived spoke well of you, and using an old expression, you came under the tongue of good report.

A school room has furniture, such as desks, chairs, etc., with appliances such as charts, maps, globes, books. These should not be confused with the object and purpose of the school; they are but means to an end; the real purpose is to convey knowledge. So a Masonic Lodge has lights, furniture, ornaments, charts, but these must not be confounded with the purpose of a Masonic Lodge, which is to give light. The appliances are but the means toward the end.

Whatever explanation or suggestions may be given in the three degrees is not intended as "ipse dixits" but merely suggestions to aid you in forming your own interpretations of the symbols, so that they may be incorporated as a part of your being. Only such interpretations are of any value. Many of the interpretations will not come to you at once, but each correctly learned will aid you in the others.

A lodge symbolizes the whole world or the universe and its dimensions are said to be in length from east to west, in breadth from north to south, and from heaven's dome to earth's center. Its covering is a clouded canopy. It is said to be supported by three pillars, denominated Wisdom, Strength and Beauty, for there must be wisdom to contrive, strength to support and beauty to adorn. Beauty is here used in its ethical sense, conveying the idea of harmony. You may never fully appreciate or understand this great symbol, but as you approach to a solution, it will widen your conception of God's work and your appreciation of the universality of Masonry.

The Great Lights may be best understood by referring to the earlier explanations of them.

Q. What makes a Lodge?

A. God and the square, with five or seven worthy Masons, on the highest hills or lowest valleys.

The highest hills and lowest valleys simply convey the idea of secrecy. Five and seven are important in Masonic symbolry; five is said to make a Lodge, seven a perfect Lodge.

Later there was added to the first two the compasses, making the three Great Lights, the Bible, square and compasses. The explanation was simply that the Bible is dedicated to God, the compasses to the Master and the square to the Craft. The monitorialists have unfortunately changed this by dedicating the square to the Master and the compasses to the Craft.

The Master wears the square not by his own right but as a gift from the Craft. It is theirs to bestow and theirs to take away. If more Masters would rightly understand this emblem, they would not try to rule a Lodge in an arbitrary manner.

The compasses are the Master's jewel. He earns it by planning and supervising the labor of the Craft, and when he has served his time and placed the Craft's emblem on the neck of another, he may be presented with the compasses, a Past Master's jewel, which he wears throughout, an honorable life and transmits to his children as a proud memento that he presided over a Masonic Lodge.

The medieval Masons were the church builders. When the ground plans had been laid out, the first building erected was a lodge or workshop. It was erected just south of the site of the church, and was rectangular in shape. It had windows in the south, east and west. There were none in the north because the rays of the sun could not reach that side, and the wall of the church as it was raised would shut off the little reflected light from that source.

Originally the Bible, square and compasses were called the furniture of a Lodge, and the lights were three windows and three burning tapers, perhaps representing light by day and light by night. In time the Bible, square and compasses, the three great lights, the windows and artificial lights were combined into a symbol of three burning tapers, arranged in the eastern, western and southern parts of the Lodge. In the earlier ritual they were said to refer to the Trinity—Father, Son and Holy Ghost. When Masonry assumed the character of a universal brotherhood, these were said to refer to sun, moon and Master Mason. The explanation of these is most puerile if taken literally. It evidently hides a deeper meaning; the interpretation is for you to make that it may become your own.

A Lodge is said to have three movable and immovable jewels; the square, level and plumb, the movable; and the rough ashlar, the smooth ashlar and the trestleboard, the immovable. The square, level and plumb are assigned as emblems to the three principal officers and are also the working tools of a Fellow Craft. They are bestowed upon the officers by the pleasure of the Craft and therefore movable.

The place of the immovable jewels is fixed in the northeast corner of the Lodge room, and consists of a drawing-board supported upon a trestle and upon each side of the rough and smooth ashlars, supported upon proper columns. Upon this board are drawn the geometric symbols of Freemasonry, with other appropriate designs used in architecture. Chiefly they consist of a point within a circle, the forty-seventh problem of Euclid, two intersecting circles in a semi-circumference; three right angle triangles are drawn on the diameter of the hypotenuse. Two of them are called oblong squares, the other a perfect square—an equilateral triangle surmounting a patee cross.

You will have no difficulty in correctly interpreting the rough and the smooth ashlar. The geometric designs on the trestle-board are most important and conceal Masonry's chief secrets.

The intersecting circles were most important to the early Masons. This was the basis for the design for the windows in the churches they built. It was called by the early Christians Ichthus, or fish and was everywhere carved on the walls of the catacombs. To them it signified regeneration. Let me give a probable help to its interpretation, using a biological illustration. A small rounded mass falls from the tassel of a corn-stalk upon the end of a silken strand. It passes through the hollow of the silk and comes into contact with another rounded mass of the same size at the base of the embryonic grain. These two coalesce and form a new mass of practically the same size as either one. This gives life to the grain, which rapidly develops into a full-grown grain of corn. Will this grain live again? Thou fool! Knowest thou not that this grain must die before it can again live?

The point within a circle is not of cabalistic origin, nor has it any reference to Phallic worship, nor is it a symbol of the sun. It is of purely geometric origin. The monitorialists have added two parallel lines, the figures of the two St. Johns and other adornments, and to the whole "give an explanation so absurd as actually to excite admiration."

In the old lecture is the following, explaining point, lines, superfices and solid:

> Point, the center (round which the Mason cannot err); line, length without breadth; superfices, length and breadth; solid, comprehends the whole.

In the revision of the lectures in 1732 by Martin Clare, for the above there was substituted the point within a circle. It is therefore based upon the fundamental definition of geometry. You may never fully solve it, yet by continual application you may approach a solution.

A point is a fit representation of God. We may conceive of this point in motion, and the resultant, the universe is created; or we may conceive of an infinite number of circles about the point, and wherever an individual may be in the universe, he will of necessity touch one of these circles.

A circle is composed of an infinite number of straight lines or infinitesimal tangents. If one of these sides is bisected by a perpendicular, it will pass through the center. Again, if an object is revolving in a circle, held to the center by a line or force, if this be snapped the object leaves the circle and goes off in a tangent. Yet however far it may travel it will always be on a circumference of one of the infinite circles that emanate from the center. If the individual will but halt, reflect and rightly bisect the tangent, he may again attain the center. Thus howsoever far a human soul may depart from God, it can never get beyond His influence and His salvation.

Note that the figure formed by the bisection of the line forms a tau cross, the crux ansata of the Egyptians, the sign that was said to have been made with the blood of a lamb on the doorposts of the Hebrews to protect them from the fury of the Pharaoh. It is a universal sign of salvation.

The same general thought may be obtained from figure on the trestle-board. This figure may readily represent the steps of perfect and oblong squares by which we hope to obtain the secrets of Masonry. A cubical stone was supposed to be in the center of the Holy of Holies, called the Stone of Foundation and symbolizing truth, the ultimate end of Masonic research. The individual standing on the porch of the Temple assumes the step of an oblong square with the longer side to the right. In bisecting this square, he goes to the right of the center, thereby failing in his attempt. He then tries the oblong square with the longer side to the left, and again fails. Not until he uses the perfect square, the bisection of which passes straight to the center is he permitted to stand on the Stone of the Foundation with Urim and Thummim upon his shoulders and light and perfection about him.

Originally the furniture of a Lodge was given as the Three Great Lights (Bible, compasses and square), and the Tarsel Board. Both were held in the highest esteem by the early Masons.

The Tarsel Board consisted of a mosaic pavement surrounded by a border and in the center a blazing star called "Glory in the Center." From the four corners hung four tassels. The monitorialists have unfortunately separated this symbol into three parts: Jacob's ladder, the ornaments of a Lodge and the four cardinal virtues. The division is unfortunate, and completely destroys this great symbol of Freemasonry.

If the universe were projected upon the plane of the ecliptic, this figure would be made; the blazing star, Polaris, the mosaic pavement, the surface of the earth, and the beautiful border about it, the zodiac. All other stars of the heavens change their apparent positions day by day and month by month save the North star, the star of constancy. It shines from the north, the Masonic place of darkness, and is fitly represented by faith. The earth, with its variegated surface, with its mountains and plains, its rushing streams and placid lakes, its forests and grassy leas, its shades and shadows, may well represent hope. The beautiful border about it may well symbolize love. The four tassels hanging from the four corners represent the four cardinal virtues, Fortitude, Justice, Prudence and Temperance.

Remember you are dealing with ethics or moral philosophy. It is well to get the correct use of these terms in an ethical sense. The four cardinal virtues were so named by Socrates. He was the founder of the science of ethics. To these St. Augustine added three cardinal virtues: Faith, Hope and Charity, and called them the theological virtues.

Cardinal is derived from "cardo," a hinge. The Latin word for heart is derived from the same word. Hence, in an ethical sense cardinal means turning. Virtue is from "vir," a man, and implies strength, power, potentiality. Cardinal virtues are those powers or potentialities that cause you to turn from the wrong to the right direction. Thus the chief cardinal virtues of Masonry consist of the four Socratic and the three theological virtues, making seven in all. Compare this with the fact that seven makes a perfect lodge.

Virtue is used in its ethical sense. When Christ turned to someone who touched His garments, He said: "For I perceive that virtue has gone out of me." Get your dictionary and familiarize yourself with the ethical meaning of these words: One example: Temperance, derived from the Latin word "Tempus," time. You temper steel, glass, mortar. What is the basic idea, for instance, in tempering steel? It is heated to a certain temperature, then plunged into a liquid for a certain time; the duration of this gives the proper degree of hardness to the metal.

While temperance conveys the idea of moderation, yet it also implies patience, and completes the formula:

"Abide your time in patience, etc." Study these virtues and apply them to your own conduct.

These Socratic virtues have been criticized by modern writers on ethics as incomplete in number. They were never intended to give all the forces that may cause us to turn from the wrong to the right direction, but rather types of these forces.

While it will be both interesting and instructive to apply the separate virtues to your own life, yet the full meaning of the symbol is in all these virtues taken as a whole.

The Tarsel Board was invented in operative Lodges, those places which have been called properly: "Parliaments of genius," where learned laymen and high prelates discussed with much freedom questions that were forbidden on the outside. If these discussions had become known, it would have lost for the prelate his cassock and for the laymen even his head. They freely spoke of faith and practice and interpreted passages of Scripture to which they had access; also the work of Plato and Aristotle and other Greek philosophers were opened to them. These expressed thoughts of great souls that had lain buried for more than fifteen centuries and almost forgotten—these great thoughts burned into their souls and could not be erased. As yeast in the right medium and proper temperature works, and unless properly contained boils over, so these ideas and thoughts just overflowed and joined with that irresistible stream of the Renaissance and the Reformation which has meant so much to mankind.

This symbol is also represented by an equilateral triangle, surmounting a patee cross: △—the triangle representing Faith, Hope and Charity, and the cross Fortitude, Justice, Prudence and Temperance. These were also represented by four tassels pendant from the four corners of the Lodge room. These seem to have been omitted in America, but are still common in English Lodges. They were also represented by the four acute angles of the patee cross, as ✠ for Fortitude, and so on.

The three theological virtues represent the religious instinct in man, and are derived from the Hebrew. The four cardinal virtues, the philosophical instinct or reason have a Greek source. Both of these are essential to the full and complete development of character. Man only attains approximate perfection when each of these is harmoniously blended and act together. If the religious instincts are predominant, we have the Middle Ages with the church supreme. If the philosophical instincts entirely prevail, we have the period of the French Revolution, when the very name of God was banished, and a woman of the streets was set up as the Goddess of Reason, with the wild orgies that followed.

The human soul unconsciously feels a separation of the divine within itself from the Great Divine; it seeks a reuniting. Darkness is about it. In its helplessness it turns its eye to the star of constancy, "Glory in the Center," and asks for succor and strength. The current of the divine enters the heart and makes contact with the divine principle within us, and a spark is produced. This we call faith.

God is attainable by all men. There can be no one so lonely or alone, but who earnestly, devoutly and rightly seeking God, he will find Him. This faith strengthens the human soul and gives it courage to fight valiantly against the evils that beset it. And when at last the time of his departure arrives, as it must, he may "wrap the draperies of his couch about him and lie down to pleasant dreams" of immortality.

If the mountain will not come to Mohammed, Mohammed will go to the mountain. Faith can indeed move mountains, but always in accord with the divine will or the law of the universe. "Seek ye first the kingdom of heaven (conform to God's laws) and all these things shall be added unto you."

"Honor and shame from no condition rise;
Act well your part, there all the honor lies."

So health, happiness and contentment, as well as sickness and despair, from no condition arise; obey God's laws, conform yourself to the divine will; there all the healing lies.

Faith may be illustrated by the radio. An impulse is given to the ether of a certain wave-length. This impulse may travel thousands of miles, but ever growing weaker and weaker. A receiving set far distant, if attuned to this same wave-length, will receive it but so weak that it could not stir an atom of air to reproduce the original sound. It is strengthened by the introduction of a powerful electric current that is attuned to the same wavelength as the original impulse, and so the air is caused to vibrate and reproduce the initial sound.

So with your own self, however weak the divine spark within; if rightly it seek the all-powerful influence of the divine and be rightly attuned to it, the divine enters to strengthen the soul.

Hope is the child of faith. It illuminates the soul and fills it with a brightness as radiant as an angel's dream. Love spontaneously pervades the human soul when faith and hope are rightly there. It answers that eternal challenge that comes to us from the grey of the world's morning: "Thou shalt love the Lord thy God with all thy heart . . . and thou shalt love thy neighbor as thyself."

Socrates in one of his dialogues develops the thought that all things are good, that God created nothing bad in itself. It is only the wrong use or abuse of it that makes it evil. The entire want of anything is often as baneful as the excessive use or abuse of the thing, however good it may be in itself.

A clock without a pendulum runs wild. So however good and beneficial may be these theological virtues, without proper restraint or balance, a one-sided character develops. The philosophical virtues or reason is the pendulum that holds the faculties into a harmonious whole and thus develops the complete man.

The tenets are that to which with confidence we hold; they are the very groundwork of the structure. By the proper application of the Masonic principles contained in the forty-seventh problem of Euclid, many of the Masonic trinities may be solved. Let one side represent love in essence (brotherly love) and the other love in action (relief), and rightly combined there is produced the hypotenuse of truth, the ultimate accomplishment of Masonic research. If thou wouldst know the truth, love the Lord thy God with all thy heart and thy neighbor as thyself.

In the early ritual it was chalk, charcoal and earthen pan. The last seemingly had reference to the tiling of

the floor. At each initiation the symbols suitable to that
degree were drawn with chalk and charcoal on the floor
of the Lodge, and later were erased. The reason of this
was to prevent any of their secrets becoming known to
the profane, since their meeting was always held in a
room in a public inn.

Let us reproduce a part of a scene at an initiation.
On the floor of the room had been drawn a rectangle
representing a Lodge, and within which were the essential emblems. There were two tables, arranged length-
wise of the room and parallel to each other. They were
loaded with the necessary eatables and drinkables, and
about them were seated the brethren in the proper order.
The Master, having found out by proper inquiry that all
the brethren present were properly charged, and raising
his firing glass, asked: "How should Entered Apprentices serve their Masters?" In unison there came from
the assembled Craft the response: "With freedom, fer-
vency and zeal." "How represented?" "By chalk, charcoal and earthen pan." "Then let us so serve. All together." The firing glasses having been emptied were
brought again to the table by proper signs and uniform
motion.

This may seem strange and improper to the American Mason, yet it was the way it was done in "ye olden
times." The spirit of this is still retained in English
Lodges. One of their last toasts is to the absent brother,
be he on land or be he on sea, be he ill or be he in
health, and so on. Then all join hands and sing with
great fervor: "Auld Lang Syne," a song written for
Masons.

The "Ancient" Masons discountenanced the toast system in old Lodges and emphasized the solemnity of the
ritual. Since they gave us our ritual, so we have departed
from the old plan and follow the customs with which
you are familiar. While we have lost much in good fellowship, yet we have perhaps saved some weak brother
from falling. We will not discuss the question as to
which is the right way; but if the one causes the weakest
of our brethren to err and fall into the pits of excess
and intemperance, then let us abandon a part of our
good fellowship for his sake.

The first section of the Fellowcraft degree is so similar to the Entered Apprentice that it needs no further explanation. The legend of the winding stairs forms almost all of the second section. You have no doubt already observed that the Masonic symbol does not at all agree with the description of Solomon's Temple. It is not so intended. Masonry erects an idealized representation of the Temple; it represents an uncovered porch with black and white square tiling; standing upon this are two pillars named Jachin and Boaz. After passing these pillars we meet a flight of winding stairs consisting of three, five and seven steps, leading into the middle chamber of Masonry, but the sanctuary of the Temple; from thence into the Holy of Holies.

There are two principal guards, one at the entrance between the pillars and the other at the top of the stairs, at the door of the sanctuary.

As a whole it may represent the human race, in its long, tortuous advance from darkness unto light, from savagery unto civilization. It may represent the masses of medieval Europe as they emerge from the bondage of feudalism to their present state of civilization. It may represent the individual as he advances from childhood to man's estate, from ignorance unto knowledge. Whatever it may typify, it represents a struggle ever upward, ever onward, until it may catch the glimpse of

"That hieroglyphic light
Which none but Craftsmen ever saw."

Man seeks a harmonious development of God and geometry, of God and reason, of religion and philosophy. To the extent that these two principles are brought into equilibrium, to that extent only has he made any permanent advancement.

The ancient Craftsmen at the building of Solomon's Temple, in making this journey received as wages, corn, wine and oil, which was currency in that day. But the symbolic pay of the human race or the medieval Mason or the individual is far nobler and more worthy of the contest than that. It can be nothing less than Liberty, Fraternity and Equality.

The two great pillars were undoubtedly erected to commemorate some important event in the history of

Israel. We can conceive of nothing more appropriate than the pillar of fire by night and the pillar of cloud by day that guided them safely through the wilderness from Egyptian darkness to the land of promise. The pillar of fire by night beckoned ever onward and proclaimed that God's love would be lamp to guide their steps in this perilous journey. The pillar of cloud may fitly represent memory or experience, for surely he walks upon the edge of a steep precipice who does not profit by the experiences of the past.

The enslavement of the Israelites by the Egyptians was not without its benefits. The Egyptians possessed the most advanced civilization of the whole world up to that time. The long residence of the Israelites on the Nile was a great school that did much to fit them to become the very ark that transmitted to mankind the idea of the oneness of God. They could not forget that tau cross made from the blood of the paschal lamb and sealed upon their door posts which had miraculously protected their first-born from destruction. Memory must have projected it into the pillar of fire that gave them hope everlasting. The recollection of a sure reward when they did right and punishment when they did wrong formed a body of experience that was an ever-present guide to them for future conduct. This cloud of experience was not only a safe guide to their future steps, but also prevented the enemy that pursued from overtaking them. The past deeds of wrong and evil are bloodhounds that follow the scent of your steps, ever ready to pounce upon and destroy. You are protected by the pillar of experience, if properly used.

The guard or warden that you meet at the very beginning of the journey may well symbolize memory or experience. The wise interpret the future in terms of the past. There is an instructive story of Woden, the great Teuton demi-god, from whose name we derive Wodensday or Wednesday. He sought wisdom and was directed to the fountain of memory, where he could find how to obtain this gift. Looking down into the clear bubbling fountain, he asked of Memory the secret of wisdom. There came from the depths this answer: "Oh Woden, the price of wisdom is thy right eye." No sooner said than done; Woden plucked out his eye and cast it into the spring of memory, there to remain as a memento of the dearness and price of wisdom. And so the expression: "A wise man with one eye is better than a fool with two."

Martin Clare in his version of the lectures changed the seven or more steps in the winding stairs to three, five and seven. To the three he assigned the trinity of Father, Son and Holy Ghost. This was evidently too sectarian, and was tacitly omitted and left blank. This was as it should be. The monitorialist later assigned to these the three movable jewels, the level, the plumb and the square, and made them represent the three principal officers of a Masonic Lodge—a childish interpretation and unworthy of Masonry.

Many great and good men who were not members of the Masonic fraternity having read these puerile, vapid explanations and interpretations, having formed and expressed an idea that Freemasonry is but an innocent trap to catch the gullible; having had their own tail cut, they sought out others that they also might have their tail shortened. They rightly felt that it would be more instructive to hear the prattle of children in the nursery than in a Masonic Lodge, listening to these silly and weak explanations of great symbols, as old as mankind and expressing man's hopes, fears and prayers.

The number three is the mystic number of Freemasonry. In it is the secret of secrets, the Master's secret if you will. In it is logos that was in the beginning, is now and shall be forevermore. It cannot be told unto you; you must find it out for yourself. It is near, very near to you. Search for it and having found it, cherish it as the priceless treasure of your possessions. It is a jewel rarer than rubies and more precious than diamonds. It is THE TRUTH that will make you free.

Three is one and one is three, is an old Masonic maxim. One is all and all is one, is equally true. This formula might be illustrated in many ways, but let us use this one.

"And the Lord God made man out of the dust of the ground and breathed into his nostrils the breath of life; and man became a living soul." This is one.

"And the Lord God caused a deep sleep to fall upon

Adam . . . and he took one of his ribs . . . and made woman." The one has become two.

"And Adam knew Eve his wife; and she conceived, and bare Cain." The one has become three, yet still one.

Thus the child is the great mystery, the mystery of mysteries. Upon his weak and puny shoulders rests the future of the human race. His cry is but the cry of the human race seeking succor and assistance. And his infant eye peering about him and understanding not, is but the eye of humanity peering into the future, knowing not whence or whither.

And He set a child in their midst and said, "Of such is the kingdom of heaven."

The kingdom of heaven may be likened unto a mustard seed, the smallest of seed, yet when planted and cared for, grows into a large tree, spreading wide its branches upon which the fowls of the air may rest.

The kingdom of heaven may be likened unto a woman who hid some leaven in three measures of meal and the whole was leavened.

The child, though small and insignificant, if rightly born, nurtured and educated will grow into manhood's estate a blessing to his generation, but if neglected and the leaven of ignorance left concealed within, will be a hindrance to mankind's progress. "If the child be saved, all things will be saved and all things saved will bless us. But if the child is lost, all things will be lost, and all things being lost will curse us."

Masonry stands for universal education and enlightenment; not only the education of your child, but of your neighbor's child as well. Whatever education is good for your child, the whole community has a right to demand for their children.

Since the public schools are the only means by which all children may have an opportunity for education, it necessarily follows that Masonry should stand squarely behind them, giving them their unstinted aid and support.

Upon the five steps are delineated the five human senses and five orders of architecture. Upon the seven are the seven liberal arts and sciences. These should not be separated, but taken as a whole to understand rightly the symbolry.

The five senses are the means and only means by which any knowledge may be obtained. The five orders of architecture represent architecture as a whole, and symbolize the means by which the human race preserved this knowledge through many generations. The seven liberal arts and sciences are the trivium and quadrivium of the medieval scholars and symbolize all knowledge which has been acquired by the human race.

By their knowledge of geometry the medieval Masons gave to the building the proper proportions, thus giving to it beauty, and by equalizing strains and stresses gave to it strength and durability. The cathedral builders revered it beyond all other sciences, and geometry and Masonry were synonymous terms. It not only had for him a practical application, but also a moral one. It was to him the basis of a system of moral philosophy or ethics.

Man's reasoning power fails to prove the existence of a God whom we may rightly call "Our Father." But when reason fails, then the human soul is partly prepared to receive an assurance which is just as real and often more so than is any other mental impression. This contact of the divine and the divine within us we call faith. We may not be able to define it or answer whence or how, but we know it is there. And in the words of old Job we may cry out: "I know that my Redeemer liveth." This consciousness that there is a God above us who watches over us has been attained by man throughout all times and in every clime. Faith in God is the first great axiom of the geometry of Masonry.

Again universal experience teaches us that a violation of nature's law brings its own punishment. Hence upon our lips and from our hearts should be the prayer: "Thy will be done on earth as it is in heaven." It is writ on the face of nature, in the stars, and in the heart of man that God's will is his law, immutable, unchangeable. Ignorance is no excuse for the violation of the law.

Half the world cannot be left in ignorance without it in turn engulfing the other half in the blackness of night.

Hence it follows as a corrollary that only through universal education and enlightenment can man's proper destiny be attained. Education must start with the child. If this period be neglected, education becomes almost impossible.

The public schools are the only means yet devised that all the children may be properly educated.

Music is an expression of harmony in sound. There are certain sensations of the human soul that cannot be expressed in words. Music, therefore, is a soul language to express its yearnings and unutterable ideas. It implies harmony and is therefore peculiarly appropriate to the Masonic system of symbolry, using the great symbol, the forty-seventh problem of Euclid, in which we represent the hypotenuse as the line of equilibrium between two forces rightly exerted upon a point. If we rightly (wisely) plan a building and give to it strength and durability, the whole when complete gives us the sense of the beautiful.

The first section of the Master's degree, like that of the Fellow Craft, is so similar to the Entered Apprentice it needs no special treatment.

The trowel as a working tool is an Americanism. In England they are skirret, pencil and compasses. In the latter country, and practically in the whole world except the American States, all the business of the Lodge, the election of candidates and officers, the installation of the officers, etc., are done in an Entered Apprentice Lodge. The Fellow Craft and Master's are only opened for degree work. This conforms to the development and history in which the apprentice is the basic degree and the other two but additional or higher degrees.

In America as you know all business is transacted in the Master's Lodge, and the Entered Apprentice and Fellow Craft are only opened for work. Since the principal duty of the Master is to design, plan and lay out a building, the skirret, pencil and compasses are most appropriate working tools in that particular system. On the other hand, in that system in which the first and second degree are but subsidiary to the Master's then the trowel is certainly most appropriate, for in such a Lodge there is need of harmony, union and "that noble contention or rather emulation of who may best work and best agree."

The pictures with explanation that we find in the monitors, such as the anchor and ark, the beehive, etc., with the sole exception of the forty-seventh problem of Euclid, should be relegated to the attic. They were introduced by some of the monitorialists who hoped to "paint the lily and add perfume to the violet." Some of them were even borrowed from the Odd Fellows and other sources. However instructive they may be, they do not conform to Masonic symbolry. The forty-seventh problem of Euclid belongs to the trestle board among the other geometric symbols. The usual explanation given to this great symbol in the monitors is inaccurate and improper.

The second and last section of the Master's degree is the Hiramic legend. It needs no additions; it is sublime in itself. However crudely it may be rendered, there is something in it that holds fast our attention and interest. Let each interpret it in terms of his own faith and respect whatever interpretation may be made by his companion. I may see in it the symbol of the Man-God, the Messiah whose body was bruised for my sake, who bore the sins of the world that the world might be free. My brother sitting by my side may see in it an example of fidelity to a trust unsurpassed and a general portrayal of immortality. The symbol is fixed, the interpretation is individual. My own interpretation will change with more light and attentive study of the symbol. Masonry is in no sense dogmatic, except as to essentials. These essentials are a belief in the fatherhood of God and the brotherhood of man. This fundamental idea is expressed in the tenets of Masonry, brotherly love, relief and truth.

While this individual interpretation and mutual respect for the opinions of each other have always been a part of Masonry, for a long period it remained in a state of dormancy. It remained for that great Masonic scholar, Albert Pike, to bring it again to light and become the liberator of Masonry from dogmatic interpretations. A Christian and a Jew may sit side by side in a Masonic body and witness a degree in which the crucifixion and resurrection of Christ are portrayed in wonderful symbolry, and even His name becomes the long-lost word.

The one may see in it the anointed of Heaven, the promise of the ages; the other a great man who taught mankind not to hate, but to love one another; who for this was cruelly slain by intolerant priests. But the principles that He taught will live and be a blessing to mankind; though they may differ in their interpretations, yet they remain brothers in the mystic tie.

Insofar as you have not conquered your pride of opinion, that you are not willing to accord to your brother the right of forming an honest judgment, the same as you assume for yourself, you are in that respect not yet a Master. Toleration is the basic principle of Masonry, and he who has not yet learned its lesson is but a beginner in the mystic art.

The Master Hiram was a servant of King Hiram's father, a man of the people who by sheer industry and application had become a skilled artisan. His proficiency was such that Solomon fetched him out of Tyre and made him chief of the workers on the House of God at Jerusalem. More than his skill as a workman, he was a man, a noble man, pure of heart and contrite of spirit. He was beset by his own fellow workers, by his own countrymen, and left prostrate. In the building of a life worthy of your dreams, with courage undaunted to do the right, you need have little fear of the enemies from without, for they can do you but little harm. It is the insidious enemies from within, hate, selfishness, greed and unholy ambition, that are most dangerous and most to be feared.

In ye olden times Masonry made much of the bone box that contained the key to an individual Lodge that was held in the heart and under the left breast. It is to be regretted that this has been dropped from the modern lectures, yet the spirit of it still remains.

Let us in some great moment visit this heart Lodge. Be sure that the seven faithful members are there—Faith, Hope, Love, Fortitude, Prudence, Justice and Temperance; that no unworthy members have been permitted to enter, such as hate, licentiousness, intolerance and selfishness. If, however, we find one of them present, let us be quick to rid our heart lodge of such. Let us upon its altar lay the confessions of a contrite spirit, and be assured that we shall be pardoned by Him to whom our Lodge has been devoutly dedicated.

In an effort to portray Masonry or the spirit of Masonry in words, many attempts have been essayed, but none has surpassed that little poem by that great genius and Mason, Johann Wolfgang Goethe. He called it "Mason-Lodge!" Thomas Carlyle, himself not a Mason, called it "The Marching Song of the Teutonic Race." It should be memorized. Below is given Carlyle's rough and rugged translation of this wonderful poem by Goethe:

MASON-LODGE

The Mason's ways are
A type of existence
And his persistence
Is as the days are
Of men in this world.

The future hides in it
Gladness and sorrow,
We press still thorow,
Naught that abides in it
Daunting us,—onward.

And solemn before us,
Veiled, the dark portal,
Goal of all mortal:—
Stars silent rest o'er us,
Graves under us silent.

While earnest thou gazeth,
Comes boding of terror,
Comes phantasm and error,
Perplexing the bravest
With doubt and misgiving.

But heard are the voices,—
Heard are the sages,
The worlds and the ages:
"Choose well; your choice is
Brief and yet endless.

"Here eyes do regard you
In eternity's wilderness;
Here is all fullness,
Ye brave, to reward you;
Work, and despair not."
—Goethe.

The lost word was only hinted in the original Master's degree, but today it has grown into a wonderful symbolry inseparably connected with Masonry. It is the logos of the ancients: "In the beginning was logos and logos was with God and logos was God." It is that unutterable something that fills yours heart when you are rightly prepared and have placed yourself in the right position. It is the secret of the ages; the Master's secret, the royal secret, if you please. It marks the ultimate search in Masonry—THE TRUTH.

There is a persistent tradition that the Master's degree has been mutilated and part of it transferred to the Royal Arch. The most careful and painstaking investigation proves this to be untrue. The Master's degree, with slight changes in the verbiage to adapt it to the legend of the Royal Arch, remains the same as when first conferred in 1725. However, the Ancients added the Royal Arch to the Master's and later separated it and made a fourth degree. From this comes the idea of the mutilation of the Master's degree.

There is a persistent rumor that this degree had its origin among the adherents of the Stuart dynasty. Charles the Second before his restoration to the throne was known as the widow's son, his mother being Maria of France, the queen of Charles the First who was beheaded. Later the two pretenders, the elder and the younger sons of the deposed king, James the Second, undoubtedly had some connection with French Masonry. A mythical valley known as Heredom in Scotland was invented, and from this source the secrets were obtained. The French called this Masonry "Eccosias" or Scottish Masonry. You must never confound the Scottish Masonry with the Masonry of Scotland. They are two different things entirely. Scottish Masonry is of French origin, and the Masonry of Scotland is derived from England.

You will be importuned soon after attaining the Master's degree to take the dependent degrees. In them is a rich store of Masonic knowledge. Through the genius and labor of many men they have been made into wonderful symbolry. Albert Pike, the greatest Mason of the century, has enriched them with great beauty. But do not join them with merely a desire to wear a thirty-second degree pin or Knight Templar charm, for you will be sadly disappointed. But if you unite with them as an earnest searcher after truth and for a better understanding and appreciation of Masonic symbolry, you will be richly repaid for your labors.

Still I would not have you confuse Craft Masonry with the Masonry of the dependent degrees. There is a sharp line of demarcation between the two. Craft Masonry grew out of the state of society of medieval Europe as affected by the Renaissance and the Reformation. Scholasticism prevailed, an artificial system of logic that could readily and effectively prove white to be black and sin to be virtue. The human mind was fettered by excerpts and sayings of the early fathers of the church and others in authority that had little if any connection with the then conditions.

Francis Bacon in his "Novum Organum," a recrudescence of Greek thought, proclaimed an empiricism based on experiments. Man's mind began to dare and investigate. John Locke asserted that ideas were not innate, but the product of experience as is taught in the Fellow Craft degree by the five human senses. He also taught that reason was a safe and sane guide. Thus you have the system of Craft Masonry; the religious instincts, represented by Faith, Hope and Charity, derived from a Hebraic source, and the philosophical or reasoning instincts represented in Masonry by the four cardinal virtues, Fortitude, Prudence, Justice and Temperance, derived from the Greeks. The right combination of religion and philosophy, of God and the Square, has given to mankind modern civilization as well as Craft Masonry.

But there is another aspect of man's history that Craft Masonry hardly touches upon; yet the dependent degrees are replete with man's eternal quest after the unknown throughout countless centuries. It portrays the earliest man looking down into the grave and asking of it: "Is there nothing beyond?" and the grave gave no answer. He turns his eyes to the stars of heaven and asks of them the secret, and they like eyes of hungry wolves glare down upon him and answer him not. We hear the chants of the early Aryan priests as they sing the praises of the great God, the source of light. We stand in mortuary temples of Egypt and listen to their ritual as they proclaim immortality and the resurrection. Again we are in the courts of Cyrus and listen to the princely Zerubbabel as he pleads for his enslaved people. We listen to their plaintive cries as they hang their harps on the willows, for they could not sing the songs of Zion in a strange land. We return with them to Jerusalem and assist in the rebuilding of the house of the Lord under the direction of Zerubbabel, Joshua and Haggai.

Stand upon the crest of the centuries and see that strange, wierd figure who dressed in camel hair, girded with the skin of wild beasts and subsisting on dried grasshoppers and the honey he gathered from beneath the rocks, crying out: "Repent, repent, for the kingdom of heaven is at hand."

We stand on a brow of Moriah, on Calvary, and witness the agonies of the crucified One, amid the rattling of dice and the sobs of a Magdalene, and hear His last words: "It is finished."

We visit Patmos and with John witness the scene of the four horsemen as they come rushing down through the centuries. We witness truth and justice striving against war and death. Today we see truth imprisoned in durance vile, bleeding from a thousand wounds; today crucified amid the jeers of the populace, but on the morrow the black and the white triumph over the red and the pale. The white merges into the black and lo! a miracle—the black is white. We join the Crusaders and witness their glittering swords raised high in the defense of destitute widows, innocent maidens and the Christian religion. We stand at the tomb of Jaques de Molay, a martyr to an unholy conspiracy of an infamous king and an infamous priest, and shed tears at his untimely fate.

These and many other interesting scenes we witness in the dependent degrees. They are enriched with drama, philosophy and the enunciation of great truths. They teach Liberty, Fraternity and Equality.

Operative Initiation

"On the day fixed, the candidate went into the house where the assemblies were held, where the master of the chair had had everything prepared in due order in the hall of the Craft. The brethren were then summoned (of course bearing no weapon of any kind, it being a place dedicated to peace) and the assembly was opened by the Master, who first acquainted them with the proposed inauguration of the candidate, dispatching a brother to prepare him. The messenger, in imitation of an ancient heathen custom, suggested to his companion that he should assume the demeanor of a supplicant. He was then stripped of all weapons, and everything of metal taken from him; he was divested of half of his garments, and, with his eyes bound and breast and left foot bare, he stood at the door of the hall, which was opened to him after three distinct knocks. The Junior Warden conducted him to the Master, who made him kneel and repeat a prayer. The candidate was then led three times around the hall of the Gild, halting at last at the door, and putting his feet together in the form of a right angle, that he might in three upright square steps place himself in front of the Master. Between the two, lying open on the table, was a New Testament, a pair of compasses, and a mason's square, over which, in pursuance of an ancient custom, he stretched out his right hand, swearing to be faithful to the duties to which he pledged himself, and to keep secret whatever had been, or might be thereafter, made known to him in that place. The bandage was then removed from his eyes, the three great lights were shown him, a new apron bound around him, a password given to him, and his place in the hall of the Gild pointed out to him." (History of Freemasonry, Findel, page 65).

THE OPERATIVE CATECHISM
(Mackey's Encyclopedia)

"Q. Are you a Mason?

A. Yes, I am a Freemason.

Q. How shall I know that?

A. By perfect signes and tokens and the first poynts of my Entrance.

Q. Which is the first signe or token, shew me the first and I will shew you the second.

A. The first is heal and conceal or conceal and keep secret by no less paine than cutting my tongue from my throat.

Q. Where were you made a Mason?

A. In a just and perfect or just and lawfull lodge.

Q. What is a just and perfect or just and lawfull lodge?

A. A just and perfect lodge is two Interprintices two fellow craftes and two Mast'rs, more or few the more the merrier the fewer the better chear but if need require five will serve that is, two Interprintices, two fellow craftes and one Mast'er on the highest hill or lowest valley of the world without the crow of a cock or the bark of a dogg.

Q. From whome do you derive your principalls?

A. From a great'r than you.

Q. Who is that on earth that is great'r than a free-mason?

A. He y't was caryed to y'e highest pinnicall of the tempple of Jerusalem.

Q. Whith'r is your lodge shut or open?
A. It is shut.

Q. Where lyes the keys to the lodge doore?
A. They ley in a bound case or under a three cornered pavem't about a foote and halfe from the lodge door.

Q. What is the key to your lodge doore made of?
A. It is not made of wood stone iron or steel or any sort of metal but the tongue of good report behind a Broth'rs back as well as before his face.

Q. How many jewels belong to your lodge?
A. There are three the square pavem't the blazing star and the Danty tassley.

Q. How long is the cable rope of your lodge?
A. As long as from the Lop of the liver to the root of the tongue.

Q. How many lights are in your lodge?
A. Three the sun the mast'rs and the square.

Q. How high is your lodge?
A. Without foots yards or inches, it reaches to heaven.

Q. How stood your lodge.
A. East and west as all holy Temples stand.

Q. W'ch is the mast'rs place in the lodge.
A. The east place is the mast'rs place in the lodge and the jewell resteth on him first and he setteth men to worke w't the m'rs have in the forenoon the wardens reap in the afternoon.

Q. Where was the word first given.
A. At the tower of Babylon.

Q. Where did they first call their lodge?
A. At the holy chapell of St. John.

Q. How stood your lodge?
A. As the said holy chapell and all other holy Temples stand (viz.) east and west.

Q. How many lights are in your lodge?

A. Two one to see to go in and another to see to work.

Q. What were you sworne by?

A. By God and the square.

Q. Whither above the cloathes or und'r cloathes?

A. Und'r the cloathes.

Q. Und'r what arme?

A. Und'r the right arme. God is gratefull to all Worshipfull Mast'rs and fellow in that worshipfull lodge from whence we last came and to you good fellow w't is your name.

A. J. or B. then giving the grip of the hand he will say Broth'r John greet you well you.

A. God's good greeting to you dear Broth'r.

Q. Peace be here.

A. I hope there is.

Q. What o'clock is it?

A. It is going to Six or going to Twelve.

Q. Are you very busy?

A. No.

Q. Will you give or take?

A. Both, or which you please.

Q. How go squares?

A. Straight.

Q. Are you Rich or Poor?

A. Neither.

Q. Change me that.

A. I will.

Q. In the name of, etc. are you a Mason?

A. I am so taken to be.

Q. What is a Mason?

A. Man begot of a Man, born of a woman, Brother to a king.

Q. What is a Fellow?

A. A Companion of a Prince.

Q. How shall I know that you are a Free Mason?

A. By Signs, Tokens, and Points of my Entry.

Q. Which is the Point of your Entry?

A. I hear and conceal under the penalty of having my Throat cut or my Tongue pulled out of my Head.

Q. Where were you made a Free Mason?

A. In a just and perfect Lodge.

Q. How many make a Lodge?

A. God and the Square with five or seven right and perfect Masons on the highest Mountains or the lowest Valleys in the world.

Q. Why do Odds make a Lodge?

A. Because all Odds are Men's Advantage.

Q. What Lodge are you of?

A. The Lodge of St. John.

Q. How does it stand?

A. Perfect and West as all Temples do.

Q. Where is the Master's Point?

A. At the East Window waiting at the Rising of the Sun to set his men to work.

Q. Where is the Warden's Point?

A. At the West Window waiting at the Setting of the Sun to dismiss the Entered Apprentices.

Q. Who rules and governs the Lodge and is Master of it?

A. Irah   )

) of the Right Pillar.

Iachin)

Q. How is it governed?

A. Of Square and Rule.

Q. Have you the Key of the Lodge?

A. Yes, I have.

Q. What is its virtue?

A. To open and shut, and shut and open.

Q. Where do you keep it?

A. In an Ivory Box between my tongue and my teeth, or within my heart where all my secrets are kept.

Q. Have you a Chain to the Key?

A. Yes, I have.

Q. How long is it?

A. As long as from my Tongue to my Heart.

Q. How many precious Jewels?

A. Three: a square Ashler, a Diamond and a Square.

Q. How many lights?

A. Three: a right East, South and West.

Q. What do they represent?

A. The Three Persons: Father, Son and Holy Ghost.

Q. How many Pillars?

A. Two: Iachin and Boaz.

Q. What do they represent?

A. Strength and Stability of the Church in all Ages.

Q. How many Angles in St. John's Lodge.

A. Four bordering on Squares.   △✠

Q. How is the Meridian found out?

A. When the Sun leaves the South and breaks in at the West-End of the Lodge.

Q. In what part of the Temple was the Lodge kept?

A. In Solomon's Porch at the West-end of the Temple, where the two Pillars were set up.

Q. How many steps belong to a right Mason?

A. Three.

Q. Give me the Solution.

A. I will . . . The Right Worshipful, Worshipful Master and Worshipful Fellows of the Right Worshipful Lodge from whence I came, greet you well. That Great God to us greeting, be at this our meeting, and with the Right Worshipful Lodge from whence you came, and you are.

Q. Give me the Jerusalem Word.

A. Giblin.

Q. Give me the Universal Word.

A. Boaz.

Q. Right Brother of ours, your Name.

A. N. or M. Welcome Brother M. or N., to our Society.

Q. How many particular Points pertain to a Free Mason?

A. Three: Fraternity, Fidelity and Tacity.

Q. What do they represent?

A. Brotherly Love, Relief and Truth among all Right Masons; for all Masons were ordained at the building of the Tower of Babel and at the Temple of Jerusalem.

Q. How many proper Points?

A. Five: Foot to Foot, Knee to Knee, Hand to Hand, Heart to Heart, Ear to Ear.

Q. Whence is an Arch derived?

A. From Architecture.

Q. How many Orders in Architecture?

A. Five: the Tuscan, Doric, Ionic, Corinthian, and Composite.

Q. What do they answer?

A. They answer to the Base, Perpendicular, Diameter, Circumference and Square.

Q. What is the right Word, or right Point, of a Mason?

A. Adieu.

THE PENDULUM SWINGS

By William B. Clarke, Past Grand Master

WATCH THE pendulum of the clock swinging from one extreme of its arc to the other, propelled by the impulses from the mainspring, and then let the clock stop. Midway between the high points of the arc the pendulum seeks its resting place. As the pendulum has two extremes to its arc, so is nature filled with extremes in life which are held in equilibrium by the will of the Divine.

The great mass of mankind seldom hesitates long enough in the mad search after the material things of the world to see or to appreciate the fact that the world is filled with extremes. Where there are men, there are also women; the presence of light is discovered because of the shadows; health is opposed by sickness; life meets its opposite in death; joy is greater because of sorrow. The fullness of life is obtained when we reach a balanced relationship between the great opposing forces in the world.

In the life of the human, the great opposites, the flesh and the spirit, are continually at war with each other and the struggle continues from the cradle to the grave. To inspire and direct these great forces, two other forces have been given to man by the hand of the Divine. Upon the one hand, we are the creature of impulse, impelled by the heart. On the other hand, there is given for our use the reasoning direction of the mind. To develop one at the expense of the other is to throw out of balance the fully rounded or complete life. True education only will enable man to obtain an equilibrium in the development of the great powers in life which were intended to give to the world a creature fully equipped to enjoy the things of life in all their fullness and to the final degree of richness and service. The spirit and the mind must work in harmony so that the desire of one must be restrained by the logic and experience of the other. Only thus may we differentiate between liberty and license, and obtain the richness and fullness of true liberty and without infringing upon the rights of others.

It is not often that men see in the history of the world the power and influence of the Divine in the affairs of nations as well as see the historical record of the accomplishments of the peoples of the nations. If we could but appreciate that fact in our nation today, if we would realize that we have a two-fold duty to perform, we would be leading a far different national life, and we would not be the ignorant victims of alternate eras of prosperity and of depression. Could we but see our two-fold duty, and live up to it, our national life would soon reach that point of equilibrium between these two duties which would bring a much greater degree of happiness and progress to our people. Our duties as citizens are fairly well known to us, but many of us fail to grasp the fact that the founders of our nation gave us another Power to which we owe allegiance and service when they placed upon the coins of the country the national motto "IN GOD WE TRUST." Here, in the very foundation of our nation, is seen expressed a clear understanding upon the part of our forefathers of duty to God and to country, the two great phases of national life which must be properly developed if we are to have a complete and happy national existence.

From the shores of sunny Spain nearly five centuries ago, the three little ships of Columbus pointed their prows out into the broad wastes of the Atlantic Ocean on their voyage to North America. Fair winds bellied out the sails of the ships and upon the rounded surfaces could be seen the crimson emblem of Him who taught men a two-fold duty in national life. He it was who said "Render therefore unto God the things which are God's and unto Caesar the things which are Caesar's." In His name it was that "In 1492, Columbus sailed the ocean blue." How few men know that "In 1492 Ferdinand exiled every Jew." This same Ferdinand who sent Columbus on his voyage of discovery under the emblem of the Cross, was the king who, in the same year, exiled from the shore of Spain every one of the chosen people of God. Only * * * just before Alfonso XIII abdicated the Spanish throne, did an enlightened public opinion force him to sign a decree annulling the five-hundred-year-old edict of Ferdinand.

Yet the Divine law demands that opposites shall counteract each other. Though Columbus sailed as the agent of despotism and of persecution, it was not the time that these forces of religious persecution should set foot upon the soil of a virgin continent which appears to have been retained by God for the habitation of other men among whom should exist a desire for a proper relationship between allegiance to God and duty to country.

As the fleet of Columbus neared the shore of the new continent, watching eyes from the mastheads of the ships reported a flock of landbirds nearing the ships. Experienced mariners knew that the sighting of these birds presaged the nearness of land and that the birds would lead them to its shores. Columbus ordered that the ships should follow the flight of the birds. A few days later, land was discovered but it was not North America. The birds had led Columbus to the island of Santo Domingo. It seems that the hand of God intervened to preserve the continent of North America until a later day when it should become the haven of those oppressed and persecuted men of all faiths, from whom and their children. came the inspiration to establish upon this continent a nation founded upon a faith in God and loyalty to a government of themselves, by themselves, for themselves.

During the seventeenth century, there came to the shores of North America from the nations of Europe the Jew, Roman Catholic, Cavaliers of the Stuart regime in England, Pilgrims, Quakers, Huguenots and Lutherans. Among all these groups was an abiding faith in the same God. They were all the victims of persecution in the countries from which they came. On the other hand, the manner of living of each group was different. Each had brought with them the manners and customs of the mother country. Little did men dream that these widely separated groups were to be brought together in a common faith, with a common ideal and were to be welded into one cohesive group from which would spring a nation which would give to men a new conception of human rights and would lead civilization one step forward in its relationship with its God.

One of the greatest contributions which Masonry has made to the world lies in the fact that it was the instrument which brought about the establishment upon the same continent which Columbus had failed to reach, of the new nation of democracy and of faith in God, the United States of America.

In the early part of the eighteenth century, Masonic lodges were organized in many of the colonies of North America. Into the lodges went fathers and sons of the Pilgrims, the Quakers, the Lutherans, the Cavaliers, the Jews, the Roman Catholics and the Huguenots. About the altars of Masonry they worshipped the same God without the many differences of denominationalism. About the banquet tables of Masonry they discussed the trials and tribulations of their existence in the mother countries. There sprung up the inspiration for and the desire to obtain the establishment upon this virgin continent of a new nation in which there would be granted the same liberties of speech, thought and conscience which they had obtained in their Masonic lodges.

In these lodges, though the extremes of religious thought met, yet the finer emotions of true hearts were tempered and directed by the experienced reason. Though the pendulum of thought might swing from one extreme to the other, harmony and equilibrium were obtained through the Impelling Power which was found about the altar of Masonry. The product which our forefathers brought forth was a nation in which was taught the duty of training and expressing both phases of our two-fold natures. It was a nation of liberty-loving people but owing allegiance to the God who gave it.

As we try to visualize the cause of our present-day difficulties; when we read of judges expelled from the bench because of corruption; when our President calls upon the people of the nation to at least have respect for the courts and the civil authorities; when the papers are filled with the news of graft in high places; when untold crimes are committed in complete defiance of law and public opinion; when our police forces are rendered impotent by the leaders of organized crime; and when the charge is openly made that the indifference of the people of the United States is the primary cause of it all, then the time has come to swing the pendulum from the extreme of the material to the high point of the spiritual. There arises the necessity of taking immediate steps to place the proper emphasis upon those things in life equally as valuable as money and pleasure. As Masonry was the instrument of the past which gave us success, so does Masonry stand today in the forefront of those forces which must be used to bring that balance in life between the material and the spiritual from which come duty to God and to country. Let Masonry use those eternal truths which are hers to bring about a regeneration within herself and the nation.

THE POINT WITHIN THE CIRCLE

By John L. Travis, Past Grand Master

IT WOULD be impossible to give a full explanation of the meaning of this venerable and wonderful symbol without first having a profound understanding of Oriental systems of thought, and of the various religions and philosophies of the various ages of the world, a knowledge the writer makes no claim to have. To the Oriental thinker, philosophy and religion are one, not separate as with Westerners.

Light comes from the East, which has chosen to illustrate spiritual truths by symbols, leaving to each individual that interpretation most reasonable to his own conscience; and frequently a symbol that at first glance has a very simple meaning proves after some thought to carry a most profound truth. Even if we could give a synopsis of the real meaning of symbols (which would be contrary to the method of teaching adopted by the Sages and Wise Men—for it is their habit to require the student to form his own conclusions), there are few men of the Western world with sufficient preparation to enable them to accept the profound truths taught by the ancient Symbols. So for these reasons we shall not attempt an exhaustive presentation of the meaning of this symbol—to do which the writer is not sufficiently advanced himself—but we shall try to give the reader a few hints in the hope of arousing a new interest in the fascinating and never dull study of the thoughts and wisdom of the Men of Before the Flood and their successors.

There are suggested several interpretations of the meaning of the Point within the Circle; but these are by no means exhaustive, for there are several, or many, more:

I

The plain Circle is said by the wise to be a symbol of that which existed before there was Creation of our present Universe—that is, Space.

This circle represents "Darkness," the "Boundless," and in our Arabic system of numbers is the cipher—Nothing.

Now when we describe a diameter perpendicularly through the circle's center, we have the number ten—10—or (|), which is the value of the Hebrew letter Jod or Yod, and initial letter of the name Jehovah, and of the name Jesus. Jacob is said to mean "supplanter", but it also means "God is my heel," the means by which he enables me to rise; but when his name was changed to Israel, it meant "God is my head," or "God is my Captain." John means "Jehovah is gracious." Joshua, said to be the real name of Jesus, means "Jehovah is salvation." Many other proper names in the Bible commencing with the letter "J" have some reference to God. It would be useless to try to give them all here. Finite humanity can never comprehend Infinity, but has to put up with a substitute.

We measure time by motion. Our year is calculated according to the revolution of the earth around the sun. Our time is figured by watches and clocks, each having some kind of motion. The Wise Men say that motion is necessary before there can be consciousness; that at regular intervals of time all life and activity in the universe cease, and all souls are absorbed into the Divinity, so that there is then no time, no motion, and apparently no life except the life of the Great Unknowable Father; then after due time there comes an Awakening, symbolized by the Point within the Circle. This Point is supposed to move and create a diameter, making the figure (|) or ten, and releasing the Forces of Nature, the Creators, represented in Genesis by the plural word "Alhim," and the Monads emerge. (Monads here may mean equally the vastest Solar Systems and the tiniest Atoms.) The various forces animated by the Divine Breath now come into action. (In the Book of Genesis the word "Alhim" translated "God," is plural, and the phrase "In the beginning" may be translated "In the head" or "By His thought," for the beginning of a stream is the head of the stream, and the starter of a conspiracy is called the head of the conspiracy. If we take that word "Alhim" and write the letters in a circle, giving to each letter its numerical value (for the Hebrew had no figures

for numbers but used letters instead), we get the
following:

$$A=1$$
$$l=30$$
$$m=40$$
$$h=5$$
$$i=10$$

Then starting at the 30, disregarding the ciphers, and
reading from right to left, as Hebrew is read, you have
the number 31415, which mathematicians call "pi," an
approximation of the relation of diameter to circumference. The same result is obtained by taking the Hebrew word for "Man," or "Aish," the letters of which
spell out the number 113, and then dividing this 113
into the Hebrew word for a lunar year, "Shanah," the
letters of which represent the number 355, and 113 will
go into 355 the same number, 3.1415. This may mean,
and probably does mean, that if a man uses his time correctly, he may arrive at as close a conception of the
Deity as humanity can. Similarly, John's Gospel, Chapter I, verses 1 and 3, says the Word was God, and made
all things. Now that Word in this Chapter is in the
Greek Language, and is "logos"; and to get its interior
meaning you must translate it into Hebrew, where you
get "dabvar," meaning "word". The numerical value of
Dabvar is 120, and if you turn 120 cubits into English
feet, you get 206.12 feet. Divide this 206.12 by 9 times
9 times 9 times 9, or 6561, and you get this same figure
"pi," or 31415, which was regarded by the ancient philosophers as representing the Christos, the Anointed, who
Christians believe has already come, but who Hebrews
believe will come in the future. Jesus said, John XIV, 2
and 3: "I go to prepare a place for you. And if I go and
prepare a place for you, I will come again, and receive
you unto myself; that where I am, there you may be also."
If the Christians are right, and Jesus was really the
Christ, the Hebrews may be also right, for Jesus said
he was coming back, and let us hope he will not wait
very long, although if he came back to this world of
hatred and greed and selfishness and cruelty, he might
possibly want to leave us to our sins and go back to his
Father. This is spoken, not irreverently, but sadly, in
view of the present condition of the world.

As just stated, the ancient philosophers regarded "pi," 3.1415, as representing the Christos, the Divine Redeemer, the Messiah. The Gnostics said that the numerical value of the Christos was 3.18, and that is not very far from 3.1415. Abram took for the rescue of Lot from the kings who had made Lot's family captive, "his trained servants, born in his own house, 318." After Abram had refused to take any part of the spoil, he was visited by Melchizedek, King of Salem (Peace), "without father, or mother, without descent, having neither beginning of days, nor end of life; but made like unto the Son of God; abideth a priest continually." Hebrews VII, 1-3 et seq. We can never get an exact value for this "pi," it has been carried to the 700th decimal, and there was still a remainer. Pi is just a substitute.

II

The Point within the Circle may also be taken to represent God, the Eternal Parent, before the creation of the Universe, God who in himself embraced Father, Mother and Son; and the Son, Logos, the Word, was one of those said to have been awakened at the beginning of the Cycle of our Universe, and he created all things, according to John's Gospel. He is called in Genesis "the Spirit of God," who called Light out of Darkness. You may ask, "how could Light come out of Darkness?" John says, "And the Light shineth in darkness; and the darkness comprehended it not." Now this word translated "comprehended" is a Greek word meaning "apprehended, slapped down, put out." To apprehend means to arrest. It is a comfort to know that the Darkness will never be able to put out God's Light, and that no matter how dark things may seem in our own lives, we can still confidently say that God's light still shines, and still know that all the efforts of wicked men will never succeed in extinguishing it. Professor Beard, the great American historian and philosopher, said, "When it gets dark enough we can see the stars."

The Egyptians had a name for the great Father God, who was "above all other Gods, and of whom all other Gods are but attributes and names." They called him "Amen." The Book of Revelation, III, 14, says: "These things saith the Amen, the faithful and true witness, the beginning of the creation of God." We invoke this Faithful and True Witness at the end of our prayers, without realizing in most cases what we are saying.

III

The Point within the Circle may also be taken to represent the Christos, the Anointed, the Messiah, the Word, the Amen who made all things and who is immortal. He has existed forever, and is always in the center of the Universe, his Creation. In John VIII, 58, he, as Jesus, the Carpenter, says: "Before Abraham was, I am." Moses asked God by whose name should he approach the Hebrews in their captivity, and was told to say "I am that I am" had sent him, or "I am." The Christos is the Light of the World, and the Point may represent that Light, ever shining, ever guiding, ever directing, ever calling humanity to heaven.

IV

But there may be another meaning of the Point within the Circle. It may be intended to refer to what we too generally forget—to the Unity of all created things, that Unity of which we Masons speak when we speak of "The Wisdom, Power and Harmony" of God and the Universe, His creation. For without Unity there can be no Harmony. All things work together for good for them that love God, which means to them that have in their hearts the love that is the proper recognition of God's Love. Jesus said, "My Father worketh hitherto, and I work." He also said, "I am the Light of the World; he that followeth me shall not walk in darkness, but shall have the light of life:" John VIII, 12. We cannot have peace in our hearts unless we have wisdom to hear the call of God. "Her ways," says Proverbs "are ways of pleasantness and all her paths are peace." Wisdom admonishes us to guard our thoughts. "Keep thy heart with all diligence, for out of it are the issues of life."

If you would be worthy of life after death, be sure that you do nothing to disturb the peace and harmony that God put in His Universe, that you never consciously break any of His laws, and particularly that you follow the New Law and learn to love all His creatures, great and small.

V

Another meaning of the Point within the Circle may be:

You are, as it were, a little spark from the great source of Life. That little spark we call the Soul. You are always in the center of your Universe. It is impossible for you to imagine a Universe in which you are not somewhere present. You are yourself, in a way, a Light to the World around you, for your life and conduct will always influence others; many people, even folks whom you do not personally know, will be imitating you, and quoting you, and somewhere there will always be a lad or two who will consider you the greatest man in the world. He will imitate your walk, use your expletives and profanity, practice your habits, and make you his model. When you have to leave this world and go to the spiritual sphere and look down on these lads who will have grown to manhood under your example, will it not be a pleasure and a delight to see them living right, dealing honestly and fairly by all men, following the Golden Rule, and for you to remember that it was your example and your teachings that started or helped to start them in the right way?

But suppose your teachings and example have been bad, suppose you have to sit in the other world and see your influence, like a poisonous stream, injuring and spoiling the lives of those you love and of those who love you, leading them into evil, or even to the pleasure of living and being evil and doing evil, destroying all kindliness and joy in their hearts, and you have to realize that your hands are tied, that you cannot go back and undo what you have done to them, that "the moving finger writes, and having writ moves on, nor all your piety and wit can lure it back to cancel half a line, nor all your tears wash out a word of it." Wouldn't that be a more terrible punishment from your own conscience that all the brimstone fires of hell?

Remorse is not a pleasant companion, but it follows us far beyond the grave.

Which makes the Golden Rule the most scientific method of living ever yet devised.

VI

The Point within the Circle may also represent the Cosmic Egg, containing the germ of all life, which is said to be broken when the great Period of Inactivity ends, and which renews and begins life in the Universe—the life that animates all Creation, from the Suns and systems of planets to the Atom with its attendant satellites, forces now demonstrated in the Atomic Bomb and other scientific discoveries of recent date. For we are told that when the Cosmic Powers wake up after their sleep or rest that may endure for perhaps millions of years, new life begins to animate the Universe and there starts a NEW Cycle of activity wherein New Life forms are started into growth and a New Race is set up to take the place of the vanished Root Races.

It is this release of new life that is symbolized by the Easter Eggs so pleasing to children, and the various colors of these eggs have a profound meaning to the student of Life.

VII

This Point within the Circle may also refer to the waking up of Nature at the Vernal Equinox, when vegetation begins to grow, flowers to bloom, and birds start singing. The Vernal Equinox generally comes about the 21st of March, when the day and night have equal length, hence equinox, which means "equal night." We celebrate this awakening of Nature at Easter, but Easter is not observed at the Vernal Equinox—there must be after the Vernal Equinox first, a full moon, in order to have the Feminine influence of Nature at work, and after that a Sunday, the day of the Sun, source of all life in this planet. In the year 1946 the Vernal Equinox comes at noon on March 21; the next full moon shows up on April 16, and the following Sunday is April 21, and that is the date on which Easter will fall in the year A. D. 1946. It is interesting to note that Easter, the great festival day of the ancient nations which was adopted by the Church, has been celebrated on various dates in the various countries of the earth. The first Christians ordered that the correct date for Easter should be calculated at Alexandria, in Egypt, the seat of the great library, and the date communicated to the Bishops of Rome and Constantinople; but later the date was calculated at Rome, and now it is calculated and published by various other authorities. Christians observe Easter, but few people know that the Jews observe the same great event in their Passover with their bitter herbs and unleavened bread. Pesach, Passover, refers not only to the passage of the children of Israel from Egypt, the land of slavery and darkness, to Palestine, the land of freedom and light. The sun has "passed over" the equator, and now has reached its beneficent influence to the countries north of that line, as it has also roused all Nature to activity. When Moses was on the mountain so long, his followers decided he was dead, and demanded gods to worship, for the human race just has to have a god of some kind. As the constellation of the Bull had been that sign of the Zodiac in which the sun had risen at the Vernal Equinox, Aaron made a golden calf (the representation of the young bull) and the people worshipped it. (We look with pity on these newly released slaves for their ignorance in adoring the golden calf, but we still worship gold and wealth, even more than the Hebrews did in that old day. No matter how a man got his wealth, he is an oracle and a power, and we read with interest his account of how he got his riches; we may be sure he never tells us the tricks and schemes by which he acquired wealth, his story is generally a sort of Frank Merriwell narrative, not the real truth.)

Through what is called the Precession of the Equinoxes, by the time when the Passover was instituted, the sun rose at the Vernal Equinox in the sign of Aries, the Ram, and the Hebrews were taught to eat a Lamb (young or rising power of the Ram) at Passover. Savages used to think that when they ate the flesh of an enemy or of an animal, they acquired some of the qualities of the animal whose flesh they ate. So the Bull represents Strength, and the Ram innocence and harmlessness. Many coins have been found in countries around the Mediterranean with a bull's head in the position of goring, but nobody could tell from the coins what the bull was preparing to gore, until a coin was found in China showing the bull goring the Cosmic Egg, and thus releasing all the cosmic forces—symbolically. It is interesting to note that these Hebrews were symbolically passed from the worship of the Bull, sacred in Egypt, and representing brute strength, to that of the kindly lamb. We had hoped that with the change from the Bull, strength, to the Lamb, innocence and kindness, humanity would have passed from wars and despotism, to peace and brotherhood, and that tyranny and despotisms had ended, particularly as the Precession of the Equinoxes had about brought us to the sign of Aquarius, the Waterman, for the sun to rise in at the Vernal Equinox. This Waterman was probably referred to in Mark XIV, 13, and Luke XXII, 10, as the man bearing a pitcher of wáter. Water is a sacred element, and coming direct from heaven in a pure state, has been used as a symbol of purification from time immemorial; and we hoped that the human race had progressed far enough in spiritual knowledge—symbolized by water—to avoid despotism, tyranny and cruelty, and that these evils had been expunged from the hearts of the nations and all men could live in peace and harmony; but the great modern World Wars have shown that men are not yet ready to accept the Law of Love, nor to practice the Golden Rule.

VIII

You may be startled and angered when you read the statement that at certain intervals the whole Universe is said to go to sleep, so to speak, and that all souls are then absorbed into the Deity. But remember that the Greeks had no word for Eternity—the most they could say was "into the Ages."

Another meaning of this symbol of the Point within the Circle may be a reference to the Atom, the constitution of which we are just beginning to glimpse. A few years ago it was positively asserted that there could be no division of the Atom, that it was so small that dividing it would destroy it; and in the same breath we were told that the Atom was matter, and that matter could not be destroyed. Just how to reconcile those conflicting statements it takes a wise man, a Scientist, to explain. We were told that neither matter nor force could be destroyed, that motion could be changed into heat, and that heat was a form of motion; yet nobody knew exactly what heat was, nor what motion was. Men discoursed learnedly about what light is, and yet in their hearts they had to admit they knew nothing of what light really is, nor what electricity is; and they could not reconcile what they saw around them with their learned scientific theories. Now we are told that the atom is not matter at all, but an aggregation of power, its component parts flying around its center at incredible speed. Whence comes this power? Recently men have learned to separate a few of the "satellite elements" of the atom, if we may call them such, and they claim now that they can thus develop, or grasp, an unbelievable amount of power; so the Atomic Bomb. We have used this power to destroy our enemies, and are still figuring to use it for that purpose. Using it for the service of mankind in the peaceful arts is still to come, they say, but they cannot tell us how. We have used nearly all of God's gifts, automobiles, explosives, airplanes, submarines, torpedoes, to destroy the people God made and loves. Just how long God will put up with our violation of His Law of Love, nobody knows. But we are tempting Him and trying His forbearance and long-suffering every day. Some day a young scientist may learn how to disrupt the atom of oxygen, without learning how to control it, and then Peter's prophecy may come true. He says: II Peter III, 10, that the elements shall melt with fervent heat and the earth be burned up, and that this shall come "as a thief in the night."

When this cataclysm happens, it will be too late to try to reform our lives, just a trifle late to make new treaties with our allies as to the use of the Atomic Bomb, and some minutes too late to use that Bomb on our enemies.

IX

Now this Point within the Circle may also represent what is going to happen when Peter's prophecy comes true, as come some day it must.

We have discovered a new destructive agent, which we call "D.D.T.", and the powers that are supposed to control that most dangerous element are now as these lines are written, preparing to distribute this deadly thing in some parts of Georgia, and possibly in other States. This stuff is so deadly that a fly that touches a wall sprayed with it, they tell us, will drop dead. All other insects, we are told, will die from its deadly influence. This includes the insects that are useful to humanity as well as those that are harmful; it slays the bees that fertilize our fruit trees, the insects that fertilize all our fruiting trees and shrubs, and about the only insect that seems to be immune is the cockroach!

The Laws of Life are being violated by this stuff's use. God made the world with the Balance of Nature, each plant and each animal having its appointed task, and some of our enthusiastic so-called scientists are going to use D.D.T. to kill mosquitoes. That will kill a useful food for our fishes, and our streams will soon be barren of life if that is kept up. Every living creature has a right to live, but some people think they know better how to run the Universe than God does. The insects that are killed by D.D.T. are said to kill the birds that eat their dead bodies, but who cares about birds if we can just eliminate the mosquito? How do we know what will happen when the Atomic Bomb is loosed over the Pacific as it is now planned to do? What is going to be done to protect the fishes of that ocean, fishes that furnish food to thousands? Who is going to pay for the losses incurred?

Now this is not intended to be an exhaustive explanation of the symbolism of the Point within the Circle, for the writer does not know enough to exhaust that wonderful subject, but it is intended to give the reader a few hints from which he may make further discoveries for himself.

It is not in books or in lectures that the divine laws are learned, for they cannot give anyone a true explanation of the Laws of Life. Those Laws must be obtained, and can only be obtained, by living, Living a Life in accordance with them.

VISITATION AND RELIEF

By N. H. Ballard, Past Grand Master

YOU ARE CAUTIOUSLY to examine him, in such a method as prudence shall direct you, that you may not be imposed upon by an ignorant false pretender, whom you are to reject with contempt and derision and beware of giving him any hints of knowledge.

But if you discover him to be a true and genuine brother you are to respect him accordingly; and if he is in want, you must relieve him, if you can, or else direct him how he may be relieved; you must employ him some days or else recommend him to be employed. But you are not charged to do beyond your ability; only to prefer a poor brother that is a good man and true, before any other people in the same circumstances.

—Anderson's Constitution, 1723.

The Masonic rules of visitation and relief should be well known not only to the individual but also to those called upon to perform the duties of an examining committee or board of relief.

In the one case it will prevent you from being humiliated by being refused admission to a Masonic Lodge or the relief you may need; on the other hand it will prevent boards of relief or examining committees from being imposed upon by those unworthy.

Both visitation and relief are comparatively easy in your own jurisdiction, or where you are personally known by Masons, but often difficult unless you are properly prepared where you are a total stranger.

Great caution is necessary, both as to visitation and relief on account of the great number of impostors, as clandestine Masons or those suspended or expelled who seek Masonic relief unworthily.

When you go visiting always be provided with a card or receipt of your current dues. It is worth the price to note the pleasure it gives a Secretary to write one. See that upon the back of this receipt is a certificate of the Grand Lodge, signed by the Grand Secretary and properly sealed, that your Lodge is regular and a constitutional member of the Grand Lodge. This is very important, for your receipt without it will not be recognized.

There is a dotted line often marked: "Ne Varietur," where you sign your name. Do this at once, for it will be too late when you present your card without signature, and again, should you lose your unsigned card, it could be used by some impostor or unworthy Mason.

Suppose you are a total stranger in some distant city and wish to visit a Masonic Lodge. By means of the city directory or inquiry at Masonic Temple you can find what Lodges are meeting on that particular evening. Don't just butt into a Masonic Lodge without knowing of their regularity, and ask for their charter. If any friends have suggested this to you, they have sent you snipe-hunting.

Having selected a Lodge, present yourself in the ante-room, handing to the tyler your card with a request that you wish to visit the Lodge. The tyler will pass your card to the Master, who in turn will appoint an examining committee. This committee will meet you in the proper room, having in their possession your card. First they will ask you to sign your name. This signature will be critically compared with the one on your card. If it is "ne varietur" the examination will proceed.

The tyler's oath is then taken together by yourself and each of the committee. It should have been committed to memory before hand.

The examination then proceeds in a way known only to Masons. Both must be satisfied, the one by the regularity of the questions asked, the other by the answers given.

Then in the proper way you will be introduced into the Lodge where you are privileged to enjoy a pleasant evening and make many acquaintances who may add much to your pleasure while you are in the city.

Do not mix the amenities of the social side of Masonry with your private business. The social proprieties of Masonry are such that not only is it bad taste but strictly forbidden. You may later have business relations with one you meet in the Lodge, but be most careful not to mix the two.

While you may never be privileged to return the favors shown to you by any member of that particular Lodge, there will be strangers within your own gates. Extend to them a most hearty welcome. Show them every courtesy and it is not at all amiss to give your card and suggest that if in any way you could add to their pleasure while in the city, not to fail to call upon you.

It need not be repeated that the true Mason would not use this introduction for any business purposes. If any one should be so imprudent, dismiss him as either ignorant or unworthy.

If you are a stranger in a distant city and need assistance, you will apply to the chairman of the Board of Masonic Relief, or in a place that has but one Lodge, to the Master or Secretary.

Just a word of caution: never give any Masonic sign or grip to a stranger that he might recognize you as a Mason. Should one be given you, show no recognition of it whatever. He is very ignorant or a base impostor. Should he ask you for assistance, do not give him anything but refer him to the Master or Chairman of the Board of Relief.

When you have found the Chairman or Master you will present to him your card and make your request. He will inquire of you your present needs as to food and lodging and will furnish you these. He will immediately wire your Lodge, giving them your name and needs and request a reply as to what to do. Your Lodge should reply at once, suggesting the aid, if any, to be rendered and to draw on them for that amount.

It is most important that your Lodge be prompt in meeting the draft that will be drawn by the helping Lodge, including telegram and immediate relief. Some Lodges have been careless in meeting these obligations, thus bringing not only themselves but their Grand Lodge into disrepute. The helping Lodge acts only as your agent. Each Lodge is responsible for its own members and has no right to impose unworthy ones on the Craft at large.

The reason of this caution in the bestowal of Masonic relief is the great number of base impostors attempting to impose on the generosity of Masons. They were very common * * * before the organization of the Masonic Service Association. By publishing pictures, descriptions and methods of these impostors, their number has been greatly reduced. They are still too numerous and must be guarded against. It is better to refuse nine worthy applicants than to grant the request of one base impostor. This is so because the worthy brother need feel no fear if he is properly healed and his Lodge stands ready to endorse him. You may well lay the failure to be aided, to your own unworthiness or else you had not taken the necessary precautions that are prescribed.

Suppose you had lost your card or left it at home; if you needed Masonic aid you would follow practically the same course as if you possessed it. Present your request to the Chairman or Master, stating why you did not have a card. Give your Lodge, location and the name of Secretary. They will consult the list of regular Lodges and finding yours all right, would follow the same course as if you had a card.

If the Chairman or Master were in the least suspicious, he would wire your Lodge through the Grand Secretary, whose name and address is easily accessible.

The possession of a card may be the means of identification. Suppose in an extreme case you were found unconscious in a strange city. This card found on your person would bring to you such assistance as money could not buy.

Most Grand Lodges provide certificates to be issued to the wives and daughters of Masons. These can be of great assistance to them by bringing that sweet and gentle ministration of courtesy as can hardly be obtained in any other way. They would always have someone to whom they may go and confidently expect that advice and assistance that would be most helpful.

THE ENTERED APPRENTICE DEGREE

By Dewey H. Wollstein, Past Grand Master

IN THE FAMOUS Masonic poem written by Goethe, and translated by Carlyle, Masonry is described as a "type of existence". It is a pattern of life. It presents the good and the bad. Masonry makes it clear that there is no royal road to spiritual success. It is a way of life because it offers one the opportunity to understand his own being, and as a result of that understanding, the opportunity to be serviceable to all mankind.

And, so, the candidate, duly and truly prepared, worthy and well qualified, and properly vouched for, offers himself, poor, blind and destitute, and as one who has walked in darkness. Prepared for what? For the reception of great truths. For an opportunity to "behold how good and how pleasant it is for brethren to dwell together in unity". Worthy and well qualified? Yes— to assume the responsibilities that must go hand in hand with the privilege of spiritual enlightenment. Properly vouched for? Yes, by those who recognize in the candidate the spark that may be fanned into a mighty flame of goodness. Poor, all outer adornment obliterated, the candidate is stripped down to the one thing that cannot be taken from him, his inner being, his character. Because he seeks a place wherein brethren dwell together in unity, material things, which are symbols of strife among men and nations, are taken from him. Blind, but not a physical blindness. It is the reverse. It is not the eyes that must first see. The heart must feel and understand. Thus in humility and in the name of God, the candidate is privileged to enter.

Before the birth of Faith there is the contact between the Creator and the Creature. Man is not set adrift from the source of Creation. He is forever a part of that Universal Power. We have the expression, "a conscientious man" which is a declaration of the fact that man has a constant awareness of his relation to the Deity. Thus the birth of Conscience is portrayed in the Entered Apprentice Degree. Now with the birth of Conscience, Faith is well founded. A point is the symbol of Deity.

The journey of the candidate is interrupted. Though he seeks that which is high and holy the proper course must be followed if he is to be successful. Here the station of the Junior Warden is a symbol of Spiritual Desire. It is the expression of willingness on the part of the candidate to march in the right direction for the privilege of having and receiving. Desire must be controlled. Man walks on earth but keeps his eyes heavenward. The station of the Senior Warden is a symbol of balance, of Emotional Stability. The candidate must have the desire for Spiritual Enlightenment and Emotional Stability before he approaches the station of Truth and Justice. The Worshipful Master has attained the East. He knows the direction one must travel in order to arrive at Truth. Therefore, Justice decrees that the candidate retrace his steps to the point where he missed the direct path—by the way of the Three Great Lights.

The candidate has now retraced his steps and kneels at the Holy Altar of Freemasonry. Let us discuss the obligation. When the candidate takes upon himself the obligation, sacred and binding, he does so with the consciousness that he also assumes the penalty for violating such an obligation. The Lodge does not inflict punishment. You cannot remove the reward which comes as the result of obedience to Divine Laws. Only the mercy of Almighty God can change the penalty for violation of a sacred obligation. If we say things which we should not say, if we divulge secrets which we swear we will not repeat, we destroy the power of speech. The penalty then is self-destruction as the result of the violation of a self-imposed obligation. The penalty is not death as we think of the natural transition from this life to another. The penalty is burying one's self in unhallowed ground.

The obligation has been taken. The candidate is now prepared in his heart for that which he most desires. The heart has conceived the beauties of Freemasonry. Now the eyes are to behold the very source of all beauty —the Three Great Lights of Freemasonry, symbols of Unlimited Wisdom, Unlimited Justice and Unlimited Mercy. And here is revealed one of the most beautiful of all symbols. The Lesser Lights make visible the Greater. God exists because man believes. Through Truth and Faith, symbols of the Sun and the Moon, God is revealed through man. Thus the Great Lights are illumined by the Lesser Lights. Man's determination to become God-like, though he sees and understands but little of the whole, reveals the Great Architect of the Universe.

The wardens are satisfied? The candidate does not repeat any part of the obligation. He makes it known that he has held within his grasp that which forever after must be his Guiding Light.

Now we come to the never-to-be forgotten experience in the journey of the Entered Apprentice. If one looks back upon that journey into Masonry he will relive the precious moment when he was presented the badge of a Mason. I am sure that every Mason has felt at this point, "Now I am truly a part of the Masonic Institution". Let us discuss the symbolism of our Masonic Apron. Light and white are associated. He who seeks in humility will find light. The word candidate comes from the word candidus, which means white. The color then reflects the spirit of humility which belongs to one who seeks Spiritual Enlightenment. Our apron is a square and a triangle, symbols of Heaven and Earth. The four corners of the Apron representing Temperance, Fortitude, Prudence and Justice, are symbols of man's strivings and yearnings for some degree of perfection upon Earth. The triangle is a symbol of man's desire for Spiritual Perfection, representing Faith, Hope and Charity.

If the color is a symbol of humility the material is a symbol of sacrifice. A definition of sacrifice is the giving up of something for the attainment of that which is nobler and finer. We sacrifice our baser desires and passions in order to give expression to our better selves. In the story of Abraham, the sacrifice is a symbol of gross passion.

The Apron is a symbol of determination and courage. Girding the loins is equivalent to our expression "take courage".

The Apron is a symbol of restraint, of temperance. It stands as the balance between what we want and what we should have.

The Apron is not a symbol of victory. It is the symbol of a glorious struggle. It should never be worn with a feeling of haughty arrogance, but always in a spirit of deepest humility.

The candidate is now informed regarding the working tools of this degree, the Twenty-four Inch Gauge and the Common Gavel. We have the word "canon" which means law, another word is "gauge". The Twenty-four Inch Gauge is a symbol of the laws of God as the means of making a happy life. Time cannot be saved; it can only be spent. We cannot take four hours from one of the divisions and use them advantageously in another. A distressed brother is not always a brother in need of material help. The law, or rule, points out that we need our brothers and that our brothers need us. The culmination of all Masonic training is not the giving of material gifts, but the giving of our love, ourselves to others. We often say that we do not have time for certain things, yet, it is generally true that we have time for the things that give us pleasure for the moment. The Twenty-four Inch Gauge tells us: "Divide the day to suit yourself, but do not expect to find happiness. Follow the Rule and find happiness."

The Common Gavel is a symbol of the driving force of the Will, that which makes one determined to follow the Laws of God. It is the force which clears away obstructions. The Common Gavel is also a symbol of authority placed in the hand of Justice for the welfare of all.

The candidate is then taught the lesson of Charity. The word in Masonry means Love. Masonry is not a benevolent society although its members individually, and the Lodge as a whole, may perform many acts of charity. Since the desire to become a Mason is prompted by the desire to be serviceable to our fellow creatures, the only way in which a Mason can enrich himself is through thoughts, acts and deeds of Love. The very proof of Man's love of God is measured by his love for his fellowman. In our Manual we read of the "clouded starry-decked heaven, where all good Masons hope to arrive by the aid of that theological ladder which Jacob, in his vision saw ascending from earth to heaven, the three principal rounds of which are Faith, Hope and Charity". Charity is the first round of the ladder in the descent of the soul from heaven to earth; it is the last round in the ascent from the soul to its former home. Thus the finite becomes the infinite through Love and the infinite becomes the finite through Love. Charity is above Faith and Hope because Faith may become fanaticism unless Love is the goal.

Hope may run wild and defeat the purpose of Faith unless its attainment is achieved through Love. Charity is the whole of brotherhood expressed in three lines:

"No man could tell me what my soul might be;

I sought for God; He eluded me;

I sought my brother out, and found all three."

Secrecy and Charity are inter-related. Love is a silent power. No man can see, hear, or touch the bond that exists between mother and child. No one can explain the Silent Power that governs the Universe. Who doubts the existence of such a Power? The profane world cannot understand the bond that joins one Mason to another. It is learned in the silence and secrecy of the Lodge. Who doubts the existence of such a bond? No sound can be heard in battle above the thunder of guns yet there is heard by the tired and despairing soldier the voice of mother, of sister, of sweetheart, a voice that gives him the courage to fight on, the courage to die with a smile. In teaching the lesson of secrecy to our candidates, we should ever be mindful of our grave responsibilities. We should never teach the lesson in a way that will bring embarrassment to the candidate and amusement to the audience.

Now the candidate has come by way of the Holy Altar to the East only to be returned to the place of darkness, the Northeast corner. He has followed the journey of the Sun, the symbol of Truth. Darkness surrounds, yet he faces the Light of the East, a symbol of Hope. We must do more than see great lessons portrayed. We must seriously reflect upon their meanings. Darkness is a symbol of quiet contemplation. Faith would perish of non-use were there no hours of darkness. Masonry presents the two great forces—Right and Wrong. The candidate has the right to choose the materials and the path. He must choose wisely. In darkness we can see God if we do not turn away from the East.

The candidate has been given precious gifts, the wisdom of the ages, a garment of humility and courage, the jewel of charity, and the tools for the erection of a mighty Spiritual Temple.

There is no turning. THE EAST IS FOREVER THE GOAL.

THE SUBLIME DEGREE

By Rev. Gilbert Dobbs, Past Grand Chaplain

SYMBOLIC MASONRY is the foundation of the whole Masonic Science. All the so called higher degrees of the York, Scottish and other rites are extensions and amplifications of these basic degrees. And contrary to the usual opinion, I think that the Blue or Symbolic Lodge constitutes a beautiful and complete philosophy of life in itself.

Philosophy may be defined as the study of God, the universe and man and their relations to one another. To study God we must look for the revelation of Himself in nature, in revealed religion and its inspired books, and the marks of the divine in man. Philosophic speculation has shown that Nature is one vast proof of the omniscience, omnipotence and omnipresence of the Creator. The countless myriads of wheeling orbs that shine afar, declare His wisdom, power and approachable glory. The mind of man staggers in the contemplation of the immensities of the visible universe, whose shining hosts seem changeless through the drifting ages as they encircle the throne of the Eternal, and yet the incredible light-years of far flaming suns and stars are but fleeting moments in the thought of God.

Yet this inconceivably transcendant God of wisdom and power is seen to be immanent in all nature as the omnipresent spirit of beauty, goodness and benevolence. Even the once indivisible atom is now seen to be a universe, a microcosm, in itself, whose core is pure energy and whose design is divine. There may be no prior proof of God, but without God the universe is not only an inexplicable riddle but an absurdity.

You may run with him who says, there is no God, no order, no design, no beauty in the world; but I walk with him, who finds "tongues in the trees, books in the running brooks, sermons in stones, and good in everything."

God's love is sung by aeolian starbeams, rippling rills as they eddy through the glade, and by rays of the golden sun as they snatch fragrant kisses from the flowers.

Does all this seem a far fetched introduction to my theme? It is not.

God is the all important postulate of Freemasonry. To find Him in the world, to see His thoughts blossoming into stars, His breath sweetening the flowers and His beauty and glory shining in human faces and enriching human experience is the true Mason's aspiration and dream.

To see God's image in man, in intellectual apprehension, in moral responsibility, and spiritual endowment; to find out man's origin and destiny and a straight path for his feet and his relation to the Supreme Being and his fellowmen; to know the truth and its manifestation of ever increasing light is the aim of Masonic philosophy.

And Masonry chooses the most ancient mode of expression and instruction in the pursuance of this object, the symbol, the allegory, the legend. There is something very pleasing and satisfactory in symbolic instruction. The symbol is so flexible and adaptable, that it furnishes the most convenient vehicle for the use of a progressive science. Thus Masonry is not handicapped by crystalized creeds, nor burdened by prosaic forms that are rendered obsolete by advancing knowledge. Symbols and legends, which offer such a wide latitude of interpretation are the most easily accommodated to the varying angles and phases of truth as advancing research and science make it completer and clearer. So the Symbolic degrees of Masonry are eminently suited to teach the highest and truest philosophy of life and conduct.

We can well leave the question of the origin and historical credibility of our legends, allegories and traditions to the antiquarian and historian. Though much of our material is hoary with age and based on proven data the worth of our system does not rest upon such historicity but upon the inculcation of those deathless principles, which our symbolism is designed to convey. Whether the ritual of the Third Degree finds its origin in the Egyptian or Mithraic mysteries or in oral traditions, that have descended by various other channels from the distant past, or are the product of the inventive genius of more modern devotees, the great value of its teachings is not impaired.

For instance it is of no great importance to know just when and where the term "Sublime" was first applied to the Master Degree. It was probably not used in

this connection until early in the last century and may
have been borrowed from the password of the old Adon-
hiramite rite. Nor is it necessary to go into the mooted
question of its relation to the similar terminology of the
Royal Arch and whether therefore the capitular system, was indeed originally a part of the Blue Lodge
work. But accepting this designation of the degree as
now universally used, we might profitably inquire, "Why
is the Master Mason Degree called Sublime?"

1. It is sublime in the scope of its philosophy. It
leads us into progressive revelations of divine truth, a
progressive understanding of life from the cradle to the
grave, and a progressive preparation for man's eternal
destiny. King Solomon's Temple, the golden house of
God on Mt. Moriah becomes the symbol of the gorgeous
temple of Creation; the great and good Builder, whose
inspired genius fashioned its glorious fabric, its brazen
pillars, and silent stones, and all the cunning handicraft
of the sanctum sanctorum, becomes the symbol of the
Supreme Architect, whose creative hand in wisdom,
strength and beauty reared the pillars of the universe
and decked the dome of night with jewel stars; and the
Holy of Holies itself symbolizes the soul, the dwelling
place of the Most High God, where the luminous flame
of Diety glows, and the oracle waits to whisper the
Word. To know God, to serve Him, to make our souls a
worthy temple for His habitation and to manifest toward the world a spirit of dauntless integrity and tireless
zeal in the prosecution of life's appointed tasks. This
is a part of the philosophy of the Master Degree, and
this is sublime.

2. It is sublime in its answer to the a g e - l o n g
quest of the soul. A comparative study of the religions
of the world, their cosmogonies, their religious rites, and
ethical codes go far toward the proof of the unity of the
race and the unity of truth. We cannot go into that, but
at the core of all religions and systems of philosophy,
we see the quest of the soul for satisfaction, for the sum-
mum bonum. Where is God? What is man? What was
his origin and what is his destiny? Whence come you
and whither are you traveling? How to live and how
to die? These are the burning questions of an immortal
soul. The Master Degree is sublime in its answer to
these and similar questions. The inspired ode falls upon

the listening ear of the pilgrim of the dark, seeking more
light, and its solemn message sings its lesson to the
thoughtful soul: "Remember now thy Creator in the
days of thy youth—or ere the silver cord be loosed or
the golden bowl be broken, or the pitcher be broken at
the fountain; or the wheel be broken at the cistern,
then shall the dust return to the earth as it was, and the
spirit shall return unto God who gave it."

And then the sublime conclusion which we often
omit:

"Fear God and keep His commandments, for this is
the whole duty of man." For obvious reasons I cannot
go into the details of the quest of the soul for light
through the mystic mazes of this wonderful symbolic
degree. But it is here the full orbed sun begins to rise
and the traveler fare forth into its drenching light. I
find a recent sonnet by Roselle Mercier Montgomery,
entitled "The New Believers" which is appropriate here:

"They who have worshipped at one shrine alone,
    The shrine of truth, they who have long assailed
    The ancient altars where old faiths prevailed,
    Begin to sense that truth and God are one,
    And grow more humble now, more reverent.
    For science, challenging the infinite,
    Describes, beyond the furthest star, a light
    That leads to worship and to wonderment.
    Let doubts bedim the minds of lesser men
    Who can not find God in the books and creeds—
    These research men derive Him from His deeds;
    Let earth-bound ones, their eyes upon the sod,
    Broadcast today the cry, "There is no God"—
    The scientists discover God again!"

3. It is sublime in its immemorial search for that
which was lost.

Here too we are dealing with a Symbol. The lost
word is not something that can be caught and enshrined
in letters, and syllables and signs. It is something more
fundamental than that, that goes down to the innermost
depths of man's nature and soul experience. Is it something that was lost in Eden's tragedy of sin? Some pris-
tine innocence and purity and power left behind the
guarding swords of the cherubim, which exiled man

might not return to recover? Some blurring of the shining image of the Creator henceforth to be but dimly discerned?

Was it the loss of conscious contact, with that guiding spirit that walked with man beneath the ambrosial bowers of paradise—now lost? Was it merely the magic name of some forgotten deity, or was it rather the knowledge and experience of buried truth that awaited a new revelation and a new discovery? Whatever the lost word may be, the philosophy of the Master degree furnishes a rational hope of its discovery. When the temple of life is completed and dedicated, when life's labors are done and the soul's holiest dreams realized, when the soul has been purified by suffering and enlightened by visions of things to be, and regenerated by some force transcending all human powers, the lost word will be found and no doubt it will be a sufficient pass into that "far country from whose bourne no traveller e'er returns."

4. It is sublime in its presentation of the ideal man and the high ideals of human conduct.

Among all the lessons to be learned from the legend of the illustrious Tyrian Architect, we will not forget that he is the Symbolic ideal of all that's great and good in character and conduct. To stand foursquare in unimpeachable integrity before God and man; to bear the ills of life with unruffled patience and calm; to offer up devotion to Deity in the holy place and then to meet with dauntless fortitude the envy and greed, the perfidy and calumny of men; to travel bravely on the rough and rugged road, where dark passions, like hell hounds unleashed spring at the white throat of nobility and honor—aye, to resist unalarmed the world, the flesh, and the devil with instruments of death in their hands; and then to yield life itself in defense of unsullied integrity; all this is an achievement and a prize that an archangel might well covet. It is sublime.

5. It is sublime in its high dramatic appeal.

The eminent tragedian, Edwin Booth has been quoted, as saying: "In all my research and study, in all my close analysis of the masterpieces of Shakespeare, in my earnest determination to make those plays appear real on the mimetic stage, I have never and nowhere met tragedy so real, so sublime, so magnificent as the legend of Hiram."

The drama of the Third Degree contains a perpetual thrill for all loyal devotees of the craft. Here is a real drama of human life. It is the portrayal of the great contrasts of human principles and human emotions; now breathing the incense of pious devotion, where descending and ascending angels seem swiftly to pass like heralds from the throne above; now crashing in the violence of brutal passions. Now vocal with the pleadings of brotherly love, now crimsoned with the stain of bloody murder. Now strong with a spirit of conscious integrity, now groaning beneath the incubus of conscious guilt and remorse. Now boastful in fancied security from detection, now trembling before the naked sword of avenging retributive justice.

What a conflict between the nobler and baser passions of the human soul!

Then what a sublime culmination in that final scene of solemn emotion when man's extremity and importunity becomes God's opportunity; when the heavens bending low, the day follows the night and the Pale Horseman goes down before the all conquering hand of the Lion of the Tribe of Judah!

6. And finally, it is sublime in its pictorial and emblematic portrayal of the deeper meaning of life, death and immortality.

Of course this is no monitory lecture but only a brief outline of things quite familiar to the craft.

Between the points of the compasses the noblest sentiments of life, character, and conduct are exemplified, friendship, morality, and brotherly love. The arc of the square marks our just relations toward all mankind. From the symbolic book is streaming light to guide our feet into all safe paths of faith and conduct.

The All Seeing Eye that neither slumbers or sleeps keeps ceaseless vigil over the world and the naked hearts of men.

Time would fail me to tell of the Beehive and its suggestion of a diligent and industrious life; of the Pot of

Incense with its fragrance of ceaseless adoration and prayer; of the Hour Glass with its fast dripping sands of this dissolving life; and the Scythe that uplifts to snap its brittle thread or to reap its inevitable harvest of all things mortal; of the celebrated Pythagorean problem with its solution of life's mystery; of the Ark that bears us safely o'er life's whelming floods and through tempestuous storms until beyond the sunset seas, we may cast anchor where rocks and storms will fear no more; of the Coffin, Spade, and Setting Maul, those somber mementos of our mortality and approaching fate; and of the Acacia that waves it immortal green beyond the narrow house of the grave to admonish us that we have within us an immortal part, which shall never, never, never die!

Thus the Sublime degree is designed to fortify us against all the "stings and arrows of mischievous fortune," to challenge us to a life of heroic faith and courage, to lead us calmly on to meet our appointed fate, and to cheer us on in the sanguine hope and expectation of a blissful immortality in the "house not made with hands eternal in the heavens."

So I close with that sublime stanza in Campbell's poem, "The Last Man":

> "Go tell the night that hides thy face
> Thou heardst the last of Adams race
> On this sepulchral clod
> The darkening universe defy
> To quench his immortality
> Or shake his trust in God."

DUTIES OF THE OFFICERS
OF A LODGE

By Raymund Daniel, Past Grand Master

The mission of Freemasonry will not be fulfilled by augumented rights for ourselves, but through the performance of our duties to God and others.

WHILE THE DUTIES of the officers of a Lodge are laid down in the regulations of Freemasonry and the Installation Ceremonies of the Grand Lodge of Georgia, those who govern and assist in the government of a Lodge can never too well comprehend the required fulfillment of their obligations to their Fraternity and to their brethren.

At all times, it must be understood that Freemasonry is a society of democracy—an organization of freemen, free to think and act with propriety and with consideration for all concerned. It must be remembered that the just powers granted to those who govern are derived solely with the consent of those to be governed, that the organization of Freemasonry is established solely on the principles of freedom, equality, justice and humanity. Any Master or other officer who assumes office with views differing from these ancient regulations is not entitled to such offices and, at best, can but bring confusion, disorder and dishonor to his Lodge and to the Fraternity he represents.

Of all officers of the Masonic Institution, the Master occupies the most important position. The success or the failure of the Lodge depends chiefly upon his discretion, judgment and ability. The effects of the supervision of his Lodge extend even to Grand Lodge, which is composed of constituent Lodges. A Grand Lodge is no stronger than its weakest Lodge.

While the Master of a Lodge is clothed with such authority as is seldom enjoyed by any other executive or presiding head, he is, at the same time, the servant of his brethren who select him as their representative to carry out the principles, laws and regulations of the Craft, of which the Lodge is an integral part.

An ideal Master is one who will "judge with candor, admonish with friendship and reprehend with justice." Such a Master first of all, must be thoroughly acquainted with the written and unwritten laws of the Fraternity. The Grand Lodge of Georgia has compiled and codified the regulations and no Master should assume office until he has these statutes engraved upon his Masonic mind. Nothing so quickly brings disregard and shame upon a lodge as a Master who is unable to dispose of matters in accordance with Masonic principles and Masonic custom.

A Master must be firm in his decisions, but he must deal fairly with all concerned in every procedure. He must at all times be mindful of the fact that the newest member has every right and privilege bestowed upon him under the laws of rights and privileges. The Master must never forget that the Lodge is not his Lodge, individually, but the Lodge of his brethren and that the law he is called upon to administer is not his law, but that of Grand Lodge.

An autocratic or tyrannical Master is as despicable as a weak and vacillating presiding officer is detestable. A Master should possess those qualities by which the Craft may be directed, but never driven. The Master should be as the shepherd of a flock, not only leading his lodge, but also protecting it from recalcitrant members as well as from foes without.

Unfortunately, in Masonry, as in all other human societies, there are occasions when situations must be met with unassailable firmness, for the Installation Ceremonies require the assent of the Master-elect to the following pledge:

You promise to pay homage to the Grand Master for the time being, and to his officers when duly installed; and strictly to conform to every edict of the Grand Lodge, or General Assembly of Masons, that is not subversive of the principles and groundwork of Masonry?

Even in such instances, firmness must not be confused with harshness and the steel hand of determination must be gloved in fraternal love.

In the administration of justice, the Master must remember his supremacy, for there is no appeal by a Lodge from the ruling of a Master except to the Grand Lodge. Only when immediate action must be taken "to protect the character of the institution and to preserve the harmony of the Lodge" would the Grand Master suspend or discipline an improper Master.

The ceremonies of Installation require the assurances that a Master must be "of good morals (proper character) of great skill (proper intellectuality) true and trusty (proof of ability) and a lover of the whole fraternity, wheresoever dispersed over the face of the whole earth (an example of brotherhood.)"

So the qualifications of a Master are four, Morality, Intellectuality, Faithfulness and Friendliness.

In Masonic ceremonies, it is stated that one of the chief duties of the Master is to set the Craft at labor under good and wholesome instructions or see that this is done by the proper officers working with him.

In the ancient Fifteen Articles it is stated specifically that "the Master must be steadfast, trusty and true," and as emphatically it is declared that "No Master shall undertake a work that he is not able to finish to his lord's profit and the credit of his Lodge." It is also said that "the Master shall instruct his apprentice faithfully and make him a perfect workman."

Not only must a Master be fair and firm in his executive duties, and well versed in ritualism, but he must also have the intellectual capacity to lift the ritualism that cloaks the beauties of Masonry's symbols and present the great truths of our Fraternity as living, breathing principles for all life—not confined alone to the Lodge room in which they are inculcated, but applied to the great World of Humanity without.

The Master who merely presides over the business sessions of Lodge—(no matter how well) and presents the ritualistic ceremonies (impressive as he may make them) accomplishes little, unless he offers to his Craft the inspiration and desire for the practical application of Masonry in doing its God-given part to make a better world in which better men shall live.

The duties and responsibilities of a Lodge Master are hundred fold—only the Heavenly Master can measure the unknown achievements that can come from the carrying out of the obligations and opportunities.

The same rigid caution and care are vitally necessary in the selection of the other officers of a Lodge. The proper fulfillment of the duties of the other officers and their general and specific behavior may some day bring for them the reward of Mastership. Every officer elected or appointed below the rank of Master should be selected with the view that they may some time be Master of their Lodge.

The early regulations—in fact two of the Landmarks, require that all Lodges shall have a Master, two Wardens and a Tiler. Other officers have been added, but the first requirements provided that the government of the Craft, when so congregated in a Lodge, shall be by a Master and two Wardens and that every Lodge, when congregated must be duly tiled.

The word Warden is derived from the Anglo Saxon "Wearden," meaning "to guard or watch." Warden signifies a guardian or watchman. In addition to their assistance to the Master and their duties in his absence— responsibilities especially grave in their character—additional service is demanded of Wardens in Lodges of the American jurisdiction on account of their specific participation in ritualistic rendition. In practically all of the ceremonials of degrees in American Lodges, impressions are made on the candidates by the Wardens prior to their appearance before the Master. Wardens ever should aid the Master in maintaining the dignity required in a Lodge.

Next to the Master, the achievements of a Lodge depend upon the Secretary. He is really the business manager of the Lodge, under the direction of the Master. He is concerned with seeing that the records of the Lodge are preserved properly and that the various orders of business move with dispatch. He should at all times keep the Master correctly informed as to what communications may come to the Secretary's desk, so as to avoid objectionable matters from being presented before the Master has had the opportunity of their knowledge.

The Secretary is the right hand and guiding support of the Master. There must be perfect harmony, understanding and accord between the Master and the Secretary. In Lodges of the British Dominions the Secretary is the appointee of the Master, as are all others except the treasurer and tiler. Although an elective office in American Lodges, the Secretary should hold the same allegiance and loyalty to the Master, permissible under administration of Masonic law.

The vital necessity of the collections of all dues and other monies is imposed in the office of Secretary. In many instances this requirement brings delicate developments and complications and the fairness and firmness required of a Master is demanded of the Secretary. Watchcare of the Craft at refreshment is also upon the Secretary by nature of his office, although not so prescribed by regulation. He must be a man of the highest moral and intellectual traits. Responsible for records and monies he is always under the observance of the membership and he is directly to be held accountable for the business administration. Next to the Master, and often perhaps more so, he has his hands on the pulse of the Craft and is in excellent position to recognize the needs of the Lodge and Craft and accordingly to make suggestions. He is a sort of liason officer between the Master and the Craft. A Secretary not in accord with the Master or out of harmony with the membership, inattentive to his duties and lax in his dealing with the membership can impair and wreck a Lodge.

To the Lodge Secretary, Grand Lodge looks for the proper reports of the Lodge and a delinquent Lodge Secretary can hamper seriously the actions and program of the Grand Body.

Equally important, in many ways, is the office of treasurer. It is he who receives all monies from the Secretary. It is he who must keep a just account of the same. He alone can pay them out by order of the Lodge and by consent of the Master. His integrity must be above reproach, with a "regard for the fraternity" that prompts him "to faithful discharge of the duties" of his office.

Often times a Lodge fails to recognize the solemn importance of the proper selection of its Chaplain. Such an officer should be a spiritual leader, even as the Master is the governing power. He should possess traits that will make him a silent as well as a speaking blessing to the Craft. It is his duty "to point to heaven and lead the way." He should possess those qualities of mind, heart and soul that will direct properly the thoughts of members as well as novitiates.

The offices of the two Deacons—Senior and Junior— require qualifications of like high standard. Not alone are these characteristics needed for Lodge ceremonies and ritualistic impressions upon the candidate, but because these two officers, with the Senior and Junior Stewards and tiler meet and mingle most with the brethren of the Lodge. The courteous and dignified demeanor of these five named officers can do much toward preserving the decorum of the Lodge and the manifestation of hospitality and cordial brotherhood.

Outside of the ritualistic ceremonies of these five officers, the tiler is the most important. It is he who meets first all members, visitors and candidates. The office is naturally one of self-sacrifice, for the tiler without the Lodge, never sees or hears what transpires within a Lodge room. The self-sacrifice, however, must bring the realization of the important duties of which the sacrifice is made. The selection of a tiler should never be made for any financial advantage, unless the one holding the office has the recognition of his sacred duties.

The first atmosphere of a Lodge is gained through the impressions of the Mason without the door. His is the first opportunity for the Lodge's demonstration of brotherly welcome and brotherly love. His manner and bearing will not only give pleasure or offense, but will influence the spirit of the member, visitor or candidate after he enters the Lodge. The tiler is the host who meets the brother at the portal.

He is also responsible for those who "pass and repass." While there should be no strangers in a Masonic Lodge, the visiting brother can not help but have a feeling of restraint or timidity. This sentiment can mostly be relieved by the tiler. Entrance by means of avouchment or committee examination can be made easy by the well qualified tiler.

Not only the entrance to the Lodge room, but the ante-room and the preparation room are under the immediate supervision of this officer. The last named two rooms are under his direct control while a communication is being held. He is also charged with the condition of the Lodge room prior to the meetings—to see that lights and heat are properly arranged—that there are cleanliness and comfort as far as possible. A dirty hall signifies a sloven Lodge. The tiler is the custodian of the Lodge furniture, furnishings and clothing.

He is the officer in charge of the ante-room, and it is demanded of him that there be no unnecessary congregating or disorder to disturb the Lodge or confusion to distract the candidates in the preparation room.

A tiler, with a pipe in his mouth, a hat on his head, propped in a chair with his feet to the wall, has no place in the Masonic organization. Friendliness, good fellowship and hospitality are tenets of Freemasonry, but levity, lack of dignity and disregard are as abominable and repulsive in an ante-room as in a Lodge hall. So, also, should the tiler see that none enter the preparation room of the candidates except the officers so assigned and the conductors so selected.

The tiler is the first officer of the Lodge officially to see the candidates.

Here, again comes the opportunity for the properly qualified tiler. From the tiler's Masonic or un-Masonic action is the candidate's first attitude toward the Fraternity. There have been instances where a candidate has left the ante-room forever on account of the flippant or gross remarks of the tiler.

When the alarm comes upon the outer door of the Lodge room, the Master orders that the tiler be requested to invite the candidates into the room for preparation. It is the TILER, who first approaches the applicants and extends the invitation. It is he who makes the first contact. Afterward, the Senior Deacon, with the Stewards meets the applicant. There responsibility shifts from the Tiler, but he has made the first impression.

From this time until the entrance into the Lodge room, the influence that is to be given comes from the Senior Deacon and the Stewards. On the first pages of the Masonic Manual and Code of the Grand Lodge is printed the "Lecture in Preparation Room." It is the lecture given by the Senior Deacon to the unprepared candidate. Questions have been asked of the applicant, but the words of the Senior Deacon constitute the first statement of facts he has heard.

Below is presented this lecture:

"Before proceeding further it becomes my duty to inform you that the ceremonies in which you are about to engage are by no means of a light or trifling character, but are of great importance and deep solemnity. Freemasonry is a beautiful system of morality, veiled in allegory and illustrated by symbols. The design of the Masonic Institution is to make its members wiser, better and consequently happier; and this is accomplished by means of a series of moral instructions taught, according to ancient usage, by types, symbols, allegorical figures and lectures. The forms and ceremonies of this Institution have come down, through a succession of ages and are all designed to impress upon the mind wise and serious truths. I will now leave you in the hands of true and trusted brethren, who will see that you proceed as all others have done who have gone this way before."

The lecture above is not published here for any applicant but for all who are now Masons—to govern them against the blasphemous jesting or frivolous conversation that might occur in the preparation of the applicants or any unforgivable burlesque attitude of officers or conductors. The Master, through his Senior Deacon must see that all solemnity shall accompany the ceremony, and that none but those taking part in the conducting should be in the preparation room. The tiler, as well, must guard also the outer door of the preparation room into the ante-room, so as to suppress all improper noises. Every caution must be taken that the applicant shall be impressed with the beauty and sacredness of his new adventure. This care must be exercised by the Deacon, Stewards and Conductors from now on, because during the greater part of the ritualistic ceremonies the material confidence of the applicant is entrusted to them.

Roughness Prohibited—Frivolty, roughness, or brutality in conferring degrees will upon the first offense subject the Lodge to severe reprimand and upon the second offense to forfeiture of charter.

Such are some of the "Duties of the Officers of a Lodge," in addition to which are many other requirements that individual experience alone will inculcate.

However, when all are learned all will be embodied in the Masonic tenets of—

Love, Wisdom, Justice.

DUTIES OF THE MEMBERS
OF A LODGE

By Raymund Daniel, Past Grand Master

A LODGE is "a place where Masons assemble and work," according to the definition of the Old Charges of 1772. Previous to the year 1717, the foundation date of the Masonic system as we know it today, a sufficient number of Craftsmen could meet, open a Lodge, transact its business and carry out its ceremonials. However, a regulation was adopted in 1717 which provided "that the privilege of assembling as Masons should no longer be unlimited, but that it should be vested in certain Lodges convened in certain places, and legally authorized by the warrant of the Grand Master and the consent of the Grand Lodge."

In our present ritual a proper Lodge is termed "just and legally constituted." By "just" is meant the Lodge has the required membership and is supplied with the authorized Lodge furniture of the Holy Bible, square and compasses. It becomes "legally constituted," when it is established under constitutional authority. Our Lodges come from the Grand Master or the Grand Lodge. When a Lodge is authorized by the Grand Master it is termed a Lodge under Dispensation; when created by the Grand Lodge it is a Warranted Lodge. A Lodge under Dispensation is only a creature of the Grand Master, as its dispensation can be revoked either by the Grand Master or the Grand Lodge. If revoked, however, Masons made in such a Lodge are recognized as true and lawful members of the Craft.

A Lodge, while sovereign with regard to other Lodges, varies in details from other societies and organizations. Every regular Masonic Lodge derives its powers and existence from Grand Lodge. While a Lodge can compile its by-laws, they must have the consent of Grand Lodge and can not conflict with the rules of the Parent Body. Therefore no Lodge is self-created and independent.

There is one principle, however, that must be remembered; as the Grand Lodge is the guardian and custodian of the character and conduct of the Fraternity in the entire territory in which it is sovereign, so also a Lodge occupies the same position in its community or local jurisdiction. Therefore, first of all else, the local Lodges are responsible for the fair and good name of Freemasonry.

In the preceding pages, was the endeavor to present the "Duties of the Officers of a Lodge." Herewith is the effort to reveal the "Duties of the Members of a Lodge."

To the reader who hears so often the reference to Masonic "rights and privileges," there may come the conjecture as to why the term "duties" is employed. Why do we speak of "duties" instead of "rights?" Rights do exist; but when voluntarily formed organizations, such as Masonic Lodges, arise, when an association is formed upon the tenets of democracy, freedom, and fraternity, there ensues the constant danger of the "rights" of one individual clashing with those of another. In a Society that presents the generous dogma that "some must of necessity rule and teach, and others learn to submit and obey," how can we hope to reconcile and harmonize such a creed, unless we do establish some ideal higher than "rights?"

If Freemasonry should teach that Freemasonry is organized and prevails for the purpose of securing to each member the exercise of his "rights," how can a member be asked to sacrifice all of his "rights" in favour of others who belong to the organization? "Rights" of each individual are equal. In what manner or by what method then can it be proven to the individual Craftsman that he is bound to drown his will in the wills of his brothers?

Freemasonry, therefore, must possess some superior principle by which its members can be guided onward toward the improvement and understanding that will teach loyalty, constancy and self-sacrifice. Freemasonry must offer the ideal which will bring the union of all individual members with their fellow members; removing from their minds and hearts the recognition of a single man or the force of the majority.

This principle that Freemasonry offers is DUTY.

The ideal required for Freemasonry today is that local Lodges shall teach members that they are the sons of one God, and expected to fulfill only one law in this world—that each is bound to live not for himself, but for God and others.

Freemasonry DOES GIVE its "rights," but its primary and supreme right is that of recognizing and fulfilling duty. The most sublime "privilege" Freemasonry can afford is the privilege of the performance of duty.

Rights will be available only through the carrying out of duty.

The statement already has been made that the local Lodge is responsible in its community for the Fraternity's character and reputation. Every Masonic Lodge is also responsible for its opportunity to present to all Humanity the exemplification of the principles of duty and service.

When we so recognize the principles of duty, it is easy to understand the manner of the government of a Lodge. There is the familiar term of Masonic subordination, but Masonic duty is a far better expression.

In the preceding chapter there has been the attempt to define the responsibilities of the Master. As the Master is only a representative selected by his Lodge to govern the members, according to the dictates of Grand Lodge, which belongs to the Craft, many of the duties imposed on the Master are self-imposed on the Craft.

Members who recognize and are familiar with these duties will give greater assistance in the proper conduct of the Lodge. Members should realize their duty in familiarizing themselves with the laws, regulations and requirements of the Fraternity. They must place harmony first in all considerations and discussions. A Lodge is a Society that affords all opportunities for conferences, and as emphatically bars controversy.

Above all things else the membership of a Lodge must place its respect for law, Masonic and otherwise. Its primary efforts must be to observe such laws. If there be this concerted achievement, there will always be peace, harmony, unity and progress. Lodge members should be well qualified for the rendition of the ritual, for "good work" is of benefit to the novitiates. Interpretation of the symbols is a necessity as the ritual exists only for the understanding and application of the symbols.

Members of a Lodge should be equipped for the varied services demanded within and without the Lodge. Future Masters are to be selected from those who render efficient service among the brethren of the benches.

In the first chapter, the importance of the various officers was designated, but the function of greatest purpose is possible only from the ranks—that of the committee on investigation of applicants. An indifferent committee or member of such a committee, which or who does not conscientiously, carefully and honorably carry out this sacred and solemn trust, threatens the fabric of Freemasonry. Membership upon any committee of a Lodge carries with it a grave responsibility. No matter how insignificant the task should appear, it should be accepted heartily and fulfilled to the best ability.

There should remain ever constant the realization of the solemnity and sublimity of the tenents of the Fraternity. Any member who looks with frivolty upon the ceremonies of a Lodge or takes an advantage of a candidate in any of the ritualism does not comprehend the purposes of Freemasonry and is that much less worthy to be called a Freemason.

Lodge duty includes other routine and technical requirements, but catalogues far greater obligations in the presentation and exemplification of the ideals of the institution. The Mason who endeavors to live clean in his own personal life, will live clean in the Masonic Lodge and also in the outside world.

The call to all Freemasons today is to realize that we are Workingmen—Brother Workingmen—and that the earth is our workshop. We shall sanctify that workshop, which after all, is God's workshop, if we carry out the Masonic ideals of Duty.

The consciousness of our "rights" will never suffice as a permanent guide on our path towards attainment and perfection. It will not even suffice to obtain for us the continuous progressive improvement and advancement in Freemasonry that we ever desire.

The chief mission of the members of a Lodge is for the mental, spiritual and social improvement of ourselves and others, and services to God, the Fatherland, the Family and Humanity. The mission of Freemasonry will not be fulfilled by augmented "rights" for ourselves, but through the performance of our duties to God and others.

Tradition, Progress, Association—these are the sacred possessions of Freemasonry.

For us is the solemn realization of our heritage and to prove that we, too, are all sons of God and brothers in Him.

Those are the duties of the members of a Lodge.

HISTORY OF FREEMASONRY
IN GEORGIA

By William B. Clarke, Past Grand Master

CHAPTER I.

Masonic Traditions in Georgia

G EORGIA WAS founded nearly one hundred years
after the colonies in New England had become prosperous. There was little inducement for men of capi-
tal to come to Georgia and the majority of the first colonists were of the poorer classes. These colonists were
carefully selected before they were permitted to em-
bark with the first consignment of colonists. Business
failures are now adjusted by bankruptcy laws, but in
those days, the prisons of England were filled by the
victims of misfortune who had been sentenced to serve
terms in prison for failure to pay their debts.

The King of England desired the establishment of a
colony to serve as a buffer between the Spaniards in
Florida and the wealthy colonies of the Carolinas and
New England. This desire, together with a sympathy
for and a desire to help the poor debtors in the prisons
of England inspired James Edward Oglethorpe to arrange for the establishment of a colony in Georgia which
would serve as a protection for the colonies of the north
against an attack by the Spaniards from Florida and, on
the other hand, would give some of the worthy men in
the debtors' prisons of England another chance in the
New World.

The Charter for the new colony in Georgia contained
clauses prohibiting the Trustees from receiving any sal-
ary, fee, perquisite or profit whatever and also prohibited them from obtaining any grants of land within
the district, either themselves or in trust for them.
Southey, the biographer of the Rev. John Wesley, states
that no colony was ever established upon principles more
honorable to its projectors. Some of the Trustees were
Masons and several of them were members of the Grand
Lodge of England.

All oppressed Protestants of every nation were eli-
gible to become members of the colony and to receive

grants of land. Jews and Roman Catholics were prohibited. This restriction was waived by Oglethorpe
shortly after the arrival of the colonists and, upon his
recommendation, protests against his leniency were ig-
nored by the Trustees.

All applicants desiring to be enrolled as members
of the colony in Georgia and who were the occupants
of debtors' prisons, were examined by two committees
appointed for the purpose. One committee ascertained
if the applicants were worthy of charity and the other
committee ascertained if the characters of the applicants
were satisfactory. Thus the statement that the founders
of Georgia were "jailbirds" is denied.

James Edward Oglethorpe, wealthy, influential, a
military and civic leader, one of the prominent men in
England and intimately associated with the highest cul-
ture of the times, sacrificed these advantages and led
the colonists to the new land. On February 12, 1733,
they landed at the foot of the bluff overlooking the Savannah River about eighteen miles from the sea and
founded the colony of Georgia.

Many attempts have been made to prove that Masonry had its birth in Georgia either before or within a
few days of the establishment of the colony at Savannah.
There is not one single fact in existence to prove this
theory. The names of the founders of the Craft in Georgia
are not known. The circumstances surrounding the
establishment of the first lodge in Georgia are not
known. Only traditions exist to shed any light upon the
beginning of the Craft in Georgia. Traditions, of themselves, are usually unreliable and seldom trusted. When
we trace the beginning of a tradition to the time of the
circumstance or event which it describes, we can begin
to give credence to it. When surrounding facts are presented which point to the proof of the tradition, its statements must be accepted as supported by fact. When
the traditions and the surrounding facts have been presented over a period of years to criticism of the most
outstanding historical minds of this country and of Europe and the traditions accepted as proven completely
and so printed in their writings, then the traditions may
be recorded as facts beyond any reasonable doubt.
These steps have been taken with the traditions herewith

given and many of the present day historical writers are so convinced of their worth that the statements contained in them have been recorded as fact by the most eminent writers of this country and of Europe, both Masonic and profane.

There stands today upon the Coastal Highway leading from Savannah to Brunswick, and near the famous old church at Midway, an iron marker placed there by the Coastal Highway Association. This iron marker states that some fifteen miles to the east is the spot upon which it is thought the first Masonic meeting in Georgia was held, with Oglethorpe as Master. This spot was once the town of Sunbury and the first meeting was said to have been held at the place which later became the site of that town. Brother Edmund H. Abrahams of Zerubbabel Lodge No. 15, of Savannah, was the Chairman of the Historical Commission which placed the iron marker directing the tourist and the lover of the historical to the spot. He has in his possession today the document which contains the tradition that the first Masonic meeting in Georgia was held on this spot.

This document is the personal diary of Mordecai Sheftall, once Senior Grand Warden (1786) of the Provincial Grand Lodge of Georgia, Past Master and for many years a member of Solomon's Lodge No. 1 of Savannah. Mordecai Sheftall states in this diary that he was captured by the British at the first siege of Savannah and placed in the prison camp some miles to the south of Savannah; that he was a member of the Union Society organized in 1740 for the support of Bethesda Orphanage (still existing in Savannah); that the laws of the Society required that in order to preserve the charter the annual meeting should be held upon a specified date; that this date fell while he was a prisoner of the British with other members of the Society; that these members being aware of the tradition that the first Masonic meeting in Georgia was held upon the spot which later became the site of the town of Sunbury, and that the first meeting was held under the leadership of General James Edward Oglethorpe, founder of the colony of Georgia, asked and received the permission of the British officers to leave the prison camp and go to this spot where they held the annual meeting of the Union Society. The Masonic connection with this event is indicated by the fact that the Masons were in the beginning and are now actively interested in the work of the Union Society and of Bethesda, the oldest orphanage in America.

Another significant thing concerning the Masonic connection with the event is indicated by the fact that Samuel Stirk, later the first Grand Secretary of the Grand Lodge of Georgia, and John Martin, Grand Steward of the Provincial Grand Lodge of Georgia, were fellow prisoners of Mordecai Sheftall, fellow members of the Union Society, and went to Sunbury with Mordecai Sheftall to hold the annual meeting of the Society. These brethren appear to have been thoroughly convinced of the accuracy of the information given them. The ready willingness of the British officers, said by Sheftall to have been Masons, to give their permission for such an unusual event gives further indication of the value to be placed upon the tradition.

Outside of the known prominence of Mordecai Sheftall in Georgia Masonry, he was called by the British upon their official lists "The Great Rebel." His Revolutionary prominence is indicated by the fact that after that conflict, the General Assembly of Georgia passed an Act now in the hands of Brother Edmund H. Abrahams, relieving Mordecai Sheftall from the payment of all taxes during the remainder of his life in appreciation of his service to the colonies in giving all his wealth and efforts in the cause of liberty. Such a man would hardly have gone to such unusual steps to indicate his belief in the truth of the tradition which he has left in his diary had he not been reasonably certain of that truth.

A second tradition is to be found recorded upon the minutes of a Masonic lodge in Georgia. From the minutes of Solomon's No. 1 for February 10, 1859, we learn that at the dedication of the new building on that date, the lodge was presented with a gavel. In the minutes of February 17, 1859, we find a copy of the letter which accompanied the gavel. This letter reads as follows:

Savannah, February 10, 1859.

Geo. W. Adams, Esq., Chairman,
Committee of Solomon's Lodge No. 1,

Dear Sir:

Please allow me, through you, to present to Solomon's Lodge No. 1 of this city, the accompanying gavel made from a piece of the oak from Sunbury, Liberty County, Georgia, under which, (Tradition says) General James Oglethorpe opened the first Lodge of Masons in the State of Georgia. I think there can be no mistake about this being so, the late Sheftall Sheftall, Esq., (my uncle) has often told me this, he having heard it from his father Mr. Mordecai Sheftall; after the tree had been burnt down Mr. John Stevens of Liberty County, knowing the veneration I had for it on account of other associations connected with it, procured a block of it for me (some fifteen years since), from that block the gavel is made. I am thus particular that there may be no cavil of its genuineness.

Respectfully,
(Signed) PERLA SHEFTALL SOLOMONS.

P. S. White's Statistics, First Edition, under Liberty County, speaks of this tree and its associations.

The "associations" mentioned by Mrs. Solomons and White's Statistics refer to the meeting held by Mordecai Sheftall and the members of the Union Society under this tree in order to preserve the charter of the Society.

Mordecai Sheftall had sources of information open to him from brethren who were in Georgia a few weeks after the event occurred and lived to tell these events to him. His father, Benjamin Sheftall, was Master of the Lodge at Savannah in 1758.

Mordecai Sheftall's next door neighbor for more than forty years was Moses Nunis who received his first degree in the Lodge at Savannah in 1734 just several weeks after the first meeting is said to have occurred. It is beyond belief that Nunis failed to know the facts and also failed to convey the information to Mordecai Sheftall with whom he associated intimately at home and in lodge meetings. They were members of Solomon's Lodge together for years. The record of the date of initiation of Moses Nunis is in the possession of Solomon's Lodge. From the information contained in the diary of Mordecai Sheftall, and from the letter of Mrs. Solomons it appears that a meeting of Masons was held on the site of the town of Sunbury in January, 1734. If true, this was the first Masonic meeting held in Georgia. We now come to the facts surrounding the organization of the first lodge in Georgia at Savannah several weeks later.

Another tradition is recorded in the minutes of Solomon's Lodge No. 1 of Savannah, where for the meeting of December 21, 1858, there appears the following:

> That as tradition has informed us that a Masonic Lodge (now Solomon's) was first organized in this City by General Oglethorpe, February 10th, 1733, we do dedicate Solomon's Lodge New Hall on the 10th of February, next, being the 127th anniversary of the organization of Masonry in Georgia.

The New Hall, at the northeast corner of Bull and Broughton Streets, was dedicated by the Grand Lodge of Georgia on February 10, 1859 in accordance with the resolution.

In considering the traditions surrounding the birth of the Craft in Georgia we are now presented with a definite date. In considering this date, it must be remembered that in 1752, the calendars were changed and we must now determine if this date refers to the calendar in use prior to 1752 or to the calendar now in use. According to the old calendar, the year began on the 25th of March. January, February and March were the last three months of the year, and not the first three months of the year as we now recognize them. To change the calendar from the old to the new, we must add one year and eleven days when considering the months of January, February and March. The tradition we are now examining gives the date as February 10, 1733. This is one of the months affected.

If this date refers to the calendar now in use, one year and eleven days must be subtracted to convert to the old calendar. The result of this would give us January 30th, 1732, two days before the colonists landed at Savannah. It being impossible for the tradition to refer to the old calendar, reconciliation with the present calendar by adding one year and eleven days will give us February 21, 1734. If the tradition is correct, this is the birthday of Freemasonry in Georgia. The source of this tradition upon the minutes of Solomon's Lodge No. 1 is not known. Because of its similarity with the tradition received from the Sheftalls, it probably came from that family. That further weight should be given it, Charles

C. Jones, Jr., probably Georgia's most profound historian, gave a chair of oak from the tree under which Oglethorpe opened the first meeting in Georgia, to Solomon's Lodge on the occasion of the dedication of the new building. This oak stood near the site upon which grew the great oaks used to furnish the timbers for the celebrated frigate Constitution, better known to history as "Old Ironsides."

Thus far, we have reviewed the traditions surrounding the birth of the Craft in Georgia. Generation after generation in Savannah has continued these traditions almost from the time of the events which they describe and explain. Their persistence until recent times was the great inspiration prompting the search for the facts which for the last ten years have been furnished to writer after writer in this country and abroad and have given to Georgia Masonry for the first time its proper place in history. That these traditions are accepted universally as true beyond all reasonable doubt is best emphasized by the fact that in all recent Masonic histories and publications, author after author has printed the dates and statements contained without further question. February 21, 1734 is universally accepted as the date upon which Freemasonry had its birth in Georgia.

CHAPTER II.

James Edward Oglethorpe

NO MASONIC record exists to prove that the founder of the colony of Georgia was a Mason. If he was a Mason, it has been impossible to ascertain the lodge of which he was a member. When we remember that the Grand Lodge of England was organized by four lodges in the year 1717, that Oglethorpe in that year was an officer in the army of Prince Eugene; that the early lodges in England and the Grand Lodge itself kept practically no records, we must realize that to prove Oglethorpe a Mason is of itself a tremendous task.

About this man and his relationship to the beginning of the Craft in Georgia, there exists several traditions, a study of which has led every Masonic author in recent years to state emphatically that he was the founder of the Craft in Georgia. This statement will be found in every history of recent years. If he was a Mason, he must have received his degrees in one of the early English Lodges in the days when records were practically unknown.

In the preceding Chapter, we reviewed the Sheftall tradition which stated that Oglethorpe opened the first meeting in Georgia at the spot which later became the town of Sunbury. History records the fact that at the time stated, Oglethorpe was in the vicinity of that spot on a scouting expedition along the bank of the Altamaha River.

Later, when we reviewed the tradition recorded in the minutes of Solomon's Lodge No. 1 that he organized the lodge on February 21, 1734, history records the fact that Oglethorpe returned to Savannah from the scouting expedition just a few days before this date.

We will now review the traditions surrounding the connection of this soldier, statesman, scholar and philanthropist with the beginning of the Craft in Georgia, leaving to the judgment of the individual reader the determination as to whether these traditions furnish the evidence which establishes beyond all reasonable doubt that Oglethorpe was a Mason.

There are still living in Savannah the descendants of the Habersham family. The founder of this family in Georgia was James Habersham, the first merchant in the colony, co-worker with Rev. George Whitfield of evangelistic fame, builder and first president of Bethesda Orphanage, once Secretary of the Province, President of the Upper House of the General Assembly of the Province, President of the King's Council and later, during the absence of Governor Wright, Governor of the Province of Georgia. He became a Mason at Savannah on August 5, 1756. To Freemasonry in Georgia, he gave a son, James Jr., Grand Secretary of the Provincial Grand Lodge of Georgia (1786) and first Grand Treasurer of the present Grand Lodge of Georgia. From generation to generation, many of the men of this family have been Masons and members of the lodge of the father of the family.

In 1911, Mrs. Eugene F. Edwards, great-great-granddaughter of James Habersham gave to Solomon's Lodge No. 1 of Savannah an oil painting of Oglethorpe made by her grandfather Richard West Habersham. Richard West Habersham was the friend and fellow art student of Samuel F. B. Morse, inventor of the telegraph. He was also a classmate and friend of General Robert E. Lee. The portrait of James Edward Oglethorpe was copied by Richard West Habersham from a miniature given to James Habersham by Oglethorpe. Because of the fact that Oglethorpe was known in many generations of her family as the founder of the Craft in Georgia and the first Master of the Lodge at Savannah, Mrs. Edwards gave the painting to Solomon's Lodge that the lodge might have an authentic portrait of its first Master and founder. The men of her family have contributed much to Masonry in Georgia and their names frequently appear upon Masonic records in this state. In one instance, a poor and visiting brother who died suddenly in Savannah shortly after the Revolution was buried by the members of Solomon's Lodge from the handsome colonial residence of James Habersham, Jr., and given a funeral worthy of the most wealthy and prominent citizen of the city. From the Masonic connections of her ancestors, Mrs. Edwards had ample opportunity to have passed down to her the tradition that Oglethorpe was the founder of the first lodge in Georgia and its first Master.

Solomon's Lodge No. 1 has in its archives a Bible printed in London in 1733. This date means that the book was printed before January, February or March. It thus had ample opportunity to be printed in London and delivered in Georgia before the time that the first lodge was organized at Savannah on February 21, 1734. Since the year 1881, the members of Solomon's Lodge have stated that this Bible was given to the first lodge in Georgia by James Edward Oglethorpe. The basis for these statements is the fact that prior to 1881 there was written upon the fly leaf of the Bible the inscription, "Presented by General Oglethorpe, 1733." In the year 1881, the Bible was on exhibition in an exposition in Atlanta, Georgia. An autograph hunter, evidently convinced of the authenticity of the handwriting, stole the fly leaf and also a part of the title page to the new Testament which bore a marginal note. That the thief would risk the danger of arrest and imprisonment strongly indicates that he was assured of the value and authenticity of the inscription. He was convinced that Oglethorpe had given the Bible to the first lodge in Georgia.

The date, 1733, means the old calendar. The Bible was therefore presented to the lodge before March 25, 1734. During this period, we have learned from several traditions that the first lodge in Georgia was organized. That the autograph was in the Bible prior to the time it was stolen in 1881 is attested by sworn statements by eye witnesses. These are in the possession of Solomon's Lodge.

Old members of the lodge at Savannah have told younger members on frequent occasions that Oglethorpe organized the lodge and was the first Master. No relic or written tradition survives to substantiate these statements other than those already mentioned and discussed. Certain facts surrounding the obtaining of a charter for the first lodge in Georgia shed interesting sidelights upon these statements.

The records of the Grand Lodge of England show that the charter for the "Lodge at Savannah in the Province of Georgia" was issued in 1735. The lists of the Grand Lodge of England show that the lodge was constituted under the authority of this charter between

October 30, 1735 and March 1, 1736. This latter date is nearly two years after the date upon which the tradition stated that the lodge was organized on February 21, 1734. Why should the Lodge have waited nearly two years to get a charter and to be constituted? This question may be partly answered by the laws of the Grand Lodge of England which were in force at that time requiring that the Master be present at the time the lodge was constituted. Oglethorpe sailed from Charleston, S. C., on a visit to England on April 7, 1734, a month after tradition states that he organized the first lodge. He returned to Savannah on February 5, 1736. Just about this time, the records of the Grand Lodge of England show that the lodge at Savannah was constituted. If Oglethorpe was the first Master of the lodge at Savannah, his presence would be necessary before the lodge could be constituted. This would account for the wait of two years on the part of the lodge before it was constituted.

The records of the Grand Lodge of England show that the charter for the "Lodge at Savannah in ye Province of Georgia" was issued by the Grand Master of England, Lord Viscount Weymouth. This fact is conclusive evidence that there was no Provincial Grand Lodge in Georgia from which a charter could be obtained. Lord Weymouth was Grand Master of England in the year 1735 and, if there had been a Provincial Grand Master in Georgia at the time, the charter would have been issued by him. Here, again, we have interesting light shed on statements made in Solomon's Lodge for many years. These statements have persisted in saying that Oglethorpe obtained the charter while in England in 1735 and brought it back to Savannah with him. The wait of two years from the traditional time of organization until the date of constitution recorded on the records of the Grand Lodge of England reveal interesting sidelights on the truth of the statements that Oglethorpe obtained the charter.

The review of the traditions concerning the Masonic connections and activities of James Edward Oglethorpe have been studied by Masonic historians in England and America for several years. In recent histories and publications, every author without exception has accepted and printed these traditions as established beyond reasonable doubt and their works contain the statement that Oglethorpe was founder of the Craft in Georgia and the first Worshipful Master of the "Lodge at Savannah in ye Province of Georgia."

CHAPTER III.

The Beginning of Freemasonry in Georgia

PRIOR TO THE organization in the year 1717 of the Grand Lodge of England, there was no known body in existence from which lodges might obtain authority for their organization. From whom came the authority to organize lodges is a question, the answer to which is one of the mysteries closely akin to the question as to how old is Masonry. A few lodges did exist before the organization of the Grand Lodge of England and four of these lodges formed that body. These lodges were laws unto themselves and conferred degrees upon any person and in any manner that they might see fit. In the armies of several of the nations were many Masons. In the guilds of craftsmen, many of the officers, aristocrats, scholars and philosophers were found. It appears that these men, when scattered over different parts of the globe, gave their knowledge of Masonry to others and, in some places, formed lodges composed of those upon whom they had conferred degrees.

After the Grand Lodge of England was organized in 1717, lodges were organized in many of the English colonies without the authority of the Grand Lodge. When a lodge was organized in this manner it was said to have come into existence according to the "Old Customs." All of the first lodges in America were organized in this manner. Meeting places were usually taverns or public houses. The ritual used must have been very simple. Practically no records were kept.

For some years after the organization of the Grand Lodge of England, many lodges were organized without authority until the laws of the Grand Lodge on the subject became known. These laws made it illegal to organize a lodge without the authority of the Grand Master of England or without the authority of the Provincial Grand Master of that district who had been appointed by the Grand Master of England for the purpose of establishing Provincial Grand Lodges and of organizing lodges within his territory. Nevertheless, the first lodges in Pennsylvania, Massachusetts and Georgia were organized without such authority. As stated before, their organization was in accordance with the "Old Customs." All of the lodges organized in America according to the "Old Customs" were later duly chartered and constituted by the Grand Lodge of England, the irregularities in their organizations being overlooked. Thus it came about that the first lodge in Georgia was organized before the Grand Lodge of Georgia came into existence.

The earliest reference to Masonry in Georgia contained in Masonic records appears upon the minutes of the Grand Lodge of England for December 13, 1733. The following resolution was ordered:

> *Then the Deputy Grand Master opened to the Lodge the Affairs of planting the new Colony of Georgia in America, and having sent an Account in Print of the Nature of such Plantation to all the Lodges, and informed the Grand Lodge that the Trustees had to Nathaniel Blackerby, Esq. and to himself Commissions under their Common-Seal, to collect the Charity of this Society towards enabling the Trustees to send distressed Brethren to Georgia, where they may be comfortably provided for.*

> *Proposed, that it be streniously recommended by the Master and Wardens of regular Lodges to make a generous collection amongst all their Members for that purpose Which being seconded by Brother Rogers Holland Esqr. (one of the said Trustees), who opened the Nature of the Settlement, and by Sir William Keith, Bart, who was many years Governour of Pensilvania, by Dr. Desagulier, Lord Southwell, Brother Blackerby, and many others, very worthy Brethren, it was recommended accordingly.*

This resolution has caused confusion in several Masonic minds. It has been assumed that a lodge of Masons had been established in Georgia and that the Grand Lodge of England was appealing for funds to assist the members. The first contingent of colonists had not yet arrived in Georgia. A careful reading of the resolution clearly reveals the fact that the Grand Lodge of England had instituted a movement to collect funds from the brethren in England to send distressed brethren to Georgia after the first contingent of colonists had arrived and had established the colony. Had any brethren already been sent, they would have found themselves in an embarrassing position because of lack of support.

On March 18, 1734, another resolution offered in the Grand Lodge of England reveals the fact that funds had not been raised to even send brethren to Georgia after the colonists had landed. The following was introduced in the Grand Lodge:

> *Resolved, that all the Masters of all regular Lodges who shall not bring in their contributions to charity, do at the next quarterly communication, give the reasons why their respective Lodges do not contribute to the settlement of Georgia.*

It is now clearly seen that the Grand Lodge of England was not yet in position to send any distressed brethren to Georgia. Nothing in the two resolutions quoted furnishes any ground upon which to assume that a lodge was in existence in Georgia.

For many years, there were deposited in the Library of the Congress of the United States at Washington, D. C., among the Georgia manuscripts, parts of a minute book for a lodge of Masons meeting during the years 1756 and 1757 in Savannah. These minutes had been obtained by the United States Government as a part of the great collection of manuscripts purchased by the Government from one Peter Force, collector. References to these Masonic minutes may be found in several Georgia histories. Until 1926, no definite attempt had been made to identify them or to claim them.

In that year, a resolution was introduced in Solomon's Lodge No. 1 identifying the minutes as a part of the records of that lodge and also requesting their return to the lodge by the Government of the United States. Copies of the resolution were sent to Brother Walter F. George of Vienna Lodge No. 324, United States Senator from Georgia, and to Brother Charles G. Edwards of Landrum Lodge No. 48 of Savannah, Member of Congress from the First District of Georgia. Joint resolutions were introduced by these brethren in the Senate and the House of Representatives authorizing the return of the minutes to Solomon's Lodge, their rightful owner.

The matter was submitted to the Senate Committee on the Library and the House Committee on the Library.

These two Committees submitted the question of identification to the Librarian of Congress. In his reply, the Librarian was satisfied with the identification and stated that he would offer no objection to their return. By an Act of the Congress of the United States, the minutes were returned to Solomon's Lodge as their rightful owner, in the year 1926.

In these minutes is a roster of the membership of the lodge which met in Savannah in 1756 and 1757. The roster gives the dates of degrees conferred on all the members of the lodge. The names of some of the most illustrious men in the early history of Georgia appear on the roster. The first initiates of the lodge, and the first Masons to be made in Georgia, are shown by this roster to have received the E. A. Degree in 1733-34. The manner of recording the dates means 1733 by the calendar used prior to 1752, and January, February or March 1734 according to the calendar now in use. In this roster, we have proof that a lodge of Masons was at work in Georgia one year after the establishment of the colony. Add to this the tradition that the first lodge in Georgia was organized on February 21, 1734 by General Oglethorpe, and proof of the tradition, as stated by M. W. Melvin M. Johnson in his "Beginnings of Freemasonry in America," is convincing. All other writers accept the tradition as proven.

The first name upon the roster is that of Noble Jones. Many of the descendants of Noble Jones are living in Savannah and one of them, Mrs. J. A. P. Crisfield, possesses a miniature of him. From this miniature, a portrait was made for Solomon's Lodge and a copy of the portrait was given by Solomon's Lodge to the Grand Lodge of Georgia. The remains of Noble Jones were interred in imposing manner in beautiful Bonaventure Cemetery at Savannah, in 1775.

Noble Jones, so far as known, the first Mason made in Georgia, was the friend of Oglethorpe. He was Master of the lodge at Savannah in 1756 and 1757, the time during which these minutes were written. Noble Jones died on November 3, 1775. Jones was a man of unusual ability. He was the first doctor of medicine in Georgia; captain of the militia company of Oglethorpe, now the Georgia Hussars; the builder of fortifications against

attack by the Spaniards, some of these fortifications still
remaining on his plantation at Savannah; he became the
first colonel of the Georgia militia in 1757; he was a
member of all the King's Councils of the Provincial Gov-
ernors, once serving as President. In 1771 he was appointed by Lord Petre as Provincial Grand Master of
Georgia although no Masonic records in Georgia recognizes him as Grand Master. He was severely ill for several years before his death and, to such an extent, that
his son, Georgia's celebrated Brother Noble Wymberley
Jones, discontinued his patriotic efforts until after the
death of his father in 1775. Since no mention is made
of Noble Jones in any Masonic document in Georgia, it
must be assumed that he never took office or used his
warrant.

Another name of note upon the roster of 1756 is that
of Moses Nunis. He also received his E. A. Degree in
1733-34. This brother was the son of Doctor Nunis who
came to Georgia just after the colony was established
and whose medical services were noted by Oglethorpe
and reported to the Trustees as one reason for permit-
ting Jews to enter the colony. Moses Nunis is probably
the first Jew ever to become a Mason in the world.
Initiated in the first three months of 1734, it appears
that his interest in the Craft never waned. For some
years after the Revolution, the minutes of Solomon's
Lodge record his attendance at meetings and his services
upon committees. The day after his death, his remains
were interred in the Jewish Cemetery near the Union
Station in Savannah with Masonic ceremonies by the
members of Solomon's Lodge. He died on September
5, 1787 at the age of eighty-two. This is the brother
who lived for more than forty years next door to Mordecai Sheftall who says in his diary that Oglethorpe
organized the first Lodge in Georgia. Nunis was initiated
just about the time mentioned by Sheftall and is probably the source of Sheftall's information.

The records of the Grand Lodge of England show
that Viscount Weymouth, Grand Master of England,
granted a charter for the organization of a lodge in
Savannah in 1735. The English records contain no information on the appointment of a Grand Master in
Georgia in that year. The appointment of Provincial
Grand Masters being a prerogative of the Grand Masters

of England, these Grand Masters frequently failed to report to the Grand Lodge of England some of their appointments. It appears that this happened in the case of the appointment of the First Grand Master of Georgia. The issuance of the charter for the lodge at Savannah by the Grand Master of England personally, direct to the lodge, gives conclusive evidence that there was no Provincial Grand Master in Georgia at the time. Had there been, the Grand Master of England would have referred the matter to him for his approval and action.

The constitution of the lodge at Savannah under the authority of the charter issued by Viscount Weymouth does not appear upon the books of the Grand Lodge of England. Very few records were kept at that time by the Grand Lodge of England. Each year, the Grand Lodge of England issued engraved lists containing the names of lodges to which charters had been issued and, when known, the dates upon which they were constituted, with the dates of meeting and the places of meeting. The lodge at Savannah appears for the first time on the list issued in 1736, this proving that it was granted a charter in 1735. The lodge bears no name, the list containing a small illustration of a town and a church with the simple statement "Savannah in ye Province of Georgia." This is evidence that there was but one lodge at Savannah, this evidently being the lodge organized and conferring degrees in 1734. The lodge at Savannah is the second lodge in America to appear upon one of the English lists of lodges.

Upon the list for 1737, the lodge at Savannah retains the same number as upon the lists for 1736, No. 139, but neither upon this list nor upon the one for 1736 is shown the date upon which the lodge was constituted. On the list for 1737, the lodge which immediately precedes the lodge at Savannah is reported as being constituted on October 30, 1735. The lodge listed immediately after the lodge at Savannah is reported as constituted on March 1, 1736. In the fact that the lodge at Savannah is placed on the list between two lodges whose dates of constitution are known we have satisfactory evidence that the lodge at Savannah was constituted between these two dates. In this period is the time of arrival of

Oglethorpe on his return to Savannah and as tradition says, bringing the charter of the lodge with him. The list of the Grand Lodge of England adds remarkable support to the tradition, together with the fact that the charter had been granted personally by the Grand Master of England, there being no Provincial Grand Master in Georgia to whom the lodge could make application. Here is evidently the explanation of the wait of the brethren in Savannah for two years. Again, light is shed upon the question as to whether or not there was a Provincial Grand Lodge in Georgia at that time. Had there been a Provincial Grand Master in Georgia, there is little likelihood that the Grand Master of England would have personally granted the charter. It appears from the known facts that a personal appeal was made to the Grand Master of England by some person authorized by the Lodge at Savannah to make that appeal. Had the appeal been made by post, the reply would never have taken nearly two years to reach Savannah. No document exists to show that Oglethorpe was the Master of the Lodge, but when we remember that the laws of the Grand Lodge of England required the presence of the Master at the time of constituting the lodge, the tradition that he was the first Master is supported by the failure to be constituted until he returned to Georgia from his visit to England.

The period from 1736 until 1756 contains no Masonic record in Georgia from which we may learn any facts concerning the Craft in the colony. All records have been lost with the exception of the minutes of the lodge at Savannah in 1756 and 1757 returned by the Congress of the United States. If we desire to learn whether or not the lodge at Savannah continued to operate under its charter, we must turn to other sources for our information.

The lists of the Grand Lodge of England continue to list the lodge at Savannah regularly until 1783, thus indicating that there must have been activity of some nature, although the number of Masons in the lodge was exceptionally small, probably not more than a dozen. This estimate of the number of members is obtained from records other than Masonic documents.

One of the interesting records concerning the brethren in Savannah in the early days of the colony is found in the diary of the famous minister, Reverend George Whitfield. Whitfield came to Georgia as an evangelist. He was the co-worker of the celebrated Reverend John Wesley, founder of the Methodist Church, who was also in the colony doing evangelistic work. While in Savannah, Whitfield conceived the idea of an orphanage and later enlisted the support of Lady Huntingdon in that enterprise. Old Bethesda Orphanage, mentioned in the previous chapters where its relationship with the Union Society has been explained, was the final result of the efforts of Whitfield. Whitfield preached and appealed throughout the English colonies in America for money for the building of the orphanage and, in Philadelphia, he impressed Benjamin Franklin so greatly that Franklin gave him all the rents which he had collected that day. In his diary, under the date of Friday, June 24, 1738, Whitfield states that he was invited to preach to the Freemasons of Savannah and, after the service, was treated most civilly by them and dined with them.

In the year 1739, William Stephens, secretary to General Oglethorpe, states in his Journal that the Masonic lodge in Savannah went in Masonic procession to church, being led by the Senior Warden of the lodge. Stephens describes the aprons and dress, the wands or staffs used by the deacons and stewards and also tells how the people gathered on the street and ridiculed the Masons. At church, Stephens states that the Rev. Mr. Norris preached to the Masons, following the custom of his predecessors. This indicates that processions to church were a regular observance of the lodge at Savannah. If Mr. Norris followed the custom of his predecessor, then the Rev. John Wesley started the custom, he being the predecessor of Mr. Norris. Stephens states that there were but a dozen Masons in the procession.

From the English lists and these two references by non-Masons, we know that the lodge in Savannah, as late as 1739 or 1740, was fully organized and was observing Masonic customs and rites. From this date until 1756, we have but the regular appearance of the lodge upon the engraved lists issued annually by the Grand Lodge of England. It does not seem plausible that the Grand Lodge of England would have regularly continued the lodge at Savannah upon the lists unless there was some reason for doing so. Just what the nature of activity may have been we have no means of finding out. In all Masonic histories where this question has been discussed, It is agreed by the writers that some form of activity must have existed.

In 1920, Brother William Mitchell of Solomon's Lodge, while repairing the foundation of Jerusalem Church at Ebenezer, Georgia, built in 1760, found the Masonic square and compasses marked upon some of the original hand-made brick. These brick may have been from the foundations of the original building erected in 1734 by the Salzburgers. Until 1925, there were a small hand-made brass square and compasses attached to the high point of the west gable of the church. These were removed when the roof was repaired.

In 1924, a search of the records of the Grand Lodge of England was made in order to determine if there existed any documents which might shed light upon the history of the Craft in Georgia in the early days. Practically nothing was obtained with the exception of the appearance upon the English lists of the lodge at Savannah regularly after the year 1735. It being recognized that the name appearing regularly upon the lists might not constitute satisfactory record that the lodge was in active existence during the period, the aid of Worshipful Brother Gordon P. G. Hills was solicited. As Librarian of the United Grand Lodge of England, Brother Hills made a diligent search of the records of that body and in 1932 discovered the By-Laws of Solomon's Lodge No. 1 of Savannah adopted in 1780 and sent to the Grand Lodge of England for record.

The By-Laws are interesting because of the preamble to the document which reads as follows:

The Rules or By-Laws of Solomon's Lodge of the Most Ancient and Honorable Society of Free and Accepted Masons at Savannah in the Province of Georgia. North America, being Number One on the List of Regular Constituted Lodges in the said Province under the Provincial Jurisdiction Constituted in the Year 5735.

This preamble is valuable because within its contents there appears the statement that the Grand Lodge of Georgia was constituted in 1735. This preamble is still more interesting because it shows that the Solomon's Lodge No. 1 reporting its By-Laws to the Grand Lodge of England in 1780 is the same lodge which was given a warrant by the Grand Master of England in 1735. It is not now necessary to doubt the English lists which show a continuous record for this lodge up to 1781. The lodge itself reports that its existence has been continuous from 1735 until the date of the By-Laws, 1780.

Shedding light upon the Craft in Georgia during the period 1736-1756, Worshipful Brother Hills discovered a petition addressed to the Grand Master of England in 1771 by the members of Solomon's Lodge No. 1 of Savannah. The opening statements of this petition are as follows:

Worshipful Brother:

Some months ago, Solomon's Lodge in Savannah, the Eldest constituted in America, except one in New England, wrote to Rt. Worshipful and Noble Brother the Grand Master of England, and to yourself enclosing you a Bill of Exchange for Ten Pounds ten Shillings, in order to obtain a Deputation for a Grand Master of our Province; and being apprehensive the same may not have reached you do now renew the application; as we have received no Accounts. And in the first place must observe that our late Brother Grey Elliott who was appointed Grand Master about Ten Years ago (and now resides out of the Province) never did congregate a Grand Lodge whereby the Craft in General suffered greatly and from that circumstance Masonry appears to be much upon the decline and unless we shall be so happy as to get a deputation for our Worthy Brother the Honorable Noble Jones, Esq., who was strongly recommended for that purpose I am afraid it will entirely drop. And therefore from The good Opinion the Brethren have of you, they flatter themselves that you will use your utmost in forwarding the Appointment to us which will give satisfaction to the Craft in general.

That Masonry may flourish and Harmony, Friend-
ship and Brotherly love ever continue shall be the hearty
wish of

> *Worshipful Brother—*
> *Your Most Obedient and*
> *Very affect'e Brother*
> *Willm Young*
> *Master of Solomon's Lodge—*
> *in Savannah.*

Here again, in this petition addressed to the Grand
Secretary of the Grand Lodge of England, we have the
brethren of the lodge at Savannah stating that Solomon's
Lodge in 1771 is the original lodge constituted in the
first days of the colony and second in age only to a
lodge in New England, (the First Lodge at Boston constituted in 1733).

The statements contained in the petition in regard to
Grey Elliott, second Provincial Grand Master of Georgia,
and to Noble Jones, appointed in 1771 by Lord Petre in
answer to this petition as the third Provincial Grand
Master of Georgia, will be discussed later when the question of the appointments of these brethren is considered.

The outstanding facts contained in the two documents mentioned are those which established the proofs
of the constitution of the lodge at Savannah in 1736, two
years after its organization and one year after its charter
was granted by the Grand Master of England in 1735;
the facts stated which establish the continuous existence
of this lodge from the time of its organization until 1781
when, Worshipful Brother Hills writes us, a note is found
on the books of the Grand Lodge of England that the
lodge made no payments to the charity fund of the
Grand Lodge of England after that year.

Worshipful Brother Hills reports that he also found
articles on the books of the Grand Lodge of England
showing that the Lodge at Savannah made payments to
the Charity Fund of the Grand Lodge of England on
November 17, 1760; again on November 28, 1771; and
again on November 24, 1775.

From 1740 to 1750, conditions in Georgia became
critical. Jews and Roman Catholics, although admitted
to the colony, were denied the rights of citizenship. To

the south, the Spaniards in Florida were massing large numbers of troops in preparation for the destruction of the colony. This continued threat kept new settlers away. Many of those in the colony, through fear, removed to South Carolina to be safe from the impending attack. Due to the restriction of slaves, the colonists had no manual labor to work their farms and Whitfield protested to the Trustees that he must abandon efforts to build the Bethesda Orphanage unless he could obtain slave labor on the project. Farms were limited in size to such areas as the farmer and his family could take care of without further help. Profit was impossible, only a bare existence obtainable. Dissatisfaction with the acts of the Trustees was inflamed by merchants of Charleston into open rebellion. Oglethorpe had spent the greater part of his time in Georgia in the vicinity of Frederica preparing for the Spanish invasion. His character was attacked by the colonists and assailed in the Charleston papers. Rum was smuggled in from South Carolina by jealous merchants and used to inflame the Indians against the Georgians. There were less than five hundred people in the colony at the time of the Spanish attack. This took place in 1742 and was the crisis in Georgia history as well as being the crisis in the history of the English colonies in America.

The battle of Bloody Marsh is one of the great epics in the military history of America. The strategy and skill of Oglethorpe in outwitting the Spanish reads like a romance. The Spanish had more than four thousand men and at least thirty-six ships of various types supporting this military force. Pitted against them was a force of less than six hundred English and Scotch assisted by the Yamacraw Indians under Tomochichi, their loyal chief. The strategy and daring of the colonists under the inspiring leadership and military knowledge of Oglethorpe completely annihilated the Spanish force and many of them perished in the marshes after the battle. Skeletons of dead Spaniards were found for many years after to mark the scene of the conflict. Had the Spaniards succeeded, Georgia would have perished and the Spaniards would have overrun the prosperous English colonies to the north. The whole course of American history might have been changed. This battle has rightly been called "the Thermopylae of America."

Shortly after this battle, Oglethorpe returned to England, never again to return to America although his sympathies were always with the colonies in their struggles with the mother country.

During the period mentioned, the lodge at Savannah must have suffered with the colonists and must have been affected by the conditions which almost destroyed the colony. Whereas, there had been but a dozen members in the lodge up to 1740, there must have been less than this number during the trying period just discussed. No record remains to tell the story except the continuance of the lodge upon the lists issued annually by the Grand Lodge of England.

CHAPTER IV.

The Beginning of the Grand Lodge of Georgia

ALTHOUGH THE statement has frequently been made that the Grand Lodge of Georgia has been in existence since the year 1733, there is no document in existence tending to give the slightest confirmation to that statement. No tradition exists to even claim such an early existence. Just how such a claim originated, no one knows. In the FREEMASONS MONITOR, a magazine published in Salem, Massachusetts in 1816, Thomas Smith Webb states that the Grand Lodge of Georgia came into existence in 1730 through the authority of a warrant issued in that year by Lord Viscount Weymouth, Grand Master of England. Webb corrected his statement in the next issue and changed the year to 1735. By changing his statement, Webb positively admitted that his first statement was an error or a misprint. Nevertheless, some writers in Georgia have persisted in stating that Webb had correct information for his statement and, they concluded that a verbal warrant was issued by Viscount Weymouth in 1730, confirmed by a warrant in 1735. In refutation of this, no reliable Masonic historian had accepted that conclusion because of the fact that Weymouth was not Grand Master of England in 1730, and, on the other hand, every old Masonic record in Georgia agrees with other records in showing conclusively that the Grand Lodge of Georgia was not organized until 1735.

The Constitution of the Grand Lodge of Georgia also states that the Grand Lodge of Georgia has existed since 1733 by virtue of a warrant issued in 1735 by Lord Viscount Weymouth. No one knows just how this statement came to be written into the Constitution. It seems to have been inserted about 1857 when an AHIMON REZON was issued by the Grand Lodge for the use of the lodges. It does not conform to the old documents in which the men who organized the Grand Lodge state that the Grand Lodge of Georgia was organized in 1735 by virtue of the authority granted to Roger Lacey by Lord Viscount Weymouth, Grand Master of England in the year 1735.

In order that documentary evidence may be the basis upon which the facts are established in tracing the history of the Grand Lodge of Georgia, the following documents are listed as the sources from which the facts are drawn:

The charter issued by the Provincial Grand Lodge of Georgia, dated July 11, 1786, and intended for a lodge in Augusta, Georgia, but never used since it lacks the signature of the Grand Master of Georgia, Major General Samuel Elbert.

The charter issued to Solomon's Lodge No. 1 of Savannah, dated December 27th, 1786, and the first charter issued by the present Grand Lodge of Georgia after its recongition on December 16, 1786.

The Act of the General Assembly of Georgia passed February 6, 1796, incorporating the Grand Lodge of Georgia.

In each one of these documents, brethren familiar with the facts concerning the organization of the Grand Lodge, evidently possessing some of the original documents which contained the facts and the authorities granted, consistently agree that the Grand Lodge was organized in the year 1735.

All of these documents agree in stating that Roger Lacey, the first Provincial Grand Master of Georgia, was granted his warrant of appointment in the year 1735 by Lord Viscount Weymouth, Grand Master of England. The English records contain no reference to the appointment of Roger Lacey. The Grand Masters of England frequently failed to inform the Grand Lodge of England of these appointments, they being prerogatives of the Grand Master and not needing the action of the Grand Lodge of England.

Two forms of warrants were issued to the Provincial Grand Masters. One form of warrant specified the length of time the Provincial Grand Master was to remain in office and, at the expiration of this term of office, gave to the brethren of the Provincial Grand Lodge the power to regularly and, at stated times, appoint or elect his successor until the power was revoked by the Grand Master of England.

The first warrant issued to a Provincial Grand Master in America, that granted to Daniel Coxe on June 5,

1730 by the Duke of Norfolk, Grand Master of England was of the form just described. The warrant granted in 1737 by the Earl of Loudoun to James Graeme of South Carolina was also of this form and for some years after the appointment of Graeme, the brethren of the Provincial Grand Lodge of South Carolina annually elected the Provincial Grand Master.

The second form of warrant issued by the Grand Masters of England to the Provincial Grand Masters in the colonies, continued the Provincial Grand Master in office until his appointment was revoked and his successor named by the Grand Master of England. It appears that the warrant issued to Roger Lacey by Lord Weymouth, as Provincial Grand Master of Georgia in 1735, was of this second form. Roger Lacey died on August 3, 1738, and the vacancy was not filled until 1760 when Grey Elliott was appointed Grand Master of Georgia by Lord Aberdour, Grand Master of England in that year.

No reference to the exact date upon which the warrant of Roger Lacey was issued was thought to be in existence until the year 1926 when a document was discovered in the archives of the Grand Lodge of Georgia which gave the exact date. This document has been mentioned in the Proceedings of the Grand Chapter of Georgia but had been thought lost. It is the unused charter issued on July 11, 1786 by the Provincial Grand Lodge of Georgia for the organization of a lodge in Augusta, Georgia. Its authenticity cannot be questioned since it bears the signature of the Grand Officers with the exception of the Grand Master. The signatures are identical with known signatures on other documents.

The officers of the Provincial Grand Lodge of Georgia at this time in 1786 can be learned from the minutes of Solomon's Lodge No. 1 of Savannah which contain the names of Samuel Elbert, Grand Master; William Stephens, Deputy Grand Master; Mordecai Sheftall, Senior Grand Warden; James Jackson, Junior Grand Warden; George Handley, Grand Treasurer; James Habersham, Grand Secretary; John Martin and Samuel Stirk, Grand Stewards. The signatures of Stephens, Sheftall, and Jackson are upon innumerable documents in Georgia, both Masonic and legal. When the signatures upon the charter are compared with these, all doubt of the authenticity of the charter is removed. The charter is issued to George Handley who was a member of Solomon's Lodge in 1785 and removed to Augusta. In 1787, he visited Solomon's Lodge and is recorded as the Master of Columbian Lodge in Augusta, Georgia. It reads as follows:

MORDECAI SHEFTALL	*JAS. JACKSON*
Grand Senior Warden	*Grand Junior Warden*

Grand Master

W. STEPHENS
Deputy Grand Master

To all Worshipful, Right Worshipful, Noble Grand or Other Brethren of Light wheresoever dispersed GREETING.

KNOW YE, that we the Honorable Samuel Elbert Esquire Right Worshipful Grand Master of all Masons in the State of Georgia and of all Lodges therein of the Most Ancient and Sublime degree of Royal Scotch Masonry of the Holy Lodge of St. Andrews, and invested with the order thereof, Past Master of Solomons and Unity Lodges in Savannah and member of the Assembly of High Priests of the Royal Arch Brotherhood, and Sir William Stephens Esquire Right Worshipful Deputy Grand Master of all Masons in the said State and of all Lodges therein of the like Most Ancient and Sublime Degree of Royal Scotch Masonry of the Holy Lodge of St. Andrew and invested with the order thereof. Past Master of Solomons Lodge aforesaid, Knight of the Red Cross and Member of the Assembly of High Priests of the Royal Arch Brotherhood, and by the concurrence of the Right Worshipful Sir Mordecai Sheftall, Senior Grand Warden of the State, Past Master of Solomons Lodge aforesaid, member of the Assembly of High Priests of the Royal Arch Order and Knight of the Red Cross; and the Right Worshipful Sir James Jackson, Junior Grand Warden of the State, Past Master and Master of Solomons Lodge, temporary High Priest of the Assembly of High Priests of the Royal Arch Order and Sublime King of the degree of the Most Noble Order of Knights of the Red Cross, in pursuance of the right and succession legally derived from the Most Noble and Right Worshipful Sholto Charles Douglas, Lord of Aberdour, Grand Master of Scotland for the years of our Lord One Thousand Seven Hundred and Fifty-seven and One Thousand Seven Hundred and Fifty-eight and then Grand Master of England as will appear by his warrant bearing date the tenth day of October in the year One Thousand Seven Hundred and Sixty directed to the Right Worshipful Gray Elliott Esquire and renewing the warrant of the Right Worshipful and Most Noble Thomas Thyne, Lord Viscount Weymouth, the Grand Master of England, dated the second day of December in the year One Thousand Seven Hundred and Thirty-five, directed to the Right Worshipful Hugh Lacey, HAVE Constituted and appointed and by this present Warrant do constitute and appoint agreeable to the wish and desire of GEORGE HANDLEY . . . . and several other brethren to us testified YOU, the said George Handley Master and . . . . Wardens of a Lodge in the town of Augusta by the name and appellation of . . . . to be formed and ruled by such forms and orders as may be agreed on by the majority of the members thereof PROVIDED they are not repugnant to the general regulations of the Grand Lodge constituting this warrant hereby empowering you to do all and everything and things usual and customary to be done as a Lodge of Free Masons, and to admit persons with the proper ceremony as such and when admitted to pass and raise to the second and sublime degrees of Masonry TO HOLD all and every the rights and ceremonies thereof to you and your successors forever AND FURTHER PROVIDED that you pay or contribute for this warrant to the general fund at the least five shillings for every admitted Mason and two shillings for every member AND LASTLY PROVIDED your officers are elected yearly and every year as nigh the Festival of St. John the Evangelist as possible and that this warrant shall only continue in force so long as punctual and true obedience is made and had to the authority thereof.

GIVEN under our hands and the seal of the Grand Lodge at Savannah in the State of Georgia aforesaid the eleventh day of July in the year of our Lord One Thousand Seven Hundred and Eighty-six and in the year of Light Five Thousand Seven Hundred and Eighty-six.

JAMES HABERSHAM   *JOHN HABERSHAM*
Secretary Grand Lodge   *Treasurer of the Arch and*
                                            Red Cross Orders.
                                                 (SEAL)

This charter states that Roger Lacey was granted his warrant on December 2, 1735 by Lord Viscount Weymouth, Grand Master of England. This date is the birth of the Grand Lodge of Georgia. It is almost two years later than the date upon which tradition says that the lodge at Savannah was organized and two years later than the time at which Noble Jones, Moses Nunis and Daniel Nunis received their degree in that Lodge.

To support the statement contained in this charter, the officers of the Grand Lodge of Georgia, on December 27, 1786, state in the charter issued to Solomon's Lodge that Lacey's warrant was granted in 1735 by Viscount Weymouth. Further strength and confirmation is obtained in the Act incorporating the Grand Lodge of Georgia, passed by the General Assembly of Georgia in 1796. This Act states that "divers lodges have existed in Georgia since the year 1735." We thus have no grounds upon which to assume that the Grand Lodge of Georgia came into existence before the year 1735. All documents agree on that year and one gives the exact date as December 2, 1735.

Like the lodge organized at Savannah, mystery surrounds the early days of the Grand Lodge of Georgia. No Masonic documents exists to tell the story of what transpired. The first reference to Roger Lacey, the first Provincial Grand Master of Georgia, is contained in the records of the Grand Lodge of England which show him to have been a Grand Steward of the Grand Lodge of England in 1730. The first reference to Roger Lacey in Georgia is contained in the COLONIAL RECORDS OF GEORGIA in the year 1736. In that year, he was sent to Augusta, Georgia to establish a trading post there. Another reference contains reports concerning his wife. She became involved in difficulties with the colonists and was charged with cattle stealing. The

COLONIAL RECORDS show that Lacey died with the rank of Captain in the militia on August 3, 1738 and that his remains were interred with military honors at Thunderbolt, Georgia, near Savannah. William Stevens, secretary to General Oglethorpe, praises the work and character of Lacey and adds that the domestic difficulties of Lacey drove him to drink. Over-indulgence in liquor together with the effects of the intense summer heat in the colony caused the death of Roger Lacey on August 3, 1738.

From that time until 1786, we have no reference to the Grand Lodge of Georgia with the exception of the appointment of Grey Elliott by Lord Aberdour in 1760 and the reference in the records of the Grand Lodge of England to the appointment of Noble Jones in 1771 by Lord Petre, Grand Master of England.

It appears that the conditions in the colony, mentioned in the preceding Chapter, affected the Grand Lodge of Georgia as they did the first lodge in Georgia. If there was life, it was extremely weak.

The second step in the history of the Grand Lodge of Georgia occurs with the appointment of the second Provincial Grand Master of Georgia. The record of this step is not contained in the books of the Grand Lodge of England and we must turn to documents in Georgia to find the information desired. Some brethren have been under the impression that there is a broken link in the record of the Grand Lodge of Georgia. These brethren have assumed that Grey Elliott, the second Provincial Grand Master of Georgia, was given his appointment by Lord Aberdour while the latter was Grand Master of Scotland. This assumption was probably inspired by the 1786 charter of Solomon's Lodge No. 1, which states that Grey Elliott was given his warrant by "Lord Aberdour, Grand Master of Scotland for the years five thousand seven hundred and fifty-five and five thousand seven hundred and fifty-six and Grand Master of England for the years five thousand seven hundred and fifty seven and five thousand seven hundred and fifty-eight." There being no mention of the exact year in which the warrant of Grey Elliott was granted, some have assumed that it was granted while Aberdour was Grand Master of Scotland. Again, Aberdour was not Grand Master of

Scotland in 1757. He was Grand Master of England in that year and served through the year 1761.

The unused charter in the archives of the Grand Lodge of Georgia states that the warrant of Grey Elliott was issued on October 10, 1760. This was during the time that Aberdour was Grand Master of England and thus establishes the fact that Elliott received an English and not a Scotch warrant. The continuity of the English record of the Grand Lodge of Georgia is thus sustained by the facts contained in the unused charter, and the broken link, or supposed broken link is completely welded into the continuous chain.

Further proof of the English appointment of Grey Elliott is contained in the petition of Solomon's Lodge No. 1 to the Grand Master of England quoted in the last Chapter. This petition states that "our late Brother Grey Elliott who was appointed Grand Master about ten years ago (and now resides out of the Province) never did congregate a Grand Lodge whereby the Craft in General suffered greatly." When we recall that this petition was dated in 1771 and the brethren of Solomon's Lodge stated that Grey Elliott was appointed Grand Master of Georgia "about ten years ago," the date of Elliott's warrant contained in the unused charter, October 10, 1760, is confirmed.

Another interesting fact is contained in the petition and this is the report to the Grand Master of England that the English Grand Master of Georgia had not functioned and the Craft desired a new appointment to be made.

From the facts contained in this petition, there can be no grounds upon which to assume that Grey Elliott received a Scotch and not an English warrant. The continuity of the Grand Lodge of Georgia is thus established by the documents.

Very little is known of Grey Elliott. His name appears upon the minutes returned to Solomon's Lodge by the Government of the United States and he is shown on the roster to have received his degrees in England. His name upon the roster and the reference to his having been "made in England," establish the fact that these minutes belonged to a regular English lodge and also testify to the fact that Elliott was an English Mason. It is known that Elliott was a Scotchman and a member of the Scotch Presbyterian Church. He was one of the founders of the Independent Presbyterian Church in Savannah, aided in the building of the town of Sunbury already mentioned in a preceding Chapter, and the Georgia Historical Society possesses a bookplate which he used. When Benjamin Franklin was sent to England in 1774 to plead the cause of the colonies at the English Court, Elliott went with him as a representative of the patriots of Georgia. It appears that he never returned to America and it is known his death took place a short time later.

We now reach an unique phase in the history of the Grand Lodge of Georgia. No document in Georgia bears the name of Noble Jones as the third Provincial Grand Master of Georgia. The records of the Grand Lodge of England show that he was appointed by Lord Petre sometime between 1770-1774.

In a previous chapter, we have considered the contents of a petition addressed by the members of Solomon's No. 1 of Savannah in 1771 to the Grand Master of England asking that Noble Jones be named Grand Master of Georgia. The lodge also advanced the fee required for a patent. That this patent or deposition was issued is now a known fact. Worshipful Brother Gordon P. G. Hills finds in the archives of the Grand Lodge of England a copy of the reply of the Grand Secretary to the members of Solomon's Lodge under the date of August 22, 1771. The reply is addressed to the Worshipful Master of Solomon's Lodge and is as follows:

Sir and Brother:

I some time ago received the letters etc. from Solomon's Lodge in Georgia inclosing a Bill of Exchange for ten Guineas which sum has been since duly paid to me as Grand Secretary. That sum transmitted being a contribution of your Lodge to the Public Fund of Charity. Mr. Jones, the Gentleman apptd. Prov'l G. M. will remain indebted to the Grand Charity here the further sum of ten Guineas and one Guinea and a half for making out and registering his patent for by a regulation of the Grand Lodge "Every Gen'n appt'd P. G. M. shall upon his appt. not only pay for the making out

*and registering his patent but shall also contribute to the
General Fund of Charity ten Guineas."—However as the
Grand Master has no doubt of Mr. Jones' complying with
every regulation of the G. L. he has ordered the patent
to be made out—which I now have the pleasure of transmitting to you—I also beg leave to acknowledge the receipt of your letter by Bro'r Seymour through whose
means this is forwarded—and to assure you that the cor-
respondence of our Brethren in Georgia will ever be ac-
ceptable to the Grand Lodge here and to no more than*

> *Sir*
>
> *Your most obed't Serv't.
> & affectionate Bro'r.*

*Doctors Canons,
    London 22 Aug't 1771.*

That Noble Jones was duly appointed by the Grand
Master of England in 1771 as the third Provincial Grand
Master of Georgia can no longer be doubted. That his
name is omitted from every Masonic document in Georgia is a fact unexplained. Whether or not he had received his warrant, whether or not he used his power
if he did receive it, are unknown. In 1774 Unity Lodge
was organized in Savannah. In 1775, Grenadiers'
Lodge was organized in Savannah. The By-Laws of
Grenadiers' Lodge are in the archives of the Grand
Lodge of England and are identical with the By-Laws
of Solomon's Lodge of Savannah. Who constituted Unity
Lodge and Grenadiers' Lodge, we do not know. Yet they
were duly reported as legally constituted to the Grand
Lodge of England. These lodges were constituted by
either Noble Jones or Samuel Elbert. In the unused
charter of 1786, Elbert states that his authority came
from the warrant of Grey Elliott who was appointed in
1760. This would indicate that Noble Jones either did
not receive his warrant or, if he did, that some cause prevented him from exercising his authority and, under the
power of Elliott's warrant, Samuel Elbert became the
third Provincial Grand Master of Georgia.

Since the name of Samuel Elbert appears upon the
unused charter as the Provincial Grand Master of Georgia and, since the 1786 charter of Solomon's Lodge states
that Samuel Elbert retired as Grand Master on December 16, 1786 when the Grand Lodge of Georgia aban-

doned the English regulations and became the present independent body, many have desired to know how Samuel Elbert became Grand Master of Georgia. The minutes of Solomon's Lodge No. 1 mention him as Grand Master in 1785 and 1786. The Grand Lodge of England has no record of his appointment. No document in Georgia states that he was appointed Grand Master of Georgia but, all documents in Georgia which mention him, admit him to have been Grand Master. None state how he received his authority with one exception. That exception is the unused charter in the archives of the Grand Lodge. This states that Samuel Elbert and his Grand Officers in 1786 were such "in pursuance of the right and succession legally derived from the Most Noble and Right Worshipful Sholto Charles Douglass, Lord Aberdour, Grand Master of Scotland for the years of our Lord one thousand seven hundred and fifty-seven and one thousand seven hundred and fifty-eight and then Grand Master of England as will appear on his warrant bearing date the tenth day of October in the year one thousand seven hundred and sixty directed to the Right Worshipful Grey Elliott, Esquire." The statement continues in order to show that the power of Elliott's warrant continued that of Roger Lacey, granted on December 2, 1735 by Viscount Weymouth.

From this charter and the statement contained there is no further doubt that whatever the authority of Samuel Elbert and whatever the manner of his becoming Grand Master of Georgia, his authority was legally derived from the Grand Master of England through the warrant of Grey Elliott. The fact that his power came through the warrant of Grey Elliott would indicate that this warrant gave to the brethren of the Provincial Grand Lodge of Georgia the right to name the successor of Grey Elliott. The forms of these warrants have been described previously in this Chapter. Since no English document states that Elbert was appointed by the Grand Master of England and since no document in Georgia claims that Elbert was appointed by the Grand Master of England, the language in this unused charter becomes very significant when it states that his authority was "legally derived from Lord's Aberdour as will appear by his warrant directed to Grey Elliott." This reference to the contents of Elliott's warrant seems to infer that the manner of Elbert's succession is contained in the warrant of Grey Elliott. It thus appears that he was either named by Elliott as his successor, or that he was elected by the brethren of the Provincial Grand Lodge of Georgia. We have a document which states emphatically that his powers were Legally Derived and that he was thus legally Provincial Grand Master of Georgia. We have no grounds or facts upon which to doubt its statements.

Two of the signatures upon this charter are of interest. They are the signatures of James Habersham, Grand Secretary; and of John Habersham, Grand Treasurer. These two brethren are the sons of the James Habersham to whom Oglethorpe gave the miniature mentioned in Chapter I; whose name appears upon the minutes of the lodge at Savannah in 1756; and whose descendant, Mrs. Edwards, gave the portrait to Solomon's Lodge with the statement that it was a tradition in her family that Oglethorpe was the first Master and founder of the lodge at Savannah, the first lodge in Georgia. The Masonic positions and records of some of her ancestors are thus established, showing them to have held high offices in Masonry in Georgia.

The record of the Grand Lodge of Georgia has been shown from the documents to have been an unbroken chain of English authority from December 2, 1735 until July 11, 1786. At this point, certain influences came into the life of the Craft which have an important bearing upon the beginning of the present Grand Lodge of Georgia. The differences between the "Moderns" and the "Ancients" in England are to be felt in Georgia. Coupled with the influences which the Revolution had wielded in Georgia, a great change was to take place.

CHAPTER V.

Reconstituting the Grand Lodge of Georgia

T HE LISTS OF the Grand Lodge of England show
that in the year 1774, Unity Lodge was constituted
in Savannah. These lists also show that in 1775,
Grenadiers' Lodge was constituted in Savannah. These
are the only two lodges, other than the first lodge at Savannah, known to have existed in Georgia prior to the
Revolution. In the minutes of the lodge at Savannah
which were returned to Solomon's Lodge No. 1 by the
Congress of the United States, there is indication of a
lodge at Augusta. These minutes show the names of
James Paris and Edward Barnard who are shown to
have received their E. A. Degree at Augusta, but no
date is given. There may have been a lodge at Augusta
and, on the other hand, Roger Lacey may have given
them the degree while he was first Grand Master of
Georgia and was establishing the trading post in Augusta in 1736 as referred to in the previous Chapter. He
may have temporarily organized a lodge while there
but this is doubtful because of the small size of the trading post and the small number of people there.

The first lodge organized at Savannah and constituted in 1736, continued to be known as the lodge at
"Savannah in ye Province of Georgia." In the year 1776,
Worshipful Brother John Lane in his LISTS OF THE
LODGES under the jurisdiction of the Grand Lodge of
England, states that the lodge at Savannah took the
name of Solomon's Lodge. Brother Lane evidently obtained this information from English sources. That his
statement is correct is indicated by the minutes of Solomon's Lodge for 1785. During that year the lodge appointed Brother William Stephens, Deputy Grand Master, to look up the records of the court judgments obtained before the outbreak of the Revolution against the
lessee of the lodge's property in Savannah. The minutes
show that the British destroyed many of the civil records
and that the lodge was hoping to collect the unpaid rents
which had been sued for in the courts and for which a
judgment had been obtained. The inference in the minutes is that the lodge was named Solomon's Lodge at the

time before the Revolution when the judgment was
obtained.

Just when the lodge at Savannah, which had been
granted a charter in 1735 by the Grand Master of England, was named Solomon's Lodge, is not known. The
change appears upon the books of the Grand Lodge of
England for the first time in 1776. That the lodge bore
the name Solomon's Lodge as early as 1771 is proven by
the petition addressed in that year by the members to
the Grand Master of England asking for the appointment of Noble Jones as Provincial Grand Master of
Georgia. This petition is the earliest record of a name
having been taken by the lodge.

In the first section of this book under the title of the
Genesis of the Ritual, it has been explained how two
Grand Lodges came into being in England in the year
1752, one called the "Modern" Grand Lodge and the
other the "Ancient" Grand Lodge. Except for the lodges
in America chartered by the Grand Lodge of Scotland,
all lodges in America prior to 1752 were "Modern"
lodges having received their charters from the mother
or "Modern" Grand Lodge of England. After
the organization of the Grand Lodge of Antients in
1752, this body also organized and chartered lodges in
America. The Grand Lodge of Antients had the active
co-operation of the Grand Lodge of Scotland. Before
the outbreak of the Revolution in America, the Scotch
were sympathizers with and active associates of the
patriots against England. The Grand Lodge of Scotland
giving its support to the Grand Lodge of Antients led
to many of the patriots in America going into the "Ancient" lodges. By the time the Revolution broke out, the
"Ancient" lodges were the patriot lodges and the "Modern" lodges were recognized as the Tory lodges.

The differences between the "Moderns" and the "Ancients," while acute in many of the colonies prior to the
Revolution, do not appear to have actually affected the
Craft in Georgia until after the Revolution. The organization of the two lodges in Savannah just before the
outbreak of that conflict, their disappearance during
that conflict and their failure to be revived, would indicate that the patriots came into full possession of the

situation through Solomon's Lodge and did not find it necessary until 1785 to take any definite steps toward legally making the lodge "Ancient" by reconstituting it.

Just who constituted the two lodges in Savannah in 1774 and 1775 is not known. It has been shown that Samuel Elbert legally became Grand Master of Georgia, perhaps immediately after Grey Elliott went to England in 1774. Elbert may have constituted these two lodges. The unused charter in the archives of the Grand Lodge of Georgia states that Elbert was the first Master of Solomon's Lodge and then Master of Unity Lodge, one of the two lodges being discussed. If Elbert did not constitute Unity Lodge, it is doubtful that it was done by Noble Jones, appointed Grand Master of Georgia by Lord Petre in 1771. No Masonic document in Georgia mentions the name of Noble Jones as Provincial Grand Master of Georgia. From this fact but one conclusion can be drawn, that is that Noble Jones did not serve as Provincial Grand Master of Georgia. In the preceding Chapter it has been explained that the illness of Jones at this time would probably have prevented him serving as Grand Master even though he received his warrant.

At the close of the Revolution, but one lodge remained in Georgia, Solomon's Lodge at Savannah. The patriots were now in full control of the affairs of the lodge and, though the minutes show that there were members who had received their degrees in the manner of the "Moderns" and some who had received their degrees in the manner of the "Ancients," the lodge appears to have considered itself "Ancient" because of the patriotic loyalty and prominence of its members, though it was still operating under the authority of a charter from the Grand Lodge of England which was "Modern."

Though practically nothing is known of what had taken place in the Grand Lodge of Georgia, the facts that Major General Samuel Elbert was Grand Master, the "Great Patriot" Mordecai Sheftall was Senior Grand Warden, another patriot William Stephens was Deputy Grand Master, and Brigadier General James Jackson was Junior Grand Warden, prove that the Grand Lodge of Georgia was controlled by the patriots and must have been "Ancient" in its sympathies although its Grand Master had legally derived his authority from the Grand

Master of England. This is the documentary evidence which does not permit of an opinion on the matter.

As is often said, Masonry has more to fear from the enemies within than from the enemies without and such was the case in Georgia in 1785. Dissension arose among the members of the Craft concerning the organization of a new lodge in Savannah. Again the documents tell the story and clearly show how these incidents and their solution laid the foundation for the organization of the present Grand Lodge of Georgia.

In 1785, a lodge was originated in Savannah known as Number 42 and working under a charter from the Grand Lodge of Pennsylvania. The first point in question is to find the reason why Masons in Georgia should seek a charter from the Grand Lodge of Pennsylvania. The answer is apparently found in the fact that the Grand Lodge of Pennsylvania had declared itself independent of the Grand Lodge of England and had reconstituted itself into an "Ancient" and independent American Grand Lodge. It granted the charter to Number 42 in Savannah on October 29, 1784.

It was not known until recently that the original petition of the brethren in Savannah to the Grand Lodge of Pennsylvania for the authority to organize Lodge No. 42 was still in existence. This petition was found in the archives of the Grand Lodge of Pennsylvania and its contents tell why the brethren in Savannah desired a charter from the Grand Lodge of Pennsylvania rather than one from the Grand Lodge of Georgia.

The brethren in Savannah state in their petition that they are "Antient" Masons, having been regularly initiated, passed and raised in a regular and "Antient" lodge. They further state that there was no body of "Antient" Masons in Georgia wherein they could receive the "Antient" degrees and that there was but one lodge of "Modern" Masons in Georgia, and only one.

Because of the facts just mentioned in the preceding paragraph, these brethren in Savannah petitioned the Grand Lodge of Pennsylvania for the authority to organize an "Antient" lodge in Savannah and that authority was granted by the Grand Lodge of Pennsylvania on October 29, 1784.

From this document, it is immediately seen that the Grand Lodge of Georgia was still "Modern," or English, and had made no change in its constitution since 1735. It was still a Provincial Grand Lodge under the jurisdiction of the Grand Lodge of England. The only lodge in Georgia, Solomon's Lodge No. 1 of Savannah was also "Modern" and a subordinate lodge of the Grand Lodge of England.

Since these brethren in Savannah did not care to be under English authority, they applied to one of the independent Grand Lodges in America, the Grand Lodge of Pennsylvania, for an American or "Antient" charter for the organization of a new lodge in Georgia. Thus it was that Lodge No. 42, under the jurisdiction of the Grand Lodge of Pennsylvania, was organized in Savannah in 1784.

From the unused charter in the archives of the Grand Lodge of Georgia we learn that in July, 1786, the Grand Lodge of Georgia was still an English and "Modern" Grand Lodge, never having declared itself legally independent of the Grand Lodge of England and its Grand Master was still using the authority of his English warrant. The brethren in Savannah who desired to form a new lodge did not want a "Modern" or English lodge apparently, but desired to organize an "Ancient" lodge. The Grand Lodge of Georgia had no authority to organize such a lodge and the brethren in Savannah were thus forced to appeal to the Grand Lodge of Pennsylvania for an "Ancient" charter. This they did.

The organization in Savannah of Number 42, an "Ancient" lodge, immediately caused trouble. As usual in such cases, slurring remarks were made. A few members of Solomon's Lodge changed their membership to Number 42. The Junior Grand Warden of the Provincial Grand Lodge of Georgia was Brigadier General James Jackson. He was also Master of Solomon's Lodge at the same time. He summoned Brother Thomas Elfe, the Master of Number 42 to appear before the Grand Lodge of Georgia and to account for his remarks. Brother Elfe refused to recognize the authority of the Grand Lodge of Georgia. The members of Number 42 doubted that Solomon's Lodge and the Grand Lodge of Georgia were "Ancient." The members of Solomon's Lodge and the officers of the Grand Lodge doubted that Number 42 was "Ancient." Thus it went for several weeks. Finally committees were appointed by both lodges to discuss their differences. Immediately after these two committees had met, Solomon's Lodge and the Grand Lodge of Georgia started to take the steps necessary to reconstitute themselves into "Ancient" bodies, independent of the Grand Lodge of England. From this significant action, the facts must have been presented by the committee from Number 42 that though Solomon's Lodge and the Grand Lodge of Georgia were "Ancient" in spirit and perhaps in custom they had not yet taken the steps to legally become "Ancient." These steps were now taken immediately.

We do not have the records to show what transpired in the Grand Lodge of Georgia. We have only a newspaper account and the charter issued to Solomon's Lodge immediately after the Grand Lodge was reconstituted in 1786. It may be that the unused charter in the archives of the Grand Lodge of Georgia was not used because steps had already been taken to make the Grand Lodge of Georgia an American Body. This unused charter is an English charter from the Grand Lodge of Georgia. George Handley may have heard what was going on in Georgia and requested delay until the Grand Lodge had been reconstituted or, Samuel Elbert may have withheld his signature until after the Grand Lodge was reconstituted and a new "Ancient" charter could be issued.

That ancient customs had crept into the Grand Lodge of Georgia during the Revolution, or shortly thereafter, is indicated by the seal upon the charter. An arch surmounting two columns, a keystone in the center of the arch, the columns resting upon three steps and the whole surrounded by a circular motto "Holiness to the Lord" forms the seal. The date is not discernible. The symbols upon this seal would indicate influences from the Grand Lodge of Antients.

Again, in the preamble of the charter, Samuel Elbert is said to be "the Honorable Sir Samuel Elbert, Esquire, Right Worshipful Grand Master of all Masons in the State of Georgia and of all lodges therein of the Most Ancient and Sublime Degree of Royal Scotch Masonry of the Holy Lodge of Saint Andrew." The term "Most Ancient" indicates "Ancient" influences. The "Holy Lodge of Saint Andrew" is not a Scotch term. It is difficult to attempt to solve the meanings of these terms. When we refer to what happened in Massachusetts, some clearer light is shed on the situation. It has been explained that the term "Ancient" in America referred to patriotism more than it did to degrees. The Masonic center of patriotism in America was Saint Andrew's Grand Lodge in Boston and St. Andrew's Lodge, the lodge of Paul Revere, Warren and the Boston Tea Party.

When Saint Andrew's Grand Lodge in Boston asked a charter from the Grand Lodge of Scotland in 1752, it did so to establish itself as "Ancient" after the Scotch custom and in order to avoid any connection with the differences between the Grand Lodge of England and the Grand Lodge of Antients in England. In its charter, it calls itself "Most Ancient" to emphasize that fact. It may be that the Provincial Grand Lodge of Georgia desired to show that its patriotic sympathizers were similar to those of Saint Andrew's Lodge in Boston and so called itself "Most Ancient" also, and in addition, to show that its sympathizers were in entire accord with Saint Andrew's Grand Lodge in Boston, it also added "of Royal Scotch Masonry of the Holy Lodge of Saint Andrew" to show too its desire not to be connected with the differences between "Moderns" and "Ancients." While there is no proof of these conclusions, they offer the only plausible solution to the problem of trying to determine what the Provincial Grand Lodge of Georgia meant by this statement. When we remember also that at the outbreak of the Revolution, the patriots of Georgia sent five hundred barrels of rice to the patriots of Boston and, in addition, gunpowder captured at Savannah in the first days of the Revolution was sent to Boston and some of it used by Warren and his patriots at the battle of Bunker Hill, we can understand the close relationship existing between the members of Saint Andrew's Grand Lodge in Boston and the brethren in Savannah in Solomon's Lodge and the Grand Lodge of Georgia.

That "Ancient" customs had entered Georgia during the Revolution is shown by the minutes of Solomon's Lodge for 1785. Some of the members of the lodge had received their degrees after the "Modern" or English manner and others had received their degrees after the "Ancient" manner, yet all were members of a lodge working under the authority of the Grand Lodge of England and therefore "Modern."

Definite steps were taken in the latter part of 1786 to set the matter right in legal manner. It appears that the committees from Number 42 and from Solomon's Lodge had called to the attention of the Provincial Grand Lodge of Georgia the cause of their differences. The Grand Lodge took the steps necessary to change the situation. In the Gazette of the State of Georgia, a newspaper published at Savannah in 1786, the issue for Thursday, December 21, contains the following:

Last Saturday, agreeable to notification, the different Lodges, either by deputation or representatives, met the Right Worshipful Grand Lodge at their lodge room at the Coffee House when the permanent appointments under the provincial regulations of England were by the Grand Officers voluntarily abolished to be communicated to the Craft that the Right Worshipful Grand Master of Georgia, the Hon. Major General Elbert resigned the chair when the following Grand Officers were elected for the year 1787:

The Right Worshipful William Stephens, Esq., Grand Master; Right Worshipful Brigadier General James Jackson, Deputy Grand Master; The Worshipful Sir George Houstoun, Baronet, Grand Senior Warden; The Worshipful Thomas Elfe, Esq., Grand Junior Warden; The Worshipful James Habersham, Esq., Grand Treasurer; and The Worshipful Samuel Stirk, Grand Secretary.

The Grand Lodge, taking into consideration the generous and Masonic behaviour of the late Grand Master, Brother Elbert, unanimously hailed him Father of Independent Masonry; and appointed a committee to present him with the thanks of the Masonic State, with a Past Grand Master's emblematical jewel, in testimony of their respect and brotherly affection.

Thus the present Grand Lodge of Georgia came into existence on December 16, 1786. On December 27, 1786, the new Grand Lodge gave to Solomon's Lodge the first charter issued by the new body. That charter states that the present Grand Lodge was organized "by virtue of and in pursuance of a Convention of the different Lodges of the said State met in Savannah on the sixteenth day of December instant when the permanent CHARTER was voluntarily relinquished by the Right Worshipful Samuel Elbert, Grand Master, and the other Officers of the Grand Lodge and annual appointments concluded on."

One of the most significant things concerning the reorganization of the Grand Lodge of Georgia is the fact that immediately after the permanent appointments under the regulations of England were abolished by the Grand Lodge and the permanent English charter was surrendered by Samuel Elbert, Lodge Number 42 returned its charter to the Grand Lodge of Pennsylvania and was given a charter from the Grand Lodge of Georgia as Hiram Lodge No. 2. Thomas Elfe, who was Master of Lodge Number 42 and had questioned the legality of the Provincial Grand Lodge of Georgia, became the Junior Grand Warden of the new Grand Lodge of Georgia. It is readily seen that here was the bone of contention. It was simply the fact that the Grand Lodge of Georgia had not legally reconstituted itself into an independent and "Ancient" Grand Lodge. No matter what its customs or rituals were, that fact remained and on that point the brethren in Number 42 stood fast. As soon as the Grand Lodge of Georgia severed its connection with the Grand Lodge of England and became "Ancient" in fact, the brethren in Number 42 surrendered their charter to the Grand Lodge of Pennsylvania and became a subordinate lodge of the Grand Lodge of Georgia under the name of Hiram Lodge No. 2.

It is interesting to note the reference in the newspaper article to the affection in which Major General Elbert was held by the Craft. It is unfortunate that there is no mention of him in the Constitution of the Grand Lodge of Georgia. The fact that the Craft hailed him as the "Father of Independent Masonry in Georgia" gives some idea of his willingness to conform to their desires and to put aside his own authority and opportunities. His voluntary relinquishment of his powers as Grand Master under the permanent English appointments in order to make clear the path for a new Grand Lodge, shows the American spirit of this patriot, and is probably one of the reasons he was termed the father of Independent Masonry in Georgia. The Revolutionary record of this brother is discussed in the next Chapter.

The last step in the organization of the present Grand Lodge of Georgia took place in the year 1796. In that year a petition for incorporation of the Grand Lodge of Georgia was presented to the General Assembly of Georgia. The Act incorporating the Grand Lodge of Georgia was signed by the Governor of Georgia on February 6, 1796. In the petition presented to the General Assembly, the officers of the Grand Lodge state that "there has existed, and still exists in this State, divers Lodges or Societies of Freemasons on an ancient establishment, since the year 1735." Thus in the final document which states the derivation of authority of the Grand Lodge of Georgia, we find the Grand Officers themselves stating explicitly that the Grand Lodge had its beginnings in the year 1735.

In this and the preceding Chapters, every tradition which has been written into a Masonic record has been brought forth and discussed. Circumstances which tended to throw light upon these traditions have been produced together with facts which furnish remarkable support to the traditions. There has been presented also every document, whether Masonic or not, which told the story of Masonry in Georgia. All of these traditions and documents show an unvarying flow of English authority in Masonry in Georgia and in the Grand Lodge of Georgia. In regard to the record of the Grand Lodge, the facts produced are unvarying in their consistency and furnish an unbroken chain from the time of the granting of the warrant to Roger Hugh Lacey on December 2, 1735 until the present time. From that date until December 16, 1786, there is not a missing link in the chain of evidence which traces the complete English record of the Grand Lodge of Georgia up to the day that Major General Samuel Elbert surrendered his authority as Provincial Grand Master of Georgia and gave up the warrant or charter from the Grand Master of England which stated his authority under the regulations of the Grand Lodge of England.

From the two lodges, which in 1786 composed the Grand Lodge of Georgia, there have grown more than five hundred. From the little handful of less than a dozen Masons who organized the first lodge in Georgia there has grown the vast army of more than seventy thousand. Where the first little band labored to build Bethesda, the first orphanage in Georgia and now the oldest in America, the Grand Lodge of Georgia has erected upon the hills of Bibb County outside the city of Macon, the great institution known as the Masonic Home of Georgia, ministering to more than one hundred and fifty of the sons and daughters of Masons who are denied the love and affection of a living father or mother. Where the Masons of Georgia since the first days of the colony have labored, fought, bled and died that there might be a nation built upon the great Masonic doctrine of the Fatherhood of God and the Brotherhood of Man whose national motto would be "In God We Trust;" where these Masons have exerted every effort to create a state which should be a component part of that nation; upon the hills of Habersham County the Masons of Georgia have erected and given to the state of Georgia an institution which is a living testimonial to their belief in that great two-fold doctrine. In that institution, the little children, doomed to a slow death from the ravages of the white plague, are renewed to health and strength, are taught by the heart of Masonry that there is a God and a human brotherhood, and are sent forth into the world with renewed vigor that they may fight the battles of life with the same advantages and opportunities that other children enjoy.

Though Masonry in Georgia has had its trials and its misunderstandings, truly has the Great God blessed us and kept us, made His face to shine upon us and has been gracious to us. May He lift upon us the light of His countenance and continue to give us peace.

CHAPTER VI.

Georgia Masons in History

IN THE EARLY days of the original thirteen colonies in America, there existed groups of Quakers, Lutherans, Puritans, Jews, Roman Catholics and Cavaliers of the Stuart regime in England. These groups had come to America where they might find that religious and political freedom which had been denied them in the countries from which they had come. In America, each of these groups to a large extent continued the customs and the living standards of the mother country.

Because of the religious and political differences of these groups, it was not to be expected that their varying interests might be subordinated to such an extent that the apparently unrelated groups could be fused into one cohesive body with a common desire and purpose. Nevertheless, this was done and the accomplishment of it forms one of the most fascinating periods of American history.

For some inexplicable reason, perhaps ignorance, historians in the United States, while telling the story of the fact that these groups became fused into one body, fail to name the medium or the instrument which inspired and then brought about this fusion and it is necessary for the student of American history to turn to the records of Freemasonry in America if he would find that medium or instrument which he seeks and which made possible the establishment of the United States during the Revolution as the great melting pot of the peoples of the world.

In the early days of the colonies in America, lodges were being formed under the authorities of the Grand Lodge of England, the Grand Lodge of Antients in England and the Grand Lodge of Scotland. Into these lodges went men of every religious faith, recognizing only the existence of one Supreme Being. Banded together in these lodges were to be found the Jew and the Roman Catholic, the Quakers and the Cavaliers, the Puritans and the Lutherans. In a Georgia lodge, we have found the records of probably the first Jews in the world to become Masons. The fact that all of these groups were bound together in faith in a common God and that all of them had been persecuted in the mother country for the manner in which they expressed that faith naturally encouraged a desire to practice the great principle of religious freedom. The only instrument available which gave them the opportunity to enjoy religious freedom while in the presence of those who differed with them in the manner of expression of their religious faith, was Masonry.

In the taverns of the early days, about the Masonic banquet table, men discussed without restraint their religious ideals and practiced the great doctrines of the Fatherhood of God and the Brotherhood of Man. The persecutions which they had suffered made them friends and brothers and the great teachings of Masonry aided and encouraged them in seeking personal and religious freedom.

Later, the unjust attitude of the English King toward the colonies became one of the topics for discussion. In their Masonic lodges, they were prohibited from discussing political subjects, but around the banquet tables and without the lodge room, they found opportunity to discuss the conditions which faced them. From these discussions there slowly arose the demand for the establishment of a nation founded upon the Masonic principles of freedom of thought, speech and conscience.

Since, as Masons, they could take no action, there came into being shortly before the Revolution, the patriotic groups known as the Sons of Liberty. These Masons were pledged to fight for the establishment of a nation built upon Masonic principles and governed after the manner of Masonic lodges. When these facts are known, it is easily understood how successful was the ride of Paul Revere. He was Grand Master of Massachusetts. The Grand Master of Pennsylvania, Benjamin Franklin was called upon to lead in diplomacy and statesmanship. The Grand Master of Virginia John Marshall, became the great Chief Justice of the Supreme Court of the United States. The leader of the patriots in Georgia was Samuel Elbert, Grand Master of Georgia. In the Grand Lodges of America today, there exists the system of Grand Representatives. Each Grand Lodge in America is in active communication with the others by personal representative. Here is a remnant of the days when Masonry struggled in the persons of her Craftsmen, to work in harmony and understanding for the common good.

Of all the colonies in America, probably none had a greater Masonic influence in its inception and its development than did Georgia. We have seen the record of the presence of Masons upon the Board of Trustees for the government of the colony. We have read of the establishment of the first lodge in Georgia and have learned the names of the first Masons in Georgia. We have also learned that these men directed the affairs of the colony and established its principles. It is impossible to separate the influences and the men governing the growth of the colony from those governing the growth of the Craft. The men who were the guiding lights in the development of the colony and of the state, were leaders of the Craft.

Religious differences had no effect upon the Craft in the early days in Georgia. From the time of the organization of the first lodge in 1734 until some years after the Revolution, we find the names of Roman Catholics, Jews, Lutherans, Presbyterians, Episcopalians and others upon the rosters of Masonry in Georgia. This continued until the edict of the Pope * * * prohibited the Roman Catholics from remaining Masons. When Georgia became a Province in 1751, an era of prosperity visited the colony. Georgia, for the first time, began to advance.

The first Provincial Governor of Georgia, Sir John Reynolds, arrived in Georgia in 1751. Shortly prior to his coming, the affairs of the colony had been directed by Brothers Henry Parker and John Graham. As soon as Governor Reynolds put the machinery of government into operation, responsibilities fell upon the members of the Craft in Georgia.

Among the offices held by Masons in the early days of the Province appear the following:

Noble Jones, Judge of the General Court.
James E. Powell, Judge of the Admiralty Court.
William Spencer, Register of the Admiralty Court.
John Graham, Lieutenant Governor of the Province.

Sir Patrick Houston, Register of Grants and Receiver of Quit Rents.

Charles Pryce, lawyer.

Charles Watson, lawyer.

James Paris, school teacher, the first in Georgia.

In the religious activities, the Masons of Georgia also were leaders. Brothers John Graham, Grey Elliott, William Wright, James Edward Powell and John Baillie were among the founders of the Presbyterian Church in Georgia. The Sheftalls and the Nunis family were active in the establishment of the first Jewish congregation in Georgia, now Mickvae Israel Congregation in Savannah and having a chapel erected to the memory of Mordecai Sheftall, once Senior Grand Warden of the Grand Lodge of Georgia.

Full development of the Province came under the direction of Governor Ellis who succeeded Governor Reynolds in 1757. Governor Ellis was received by the Masons of Georgia upon his arrival and reported to the King the agreeable manner in which the Craft welcomed him. The Masons paraded to his home and delivered to him a welcome address. Ships in the harbor of Savannah fired three guns when the parade left the lodge room; three guns when it arrived at the home of the Governor; three guns upon the return to the lodge.

Sir James Wright, Past Grand Master of South Carolina, succeeded Governor Ellis in 1760. Brother Wright was a man of exceptional ability. He developed every opportunity for progress in the Province. On his King's Council for the government of the Province he named Brothers James Habersham, President; John Graham, John Morel, James Parker, Benjamin Goldwire, Charles Watson, Grey Elliott, Sir Patrick Houstoun, Noble Jones and James Edward Powell. Sir George Houstoun, son of Sir Patrick Houstoun, later became Grand Master of Georgia and welcomed George Washington on his visit to Georgia.

About this time, as stated at the beginning of this Chapter, there were being organized in the American colonies the patriotic groups called the Sons of Liberty. These groups were organized in Georgia and we have the names of several of the leaders although the rosters of the groups were secret. These leaders were Masons and among them were Brothers Noble Wimberly Jones, Joseph Habersham, George Walton, John Houstoun, and James Jackson. Protest against the Stamp Act, support of the Circular of the Massachusetts Colony which expressed the grievances of all the colonies against the acts of the English government; agreement to forbid the import of taxed products into the Province were some of the steps taken by the Sons of Liberty. This group of patriots obtained the support of the members of the General Assembly in Georgia and thus aroused the wrath of Governor Wright.

The Assembly came to the election of a Speaker in 1770. Brother N. W. Jones, son of the man who was shortly after appointed Provincial Grand Master of Georgia, was elected. Because of his leadership in the Sons of Liberty, Governor Wright refused to accept him and ordered another election. Brother Jones was this time unanimously elected and was again refused by the Governor. The refusal of the Assembly to elect a Speaker other than Brother Jones, coupled with the dissatisfaction in the Province with the acts of the English government, led Governor Wright to dissolve the Assembly and to go to England for a rest. Brother James Habersham, President of the Council, directed the affairs of the Province during the absence of the Governor.

Events were fast shaping themselves toward the outbreak of the Revolution in Georgia and the great majority of the Masons in the Province were openly and actively sympathizing with the patriots. Just after Governor Wright returned from England, the Boston Port Bill was passed by the English Parliament. The famous speeches of Edmund Burke, Lord Pitt and Lord Chatham had been made and had awakened echoes in Georgia. July 29, 1774, Brothers N. W. Jones, John Houstoun and George Walton called the citizens of Savannah in meeting to discuss the situation. In spite of dire threats by Governor Wright, the meeting was held, indorsed the action of the Boston Tea Party and the actions of the Massachusetts patriots. In this meeting and taking active part as leaders were Brothers John Morel, H. Bourquine, Joseph Habersham, George Walton, N. W. Jones and John Houstoun. Five hundred barrels of rice were shipped to the patriots in Boston.

Governor Wright had printed and circulated through Georgia a protest to the action of the patriots. Because of Georgia's distant removal from the events which were inflaming the patriots of the north, Georgia being only slightly affected by these events, many people signed the protest of Governor Wright, but when better informed later, joined the patriots in their struggle. The Masonic leaders in Georgia appear to have been well informed of the progress of events in the Massachusetts colony.

When news arrived in Georgia of the Battle of Lexington, Brothers N. W. Jones, Joseph Habersham, George Walton and James Jackson waited until night, then broke into the powder magazine of the King at Savannah, stole the powder and concealed it. It is said that Brother Habersham hid the powder in the cellar of his father, Brother James Habersham, President of the King's Council. The British did not dream of looking for it there. Some of the powder was later sent to Boston and used at the Battle of Bunker Hill.

During this trying period, many posts of honor and responsibility were held by Masons. Among them were the following:

James Habersham, Counsellor; John Graham, Counsellor; Grey Elliott, Grand Master, Counsellor; J. E. Powell, Counsellor; Noble Jones, Member of Assembly; Sir Patrick Houstoun, Member of Assembly; John Simpson, Member of Assembly; Thomas Vincent, Member of Assembly; Edward Barnard, Member of Assembly; N. W. Jones, Member of Assembly; Charles Watson, Provost Marshal; Matthew Roche, Provost Marshal; Charles Pryce, Notary; William Stephens, (later Grand Master) Clerk of Assembly; James Whitfield, Quartermaster; George Walton, Solicitor; Charles Pryce, Deputy Register and Examiner in Chancery; John Simpson, Clerk in the House; Moses Nunis, Searcher for Port of Savannah; Samuel Elbert, Grand Master, Joseph Habersham, George Houstoun and William Stephens, Captains in the militia.

June 17, 1775, at the meeting of the citizens of Savannah who decided to stand with and support the patriots of the other colonies we find Brothers John Simpson, N. W. Jones, Josiah Tattnall, John Graham, George

Houstoun, J. E. Powell, Francis Courvoisie and William O'Bryan. In the first Council of Safety, organized five days later to guard against British attack, we find Brothers Samuel Elbert, Joseph Habersham, George Walton, George Houstoun and John Morel. Masonic leaders were named to direct the affairs of the patriots. The plan are now made for active participation in the revolutionary events which are to come.

The first Provincial Congress met in Savannah on July 4, 1775. Brother Archibald Bulloch was president. Brother George Walton was made secretary. The Congress took over the affairs of the Province and ordered the arrest of Governor Wright. In this Congress were Brothers N. W. Jones, Joseph Habersham, Samuel Elbert, John Houstoun, Oliver Bowen, George Houstoun, John Martin, William O'Bryan, Matthew Roche, George Walton, John Morel and William Maxwell. Four delegates were sent to the Continental Congress in Philadelphia including Brothers N. W. Jones and John Houstoun. These brethren voted in the Continental Congress to make Georgia one of the original thirteen States.

The arrest of Governor Wright was made in Savannah by Brother Joseph Habersham, Major of the militia. An interesting sidelight to this event occurred after the Governor had been made a prisoner in his house. Having been Grand Master of South Carolina and having been intimate with the brethren in Georgia who were now patriots and in command of the situation in Georgia, the brethren desired to have Governor Wright off their hands and hatched a plan to make him attempt escape to the British. In order to persuade him to do so, they very casually fired shots through his house until he was distracted with fear for his safety. He made a break to escape. No attempt was made to stop him as he made his way to Thunderbolt and was taken by boat to a British ship. The patriots were thus rid of a liability on their hands.

A British ship laden with gunpowder was captured on July 10, 1775, as it arrived at the mouth of the Savannah River. This was the first naval capture of the Revolution and was made after a brisk fight by the American forces under command of Brother Commodore Oliver Bowen and Brother Major Joseph Habersham.

Two English men-of-war and a transport sailed up the Savannah River on February 28, 1776 and attempted to capture some ships loaded with rice. During the night, three hundred English soldiers landed on an island just below Savannah which made it possible for them to reach the rice ships. The ships were captured by the British and when the news reached Savannah, every patriot was called to arms. In the night, one of the British men-of-war had run aground at low tide. Before she could be floated clear, the patriots under command of Brother Joseph Habersham, Major, attacked and many of the crew were killed or wounded. A rice ship was manned by troops under command of Brothers Oliver Bowen, Commodore, James Jackson and John Morel, floated down near the rice ships captured by the British, then set afire and drifted toward the British ship. Six British rice ships were burned, three captured and two set adrift by the British and later captured by the patriots. Some of the patriots were captured in the fight but these were at once released by the British when they learned that the patriots had captured all members of the King's Council and were holding them as hostages. These arrests were ordered by Brother Samuel Elbert, Grand Master of Georgia, and in charge of the Council of Safety.

The Provincial Congress established by the patriots had now elected Brother John Houstoun as the first Governor of Georgia. With Brother George Walton and Messrs. Lyman Hall and Button Gwinnett he attended the meeting of the Continental Congress at which the great Declaration of Independence was prepared. Brother Houstoun was called back to Georgia because of dissension in the patriot ranks and did not sign the Declaration. That immortal document was signed by Brother George Walton and Messrs. Hall and Gwinnett.

1776 saw the beginning of actual warfare in Georgia. The British troops in Florida began a movement northward and, although the patriots were greatly outnumbered, they engaged the British at Midway Church in Liberty County and fought a bloody and losing battle with them. In this engagement, Brothers James Jackson and John Habersham distinguished themselves for their bravery.

The siege of Savannah by the British took place on December 27, 1778. The patriots were under command of General Howe. He failed to take the advice of Brother George Walton, Colonel, and defend a path across the marsh in the rear. The British found this path. The line troops were under command of Brother Samuel Elbert, Colonel. Although greatly outnumbered, the Americans ably defended the city until the British attacked over the unprotected path across the marsh. The resulting conflict would have been a rout had it not been for the bravery and strategy of Brothers Samuel Elbert, George Walton and Joseph Habersham. Brother Elbert held his troops in line until the Americans on the right and center had retreated to safety. Brother Joseph Habersham and the men under him fought their guns until every man had been killed or wounded. Brother Walton and his troops held the rear under heavy losses. All three of these brethren were severely wounded and Brother Walton received a grape shot in the thigh. Later, when his remains were to be removed some years after the Revolution to be reinterred in Augusta under the monument of the Signers of the Declaration of Independence, his remains were identified by the presence of this grape shot in the thigh of the skeleton.

After the capture of Savannah, the British published a list of prominent patriots whose capture was desired and for whom rewards were offered. On this list appears the names of the following Masons: Samuel Elbert, John Houstoun, N. W. Jones, Mordecai Sheftall the great rebel, William O'Bryan, George Walton, William Stephens, John Martin, James Houstoun, James Habersham, John Habersham, Sheftall Sheftall, Benjamin Lloyd, Samuel Stirk, Oliver Bowen, Joseph Habersham and Sir Patrick Houstoun. In connection with this list, it is interesting to recall that when Grey Elliott, Provincial Grand Master of Georgia, left the province in 1774 to go to England and, with Benjamin Franklin, Grand Master of Pennsylvania, represent the cause of the colonies at the English Court, Samuel Elbert apparently succeeded Elliott as Grand Master of Georgia. On this list of patriots appear the names of brethren who, five years later, are known to have been the officers of the Grand Lodge of Georgia. They were probably the officers at the time of the siege of Savannah and the list thus contains the names of Samuel Elbert, Grand Master; William Stephens, Deputy Grand Master; Mordecai Sheftall, Senior Grand Warden; James Jackson, Junior Grand Warden; Joseph Habersham, Grand Secretary; James Habersham, Grand Treasurer; John Martin, Oliver Bowen, Grand Stewards. It is readily seen who were leading patriots in Georgia in their struggle for liberty.

A year later, the Americans, with the aid of a large French force and of the French fleet, attempted to recapture Savannah. One of the bloodiest battles of the Revolution resulted. In this battle, the brethren named in the above paragraph served bravely. The attacks against the strong British positions failed at the cost of thousands of dead and wounded and the Americans were beaten off. In this battle, the brave Polish leader, Count Pulaski, lost his life. In reference to him, many have asked whether or not he was a Mason. All known in regard to his Masonic connection is contained in the records of Georgia Chapter of Savannah. When his monument was erected, the Masons of Savannah laid the cornerstone. On return to the Chapter, Companion Richard T. Turner, Excellent High Priest, reported in the minutes that they had laid the cornerstone of the monument to "Brother Count Pulaski." Brother Turner may have had information not now known.

After the disastrous siege of Savannah had been abandoned by the French and Americans, the patriots in Georgia joined forces with the troops of General Nathaniel Greene and General "Mad Anthony" Wayne. Throughout the guerrilla campaign of these two brilliant leaders, the brethren in Georgia served nobly. The minutes of Solomon's Lodge in Savannah contain references to meetings of that lodge held while the members were fighting with the troops of General Greene. Largely through the military skill and the bravery of Brother James Jackson, now the youngest Brigadier General in the American Army, the city of Augusta was captured from the British. Letter and diaries which still exist tell of the attempts on the life of this brilliant brother Mason by British spies sent to kill him. He was the inspiring example which kept ablaze the waning spirits of the patriots in the face of successive defeats.

With the permission of General Greene, Brother Jackson brought his troops into southern Georgia and struck telling blows at the British troops located there near the coast. He attacked the troops, burned British property and the house of the British Governor and wrecked such havoc that Governor Wright was forced to sue for peace. The Governor originated a clever scheme to sow discord in the ranks of the tired patriots. He proposed to make peace on the condition that the British were to retain the property held by them and that the Americans were to hold the property which they occupied. This was tempting bait for the ragged and starving patriots. Brother George Walton destroyed the effectiveness of this proposal by the circulation of a pamphlet prepared by him which disclosed the cunning of the enemy. The peace offer was refused and the patriots decided to fight to the finish.

General Greene had now begun the campaign which was to rid the South of the British. One of his most reliable commanders was Brother Samuel Elbert. The little army of General Greene met the superior forces of the British at Briar Creek, Georgia. In the ensuing battle, the right and center broke, but the left under Major General Elbert held firm until every man was either killed, wounded or captured. Brother Elbert was severely wounded, and, while lying upon the battle field in imminent peril of death, gave a Masonic sign which was recognized and answered by one of the British officers who came out in the face of fire and dragged him to safety. Brother Elbert was later exchanged, was ordered to join Washington and became one of Washington's trusted staff officers. Washington placed him in command of the central store of arms and ammunition at the siege of Yorktown.

The patriots having cleared the rest of the state of British forces and having assumed control of the situation in Georgia, the British troops in Savannah were left in a dangerous position. In 1782 they decided to evacuate Savannah. Major General Wayne selected Brother James Jackson, Brigadier General in command of a part of Wayne's army, to receive the surrender of the British. The terms of surrender were arranged by Brother Joseph Habersham, Major. The selection of

Brother Jackson was by election of the army and is a testimonial of the high esteem in which he was held by his troops. The command of the city was turned over to him by General Wayne after the surrender.

The surrender of the British at Yorktown had now ended the Revolution. The patriots had won the great principles for which they had fought. The time now comes for the establishment of a nation upon those principles and again the nation called upon the members of the Craft for leadership. William Pierce, William Houstoun, George Walton and Nathaniel Pendleton, Georgia Masons, were selected by the people of Georgia to attend the Continental Congress at which the Constitution of the United States was prepared. The Convention called in Georgia to ratify this first Constitution of the United States contained Brothers William Stephens, Joseph Habersham, James Powell, George Handley and Henry Osborne. George Handley is the brother to whom the unused charter now in the archives of the Grand Lodge of Georgia was issued for the organization of a lodge at Augusta, this charter containing the complete story of the derivation of authority of the Grand Lodge of Georgia from the Grand Master of England. The full story of this charter has been told in the previous Chapters.

It is interesting to note that when the city of Savannah was incorporated, the first mayor was Brother John Houstoun. The eight mayors following him were also Masons.

General George Washington, first President of the United States, and one of the greatest Masons in the world, visited Savannah in 1791. On the committee to receive him were Brothers N. W. Jones, John Houstoun, and Joseph Habersham. President Washington had appointed Brother Habersham Postmaster General of the United States. The Grand Lodge of Georgia visited the President in a body and the Grand Master, Sir George Houstoun, addressed him as follows:

Sir and Brother:

The Grand Master, Officers and Members of the Grand Lodge of Georgia, beg leave to congratulate you on your arrival in this city.

Whilst your exalted character claims the respect and deference of all men, they, from the benevolence of Masonic principles, approach you with the familiar declaration of fraternal affection.

Happy indeed that Society, renowned for its antiquity, and prevading influence over the enlightened world, which having ranked a Frederick at its head can now boast of a Washington as a Brother—a Brother who is justly hailed the Redeemer of his Country, raised it to glory, and by his conduct in public and private life has evinced to Monarchs, that true Majesty consists not in splendid royalty, but in intrinsic worth.

With these sentiments they rejoice at your presence in this state, and in common with their fellow citizens, greet you thrice welcome, flattering themselves that your stay will be made agreeable.

May the Great Architect of the Universe preserve you, whilst engaged in the work allotted you on earth, and long continue you the brightest pillar of our temple; and when the supreme fiat shall summon you hence, they pray the Mighty I Am may take you into His holy keeping.
GEORGE HOUSTOUN,
(Grand Master of All Masons in the State of Georgia).

Grand Lodge in Savannah 14th May 1791.

The President responded in the following words:

Gentlemen:

I am much obliged by your congratulation on my arrival in this city, and I am highly indebted to your favorable opinions.

Every circumstance concurs to render my stay in Savannah agreeable, and it is cause of regret to me that it must be so short.

My best wishes are offered for the welfare of the Fraternity and for your particular happiness.
G. WASHINGTON.

The Grand Master then introduced to the President the officers, Past Grand Masters and members of the Grand Lodge.

In the newspapers of the time, references are made to the Masons on several occasions. They were active in all the affairs of the State. The period demanded men of readiness. The times were trying and tested men's souls. No police forces existed to protect the citizens. Men defended themselves and wrongs were settled by the duel on the field of honor. Though duels were frequent, no records exist to show that one Mason drew the blood of another. They challenged but they did not fight. Reason and Masonry prevailed.

The records of that day show that the Masons were men's men; they worked like men, they fought like men, they served like men; and in following the rough and ready customs of the time, lodge records show from the tiler's bills that at their lodge banquets they drank as the men of their day. Above it all they built lastingly and well and we of today enjoy the privileges for which they sacrificed.

To the glory of Masonry in Georgia may it be said that its members have served well the colony, the province, the state and the nation. In their capacities as public servants rarely have they failed to impress publicly upon the minds of their fellow citizens the fact that they were Masons. The Craft has furnished to the State the great majority of its leaders, men who have put into the affairs of the state the great principles for which the Craft has struggled to give expression. Thus it is that the histories of the Craft in Georgia and of the state of Georgia are inseparable. The Masons of Georgia have breathed into the state its very breath of life. That breath had come to them from the Eternal Source and thus it is that we may, with the prophet Ezekiel pray.

Come from the four winds, O Breath, and
Breathe upon these dead that they may live.

TYLER & COMPANY, PRINTERS, HAPEVILLE, GA.

www.ingramcontent.com/pod-product-compliance
Lightning Source LLC
Chambersburg PA
CBHW050112280326
41933CB00010B/1068